FootprintItalia

Italian Lakes

D1022719

Terry Carter
Lara Dunston

4 About the authors
4 Acknowledgements
4 About the book
5 Picture credits
280 Index
288 Credits

Milan

152 Lake Orta
154 Listings:
154 Sleeping
156 Eating
159 Entertainment
160 Shopping
161 Activities & tours

Introducing
the region

8 Map: Italian Lakes
9 Introduction
10 At a glance
14 Best of Italian Lakes
18 Month by month
22 Screen & page

79 Introduction
80 Map: Milan Metro
82 Map: Milan
84 Sights
88 Map: Central Milan
94 Great days out:
   A walk through
   the centro storico
104 Great days out:
   Milan fashion walk
118 Great days out:
   Certosa di Pavia
120 Listings:
120 Sleeping
124 Eating
128 Entertainment
130 Great nights out:
   The Navigli
135 Shopping
138 Activities & tours

Lake Como

167 Introduction
168 Como
170 Map: Como
172 Great days out:
   Lakeside promenade
174 Southern &
   western Como
176 Great days out:
   Outdoor activities –
   Lake Como
180 Great days out:
   Lake Como gardens
182 Northern & eastern Como
186 Listings:
186 Sleeping
187 Eating & drinking
190 Entertainment
190 Shopping
191 Activities & tours

About the region

28 History
38 Art & architecture
44 Italian Lakes today
48 Nature & environment
52 Festivals & events
56 Sleeping
60 Eating & drinking
66 Entertainment
68 Shopping
72 Activities & tours

Lakes
Maggiore & Orta

143 Introduction
144 Lake Maggiore
146 Great days out: Island
   hopping – Lake Maggiore

Lake Garda

195 Introduction
196 Southern Lake Garda
198 *Map: Lake Garda*
200 Western Lake Garda
204 Northern & eastern
    Lake Garda
206 Great days out:
    Outdoor activities –
    Lake Garda
208 Listings:
208 Sleeping
210 Eating & drinking
212 Entertainment
212 Shopping
213 Activities & tours

Towns of
the Po Valley

217 Introduction
218 Bergamo
219 *Map: Bergamo*
224 Brescia
225 *Map: Brescia*
230 Cremona

236 Mantua
240 Verona
242 *Map: Verona*
246 Great days out:
    An amble around
    romantic Verona
248 Listings:
258 Sleeping
252 Eating
257 Entertainment
260 Shopping
264 Activities & tours

Practicalities

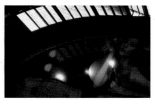

268 Getting there
270 Getting around
272 Directory
276 Language

Contents

About the authors

Australian-born, Dubai-based, husband and wife travel writing team, Terry Carter and Lara Dunston, have experienced some 60 countries and authored more than 40 guidebooks for the world's best publishers, many of which Terry, a travel photographer as well, has also shot. Their words and pictures have been published in magazines and newspapers all around the globe, including *National Geographic Traveller, Wanderlust, Lifestyle+Travel, Get Lost, USA Today* and *The Independent*. Terry has degrees in communications and media studies, while Lara's qualifications are in film, screenwriting and international studies. Terry's career wanderlust has seen him drift from technical writing to graphic design to new media and back to writing with an ever-increasing side serving of photography. Lara's serendipitous 'career' has taken in filmmaking, public relations, teaching, and travel writing. Lara and Terry have been travelling to Italy for 12 years. Their first destination was Milan because that's where the plane landed, but they've been frequent travellers to Italy's hippest city and its nearby lakes and towns ever since. An obsession with food, wine and design has kept them coming back to explore – as has the temptation to smuggle back various hams, cheeses, olive oils and truffles, and the odd fashion bargain to boot. They spent three months in Italy researching this book.

Acknowledgements

Molte grazie to everyone in Italy who assisted us, especially those who kindly helped arrange the permissions so necessary for photography in Italy and generously gave us their precious time for photo shoots, especially Chef Pietro Leemann from Joia, Chef Ettore Bocchia from Mistral, and Chef Antonio Cannavacciuolo and his lovely wife Cinzia from Villa Crespi, as well as their very helpful management, colleagues and staff, including Francesca Blench from Villa Crespi, Antonio Calzolaro from Villa Serbelloni, and Francesco Sagliocco from Mistral. Immense thanks also to Carlo Maria Cella, Chief Press Officer at Teatro alla Scala and Francine Garino, La Scala's most passionate tour guide; master violinmaker Stefano Conia in Cremona and the fantastic staff from the Consorzio Liutai Antonio Stradivari and Cremona tourist office; Stefano Stoppani from Peck; Roberta Davanzo and Francesca Govoni from the Sheraton Diana Majestic; Marco Novella from Starwood Hotels; Claudio Ceccherelli, Anna Montanaro, Christelle Zucchelli, and Serena at the Park Hyatt Milano; Laura Doronzo and Federica Manoli at Museo Poldi Pezzoli; Antonella La Seta at The Triennale; Eleonora Corona of Sermoneta Gloves; Serena Bertolucci from Villa Carlotta; Cristina Zucchi from Albergo Terminus Como; Luciano Guidetti from Grand Hotel Gardone; and Stefania Gatta at the Italian Tourism Board. Thank you also to Alan, Alice, Kassia and the Footprint team for their patience, and a special thanks to George, Tamara, Griselda and family for shelter, comfort and support during write-up. *Fino alla prossima volta!*

About the book

The guide is divided into four sections: Introducing the region; About the region; Around the region and Practicalities.

Introducing the region comprises: **At a glance**, which explains how the region fits together by giving the reader a snapshot of what to look out for and what makes this region distinct from other parts of the country; **Best of Italian Lakes** (top 20 highlights); **A year in the Italian Lakes**, which is a month-by-month guide to pros and cons of visiting at certain times of year; and **Italian Lakes on screen & page**, which is a list of suggested books and films. **About the region** comprises: **History; Art & architecture; Italian Lakes today**, which presents different aspects of life in the region today; **Festivals & events; Sleeping** (an overview of accommodation options); **Eating & drinking** (an overview of the region's cuisine, as well as advice on eating out); **Entertainment** (an overview of the region's cultural credentials, explaining what entertainment is on offer); **Shopping** (what are the region's specialities and recommendations for the best buys); and **Activities & tours. Around the region** is then broken down into five areas, each with its own chapter. Here you'll find all the main sights and at the end of each chapter is a listings section with all the best sleeping, eating & drinking, entertainment, shopping and activities & tours options plus a brief overview of public transport.

Map symbols

Picture credits

Contents

8 *Map: Italian Lakes*
9 Introduction
10 At a glance
14 Best of Italian Lakes
18 Month by month
22 Screen & page

Nightlife of Milan's Navigli area.

Introducing the region

Introduction

The Italian Lakes are a compelling part of Italy. Milan can appear to be a dispassionate capital of cool, where the blinkered worlds of fashion, design and finance take precedence over the Italian notion of living *la dolce vita*. However, while it may be the city that drives the Italian economy, it also takes time out to appreciate the sweet life. Once work is over, the Milanese know how and where to relax; they did, after all, invent the aperitivo ritual – they just plan it like a military operation. The world-famous La Scala theatre, splendid museums and galleries, and fine-dining restaurants featuring the wonderful wines and produce of northern Italy are all a focus of Milanese life – as they should be for your stay too!

But when the weekend and holidays arrive, the Milanese and residents of other towns and cities of the region know that their reward is right on their doorsteps – the treasures that are the Italian Lakes. With their grand hotels, luxuriant villa gardens, boating, biking and hiking, brilliant restaurants and laid-back cafés and bars, the lakes are the reward for the hard-working northern Italians. Near every lake there is a wonderful city to explore, such as Bergamo with its atmospheric streets and fine food, Cremona, where the air is filled with classical music and the sounds of stringed instruments being handcrafted, and Verona, with its unique outdoor opera season and frequent festivals celebrating the bounty of the region. Hard work, after all, should have its pay-offs.

At a glance
A whistle-stop tour of the Italian Lakes

Milan is the most stylish of Italian cities; a fashion, art, design and gastronomic hub where the everyday is elevated to an art form. When the Milanese want to relax, the Italian Lakes – a fashionable travel destination since Roman times – are Milan's playground. Scattered across Lombardy and straddling the borders with Piedmont and the Veneto, the most popular lakes – Maggiore, Orta, Como, Iseo, and Garda – are beautiful, their banks dotted with grand hotels, luxuriant gardens, and gourmet restaurants that satisfy the perfection-seeking Milanese. The region is also home to some of Italy's most absorbing towns: Bergamo, Brescia, Cremona, Mantua and Verona, destinations that reward the curious visitor to this rich region of Italy.

Milan
Milan may have given birth to the world's most iconic fashion houses and some of the planet's most cutting-edge furniture, lighting and product designers, but it's also home to some of history's most important works of art and architecture, from Leonardo da Vinci's *The Last Supper* to the city's splendid Gothic Duomo. Unlike Rome, Venice and Florence, Milan is not overrun with tourists, and its laid-back atmosphere, low-key neighbourhoods and pleasurable rituals, such as aperitivo hour, make it a delight to explore. Equally pleasing is just how close the nearby languid lakes and enchanting surrounding towns and cities are to this important travel hub.

Top: Detail of Milan's Duomo. Below: Boating on Lake Orta.

The lowdown

Money matters

Allow an absolute minimum of €100 per day per person if eating and sleeping on a budget, sharing accommodation and self-catering, and a minimum of €250 per person per day for a taste of Milan and the lakes' luxe life. While accommodation is rarely a bargain here, skipping dinner at the expensive restaurants, and opting for fixed price lunch menus, snacking standing at a bar like the locals, and doing some self-catering from the mouth-watering delicatessens, can keep budget travellers happy. Unless you're taking sporting lessons or hiring a yacht, water-based activities are quite reasonably priced on the lakes.

Opening hours & holidays

Nearly all churches close for a few hours from noon, while many museums and attractions close on Mondays. Even in the efficient industrious north you can occasionally expect to be greeted by the closed doors of a sight that is meant to be open – welcome to Italy! Remember that the month of August is not only quite hot and humid in Milan, but that many restaurants shut for a month (most Milanese evacuate to the coastal beaches) so the vibe is infinitely better on the lakes, but it's very crowded with tourists, so book well ahead. The lakes are definitely a warm-weather phenomenon. They're at their most beautiful in summer, while spring is also lovely, and probably the best time to go (fewer tourists). Autumn can also be picturesque, but locals are tired and wishing the season would come to an end. While the lakes can be pretty in winter, they're also deserted. Many hotels and restaurants close up completely for the season and places such as Bellagio are like ghost towns.

Tourist information

Nearly every town or village has at least one tourist information office or booth, while the larger cities boast at least two (local and provincial), usually located on the main squares. Most have plenty of information to hand out, as well as having websites, although sometimes these are only in Italian or barely decipherable English. Also check out these helpful websites for more information:
Milan: provincia.milano.it
Italian Touring Club: touringclub.it
Italian Tourist Board: italiantouristboard.co.uk
Bed and Breakfasts in Italy:
bed-and-breakfast-in-italy.com

Top: Waterfront at Salò. Below: A wine bar in Bellagio.

Introducing the region

Lake Maggiore & Lake Orta

With the Alps providing a dramatic backdrop, colossal old hotels gracing its shores, and four beautiful islands – the Isole Borromee – afloat on its tranquil waters, it's no wonder Lake Maggiore has a certain grandeur the other lakes find hard to match. By stark contrast, its little neighbour Lake Orta is the most exclusive lake of all. Surrounded by undulating hills and wooded forests, and with pretty Isola di San Giulio a short boat ride away from the charming village of the same name, Lake Orta is the most enchanting lake in the region.

Lake Como

The quintessential northern Italian lake, Como is the most beautiful, most romantic and most glamorous of lakes, with its majestic mountains and shores lined with atmospheric old hotels, palatial villas, pretty lakeside parks and gardens, and superlative restaurants. Light planes fly overhead, speedboats whizz by, and ferries criss-cross the water, yet the lake has in no way given over completely to tourism. This is still very much a living, breathing lake with the elegant town of Como's shops, cafés and restaurants frequented more by locals than tourists, and villages such as Varenna and Menaggio still retaining an authentic laid-back charm. Bellagio is one of the most popular villages, yet it also remains one of the north's most delightful. Como is the must-visit lake if you only have time to visit one.

Lake Garda & Lake Iseo

The largest of the lakes, Lake Garda has a bit of everything for everyone. Its faded charm, historic hotels and Michelin-starred restaurants appeal to an older, more affluent traveller, while its water sports, good beaches and theme parks attract families en masse throughout the summer months. Gardone Riviera and Salò are the places to visit for refined hotels and restaurants and loads of lakeside

Dante looks over piazza dei Signori, Verona.

ambience, while Sirmione's traffic-free streets, striking castle and Roman ruins attract the sightseers, and Riva del Garda's windsurfing is a magnet for sporty types. Not far away, low-key Lake Iseo, with its picturesque waterside promenades, pretty squares and plenty of camping opportunities, is the least tourist-driven of the lakes, making it the most alluring for some.

Towns of the Po Valley

Bergamo, **Brescia**, **Cremona**, **Mantua** and **Verona** are all conveniently located near the lakes, making great bases for day trips to the lakes when accommodation is hard to come by during summer or when hotels are closed during the cooler months. Boasting a beautiful medieval upper town and an elegant lower town, Bergamo is bang in the middle of all the lakes, between Lake Como and Lake Iseo. Only 50 km from Milan (handily located off the A4), Bergamo's airport, Orio al Serio, is a bit of a hub for low-cost airlines. The closest town to Lake Iseo, Brescia is a hidden gem with elegant *palazzi* (palaces/mansions) and lovely piazzas that rarely get crowded with tourists, even during the peak summer period, and yet it's conveniently located on the Milan-Verona train line. The small laid-back Lombardy cities of Cremona and Mantua ooze atmosphere and charm; both are connected to Milan, Brescia, Bergamo and Verona by train and freeway. Romantic Verona, the closest city to Lake Garda, is an excellent departure point for exploring this lake. Verona is home to the Arena, the legend of Romeo and his Juliet and the Scaligeri family, and is truly captivating. History and romance, both real and imagined, ooze from every marbled street and cobblestone laneway.

Not far away, low-key Lake Iseo, with its picturesque waterside promenades, pretty squares and plenty of camping opportunities, is the least tourist-driven of the lakes, making it the most alluring for some.

Top: Bergamo Alta. Below: Summer reflections on Lake Orta.

Best of Italian Lakes

Top 20 things to see & do

❶ Duomo
You'll find yourself circling this colossal cathedral time and again to gawk at its 3,400 intricately carved statues, but nowhere is Milan's Duomo more magnificent than from its lofty rooftop. There you can get close to the 135 towering spires and gaze up at the gold *Madonnina* statue – although the views of Milan will also compete for your attention! Page 84.

❷ Teatro alla Scala
Milan's sumptuous opera theatre, with its gilded balconies and plush private boxes, is one of the world's most magnificent. While La Scala's engaging museum and tour of the theatre is fascinating, there's nothing like dressing up for a night at the opera and sipping champagne in between acts. Page 90.

❸ Castello Sforzesco
Allocate a day to explore this enormous red-brick 15th-century fortress and its many compelling museums, from the Pinacoteca, with its impressive exhibition of art from medieval times through to the 18th century, to the Museo d'Arte Antica, with da Vinci frescoes and Michelangelo's *Rondanini*

2 **Teatro alla Scala, also known as La Scala.**

1 Milan's Duomo.

9 The exquisite cuisine of Villa Crespi.

Pietà. Then there's the Museo Egizio with a fascinating display of Egyptian mummies and the Museo degli Strumenti Musicali, with a mind-boggling collection of musical instruments, one of Europe's largest. Page 96.

❹ *Il Cenacolo* (The Last Supper)
Dominating a wall of the refectory at Santa Maria delle Grazie, *Il Cenacolo* (The Last Supper) is Milan's most popular sight for a reason. Painted between 1495 and 1498, Leonardo da Vinci's famous mural is simply mesmerizing. Once in there, it's hard to tear yourself away from it. It demands that you look at it. Page 102.

❺ Aperitivi on the Navigli
Joining the Milanese for their evening aperitivo ritual is one of the region's essential experiences, and there's no better place to try the local aperitifs and terrific complimentary snacks than at one of the many casual bars that line the canals in the city's most authentic neighbourhood. Page 130.

❻ Galleria Vittorio Emanuele II
Milan's most extravagant work of architecture after the Duomo, the sumptuous galleria, one of Europe's first iron and glass buildings, is a must-visit for architecture buffs. Shopping enthusiasts will be in heaven, as the arcade houses some of the city's most elegant stores, from Prada to world-famous hat-maker Borsalino. Page 86.

❼ Quadrilatero d'Oro
Fashionistas and shopaholics understandably make a beeline for Milan's famous fashion quarter, but the stylish neighbourhood is vital even for those uninterested in shopping. The cobblestone streets are charming to explore and the window displays are jaw-dropping, especially at night, when they are stunningly illuminated. Page 104.

❽ Certosa di Pavia
The exuberant Certosa di Pavia, an extravagant Renaissance Carthusian monastery dating to 1396, houses enough riches to keep you awestruck for a couple of hours while the serene cloisters and exquisite gardens allow you to ponder the extraordinary wealth in peace. Page 118.

❾ Lombardy's gastronomic restaurants
Dining is one of the real delights of the area, whether it's tucking into a hearty pasta at a rustic trattoria like Bagutta in Milan, enjoying fresh regional flavours at Agli Angeli at Gardone Riviera, or savouring a cavalcade of divine dishes on a degustation menu at one of the many Michelin-starred restaurants; highlights of these are chef Pietro Leemann's vegetarian Joia and Carlo Cracco's creative Ristorante Cracco in Milan, Ettore Bocchia's magnificent Mistral at Bellagio and Antonino Cannavacciuolo's exotic Villa Crespi on Lake Orta. Page 201.

Introducing the region

10 Bellagio's Villa Serbelloni.

⑩ The lakes' grand hotels
An essential part of the regions experience is a stay (or two or three) at one of the many enormous, elegant old hotels that preside over Italy's northern lakes. From Bellagio's Villa Serbelloni, with its gilded interiors and stunning lakeside pool, to the fairytale-like Moorish fantasy that is Villa Crespi at Lake Orta, the options are endless.

⑪ The lakes' gardens
Dramatic staircases leading to ornate fountains, tranquil ponds hidden within wild vegetation, and pretty terraces of rose gardens – one of the delights of visiting the lakes is strolling the luxuriant gardens of the many sumptuous lakeside villas open to the public, such as Villa del Balbianello (Lenno, Lake Como), Villa Carlotta (Bellagio, Lake Como), Villa d'Este (Cernobbio, Lake Como) and Villa Pallavicino (Stresa, Lake Maggiore).

⑫ Lake Orta
Surrounded by softly undulating hills covered in thick forest, its shores lined with graceful villas and verdant gardens, this tiny cobalt blue lake must be Italy's most alluring. If that wasn't enough, it's blessed with one of the region's most characterful villages, Orta San Giulio, with charming little Isola di San Giulio a short boat ride away. Page 152.

⑬ Lake Como
Cruising on or around romantic Lake Como, by boat, bike or car, is addictive. While kicking back with a good book on a bougainvillea-framed café terrace or by your hotel's splendid lakeside pool is enticing, Lake Como, with its bewitching villages, demands to be explored – any which way you can. Page 164.

⑭ Como
One of northern Italy's most sophisticated towns, Como makes an excellent base for exploring its eponymous lake. With elegant old hotels, imposing marble Duomo, labyrinthine *centro storico*, chic shopping and lively restaurant scene there are plenty of reasons for staying a while. Then there are the leafy parks, the waterfront promenade, wonderful gelaterias, and everywhere you look, lovely views of the lake. Page 168.

⑮ Bellagio
A visit to this breathtakingly beautiful village located at the end of a wooded peninsula is a must for the quintessential Lake Como experience – check into a grand lakeside hotel, stroll through lush parks and elegant gardens, shop in charming stores on skinny lanes, and dine at romantic waterfront restaurants. Page 178.

⑯ Bergamo
Sited in the foothills of the Alps, Bergamo's medieval walled upper city, or *città alta*, is simply beguiling. While the tangle of cobblestone streets of the *centro storico* are a delight to explore, and its charming shops are worth a browse, the greatest pleasure is to be gained by enjoying the local gastronomic specialities in the town's great restaurants. Page 218.

⑰ Cremona

Celebrated as the birthplace of serious violin making and home to the famous *Stradivari*, the atmospheric city of Cremona with its impressive Museo Stradivariano and Collezione Gli Archi, its hundreds of violin-makers' workshops, and the sound of music in the streets, is equally as rewarding for ordinary travellers as it is for music aficionados. Page 230.

⑱ Cattedrale di Santa Maria Assunta

The colossal 12th-century cathedral that dominates the main square of the illustrious violin-making city of Cremona is simply astonishing. A stroll or two around its base is a must to take in its monumental size, followed by a visit inside to absorb its splendour. It's especially stunning at night when it is splendidly lit, providing an atmospheric backdrop for the music students socializing on the square. Page 231.

⑲ Mantua

Stunningly set on a peninsula surrounded by small man-made lakes, the compact city of Mantua – Mantova to the locals – may boast some of northern Italy's most impressive 12th-century fortresses, but this splendid little city remains one of the region's hidden gems, receiving few visitors when the rest of the region's cities are overrun with tourists. Page 236.

⑳ Verona

The *Romeo and Juliet* myth aside, Verona is one of the region's most romantic cities, with elegant squares boasting vibrantly frescoed buildings, a perfectly preserved Roman arena, and a splendid crenellated castle. If that wasn't reason enough to visit, it makes an excellent base from which to explore Lake Garda. Page 240.

17 Cremona is home to the best violin-makers in the world.

Month by month

A year in the Italian Lakes

January & February

At some time during January, the coldest month of the year, many Milanese head off to the Dolomites for a week in the snow. *Mezzanotte Di Fiaba* (see page 53) at Riva del Garda welcomes in the New Year with fireworks. Back in Milan, Epiphany (6 January – see page 52), is celebrated with a Nativity procession. Keep in mind that it can snow in Milan – either a massive inconvenience or a winter wonderland. In Verona, one of the oldest celebrations takes place with the Carnevale – and yes, the locals wear those sinister masks around the streets.

A very dry but cold month, February sees Milan's Carnevale hit the streets – it's great fun for kids. It's also the month of *the* fashion week of the year for Milan: *Milano Moda Donna Autunno/Inverno* (see page 53), where next season's Autumn/Winter fashions are shown to crowds wearing the current season's offerings. The city buzzes with bling-loving celebrities wearing sunglasses regardless of the state of the sun, emaciated models shivering in the cold, and plenty of action in the bars, clubs and restaurants. Boys with razor-sharp cheekbones abound for the men's Autumn/Winter fashion week too. Book hotels well in advance.

March & April

As things start to warm up a little, Milan's March antiques fair gets underway (biennially, even-numbered years). Late in the month, many of Milan's historic palaces open to the public thanks to the Fondo Ambiente Italiano (fondoambiente.it). Easter falls at this time, and the processional celebrations are worth witnessing. At last the hotels and restaurants on the lakes start to open the shutters after winter and as long as you're not keen for a dip (it's *very* cold), it can be a good time to visit from late March.

The April flower fair on Milan's Navigli signals the start of spring. *Salone Internazionale del Mobile* (see page 53), held late April, is the best furniture fair held anywhere in the world and it has a public day (the Sunday) for hopeful homemakers. The city is packed to its designer-crafted rafters and room rates reach the same heights. The upside is that the city is lively and the aperitivo scene is excellent – you'll see more designer eyeglasses in one hour than you'll see in a visit to an optometrist.

At last the hotels and restaurants on the lakes start to open the shutters after winter

Navigli antiques market.

Introducing the region

Summer brings out the music festivals.

May & June

Often the rainiest month in the year, May is the time of art exhibitions across Milan as well as another flower show. Early in the month in Verona, *Le Piazze dei Sapori* (Squares of Flavours, see page 53) celebrates the local food and wine, while in Brescia, the sound of vintage sports cars' tuned exhaust systems reverberates through the streets with the *Mille Miglia* (see page 53), a classic car race. Around the lakes the anticipation of the summer rush starts, but it's a good time to visit to avoid the summer holiday crowds that will start to arrive in June.

June marks the beginning of the summer season and there are plenty of events to celebrate it. It's a good time to visit *all* of the region. *Festa del Naviglio* (see page 53) sees the Navigli come alive with concerts and markets, while *Milano d'Estate* (see page 54) offers concerts in Parco Sempione and Castello Sforzesco. On the lakes, the *Festa di San Giovanni* (see page 54) sees a spectacular fireworks display on Isola Comacina. Garda Jazz Festival takes place on Riva del Garda and Verona sees the beginning of its busy summer opera festival start. Long lines of tall, tanned and terrific-looking men outside fashion designers' workshops signal the start of the next men's fashion week.

July & August

Summer is in full swing, and so is Milan's Navigli nightlife. Shopping excursions can be thwarted by the heat, so take plenty of water when you head out for the day! *Notturni in Villa* concerts (see page 54) are on, as is the *Festival Latino Americando* (see page 54) and the concerts of *Milano d'Estate* continue. The lakes are fantastic at this time of year and events are on wherever you float your boat. The Garda Jazz Festival should be in full swing. Verona comes to life with a Shakespearean festival as well as the fantastic operas – book accommodation well ahead.

Even if your excuse for being in Milan in August is a business trip, you'll be lucky to be able to set up a meeting as everyone who can manage to escape the city is at the beach or on the lakes. Why? The heat and humidity is palpable. Your saving grace is the Navigli nightlife but the mosquitoes love it there as well. *Ferragosto* (Feast of the Assumption, see page 54) on 15 August marks the halfway point of the month, but you're better off at Riva del Garda for the *Rustico Medioevo* (see page 54) at this time.

September & October

The end of summer sees more frequent rain that, ironically, after October lessens as winter moves in. As everyone's tan (and we mean *everyone*) begins to fade and more clothing is grudgingly draped over toned bodies, the *Festival Milano* gets into full swing. September also marks the month that Monza becomes the centre of the Formula One world with the Grand Prix and red Ferrari jackets begin appearing on the streets. The Spring/Summer fashion week for women takes place around the end of the month, filling restaurants, bars and hotel rooms.

Temperatures cool off quite decidedly, giving women in the region an excuse to purchase a new pair of knee-high boots and for men to break out that overcoat. While the month has a lot of rain, the good days are wonderful on the streets and winter menus start appearing on the blackboards of restaurants. The rain makes for a good time to visit the noteworthy Milan International Film Festival. On the lakes, things start winding down as soon as the temperature drops, but Lake Maggiore still does decent business. Temperatures are ideal for walking and trekking in the hills or around the lake. Cremona comes alive with a musical festival to honour the city's obsession with things with strings.

November & December

As winter sets in, Milan is really in its element. *Tutti Santi* (All Saints Day) starts off the month of November with religious festivals. Heavy dishes in restaurants, that have you breaking out in a sweat in summer, begin to make sense and a quick stand-up espresso on a shopping sojourn becomes mandatory. The ludicrously long football season becomes more heated as the temperature drops and it's a good time to witness a match at the Stadio San Siro. The cool weather also means it's time for the *Milano Marathon* (see page 55).

Chilly December is a busy month in Milan. Two of the biggest events of the year occur on 7 December: the celebration of the *Festa di Sant'Ambrogio*, the patron saint of Milan (see page 37) and the start of the opera season at La Scala – for which you'll need to get tickets well in advance and pack a suit and a glamorous dress. In Verona, the stalls of Santa Lucia (see page 55) signal the Advent period, with a lively Christmas market. Attention turns to the mountains, and people begin planning their ski holidays and watching weather charts with fingers crossed for a white Christmas.

Festival Latino Americando, at the Navigli.

Screen & page

Italian Lakes in film & literature

Milan and the wider Lombardy region, especially the shimmering lakes of the region's north, have served as the setting for an array of Italian and foreign books and films, providing inspiration to travellers exploring the region, and a bit of fun for visitors intent on identifying the locations and backdrops.

Films

Miracle in Milan
Vittorio di Sica, 1951
The great Italian neo-realist filmmaker Vittorio di Sica directed this magical-realist fable about a dove that grants wishes. Offering a moving insight into the harsh realities of the time, Milan is represented in gritty black and white. The extraordinary story of Toto, found in a cabbage patch and sent to an orphanage – which he leaves at 18 to live in a Milan shanty town – is as heart-wrenching as it is delightful. In the film's most memorable scene, Toto and his friends escape their difficult existence by flying to heaven on broomsticks stolen from the street sweepers in Milan's piazza del Duomo. Milan's Duomo serves as a backdrop for most of the film's action and is as

much a star of the movie as the impressive cast. The movie, which won, among others, the Grand Prize of the 1951 Cannes Film Festival, remains an Italian classic.

La Notte
Michelangelo Antonioni, 1961
The atmospheric streets of a fast-growing industrial Milan set the scene in this stunningly shot black and white film. Starring Marcello Mastroianni, Jeanne Moreau and Monica Vitti, the award-winning film begins with a tour through the streets of Milan after wife Lidia sneaks out of her writer husband's book launch, and follows the couple through Milan during the course of a long night out, examining their relationship breakdown on the way.

Teorema
Pier Paolo Pasolini, 1968

An industrializing Milan (and indeed a factory in parts) provides the backdrop once again for this exploration of human relationships, individual psychology and even psychosis. A young stranger, played by British actor Terence Stamp, arrives in Milan and embarks on a series of sexual relationships with members of an upper class Milanese family. The impact of his unexplained disappearance is devastating, with individuals (and the family) falling apart in spectacular ways.

The Spider's Strategem
Bernardo Bertolucci, 1969

The Italian lakes feature far less in Italy's finest films than Milan does; however, the splendid 16th-century town of Sabbioneta on Lake Garda serves as the setting for Bernardo Bertolucci's *The Spider's Strategem* (1969), a psychological drama about a dysfunctional family haunted by their fascist past.

Star Wars Episode II: Attack of the Clones
George Lucas, 2002

The lakes provided picturesque settings for several Hollywood blockbusters in the 1990s and early 21st century. American director George Lucas chose the ethereal beauty of Lake Como for *Star Wars Episode II: Attack of the Clones* in 2002, with some of the romantic action set in the luxuriant gardens of Villa del Balbianello (see page 180), which are a delight to explore.

Ocean's Twelve
Steven Soderbergh, 2004

The beautiful lake scenery, grand old villas and olde world glamour no doubt inspired the choice of Lake Como for scenes in the American heist film *Ocean's Twelve*, directed by Steven Soderbergh and starring George Clooney, Brad Pitt and Matt Damon. Some of the action of the caper film is centred at Lake Como's Villa Erba, which serves as the home of the film's big-time thief Francis Tabour, known as The Night Fox, played by Vincent Cassel. Fights ensue at the Villa between the Fox

and rival thief Daniel Ocean (George Clooney) over the famous 1897 Carl Fabergé Coronation Egg. Clooney obviously enjoyed his lakeside scuffle so much he bought a villa there. Indeed, a focus of many American travellers' visits to Lake Como seems to be Clooney-spotting. The Italians are a lot more casual about Como's charming resident; for them the real star is of course the lake itself.

Casino Royale
Martin Campbell, 2006

Lake Como starred once again on the big screen, alongside one of cinema's most famous characters, James Bond, in the 2006 Bond film *Casino Royale*. After being horrifically tortured, Daniel Craig's Bond recuperates in the lush gardens of a private villa clinic on Lake Como. There he quickly recovers to begin a love affair with treasury agent Vesper Lynd, and once again Lake Como's sparkling cobalt waters provide a perfect backdrop for blossoming romance.

Literature

I Promessi Sposi
Alessandro Manzoni, 1827

Opening with an evocative description of Lago di Como's lakeside town of Lecco, the hometown of its author, *I Promessi Sposi* (The Betrothed) is considered to be one of Italy's greatest literary masterpieces, so much so that it's required reading at Italian schools. Written by the city's most beloved writer, Alessandro Manzoni (1785-1853), the three-volume historical epic is set in Milan and the Lombardy region in the early 1600s during the time of Spanish rule. Acclaimed for its intricate detail, the extraordinary description of Milan during the plague is not something a reader forgets easily.

Manzoni was recognized as the literary father of the Italian Verismo movement which emerged after Italian unification – it was rooted in Realism, and associated with the operatic movement of the same name. Statues and busts of Manzoni abound across the region, often in piazzas named in honour of the author, including his birthplace Lecco where a monument stands in largo Manzoni. There, his family home Villa Manzoni has been turned into a museum. In Milan, there is a statue of the author striking a thoughtful pose on piazza Fedele near La Scala, while Manzoni's remains are at Milan's main cemetery, Cimitero Monumentale, along with other notable figures (including Giuseppe Verdi who wrote his *Requiem* as a tribute to Manzoni).

The Innocents Abroad
Mark Twain, 1869

Lombardy's landscapes and lifestyle have inspired many foreign writers including Mark Twain, who visited Lake Como in 1867, and described the area at length in his novel *The Innocents Abroad*, which was compiled from the newspaper columns he sent back to America. He also traces his journey along the Mediterranean coast, through France and up to Paris.

A Farewell to Arms
Ernest Hemingway, 1929

Ernest Hemingway set this classic, tragic, semi-autobiographical love story partly in Milan and Lake Maggiore during the First World War. The book was made into an Academy Award-winning film by the same name in 1932, starring Gary Cooper and Helen Hayes. The story traces the romance of an American soldier serving on the Italian front, injured by a shell, who finds himself reunited with his lover Catherine who is serving as a nurse at Milan's hospital. She falls pregnant, he defects and the couple escape to Switzerland via Lake Maggiore where Catherine dies in childbirth, delivering a stillborn baby. While it's a real tear-jerker, the scenery is stunning. Travellers will recognise Stresa and the Grand Hotel des Iles Borromées, which actually served as a military hospital during the war.

Foucault's Pendulum
Umberto Eco, 1988

Set in Milan, Eco's book is a riddle of philosophical and political intrigue. A tale of conspiracy in a publishing house and involving Freemasons, occultists, Jesuits and more, it's an absorbing read and was the inspiration for the 2003 Dan Brown book *The Da Vinci Code*, which was made into a popular film of the same name in 2006 starring Tom Hanks.

DH Lawrence and Italy
DH Lawrence, Anthology 1997

DH Lawrence not only translated the works of writer Giovanni Verga, but he also wrote his own travel essays while travelling through Italy, of which three different pieces are available in a collection called *DH Lawrence and Italy*, which contains *Twilight in Italy* (1916), an evocation of Lawrence's stay on Lake Garda, and *Etruscan Places* (1932), a study of Italy's ancient life in the Lombardy region. The other is *Sea and Sardinia* (1921).

Contents

28 History
38 Art & architecture
44 Italian Lakes today
48 Nature & environment
52 Festivals & events
56 Sleeping
60 Eating & drinking
66 Entertainment
68 Shopping
72 Activities & tours

About the region

Papiniano market.

History

The northern Lombardy region of Italy, encompassing Milan and the glimmering Italian Lakes, has an action-packed history of battles, takeovers and power struggles. The region's geography has ruled its destiny and shaped its history. The Alps and Dolomites guard the northern, Germanic border and are believed to have formed each great glacial lake at the end of the last ice age. The longest Italian river, the Po, rushes through the region from the western Alps before emptying into the Adriatic, creating rich (and enviable) alluvial plains, valleys and fertile deltas along the way. Centrally located in Europe, and gateway to the Italian peninsula, the region's bounty and beauty have long attracted invaders and, when not consumed with in-fighting, the area has often found itself a pawn in power battles between foreign rulers.

Below: One of the first Christian churches, San Lorenzo Maggiore. Opposite page: Arena di Verona.

Visit the ancient rock art sites in Valcamonica, Brescia, and you'll be met with one of the world's richest collections of prehistoric petroglyphs – depictions of day-to-day life, warfare and belief – crafted by some of the earliest humans. Findings of arrows, axes and ceramics provide evidence that the region has been settled for millennia; artefacts and rock art show that a militaristic mindset was integral to the success of these early people.

Further south, and dating back to the seventh century BC, hardy Celtic peoples settled along the Po River (which, amazed by its scale, they called *bodincus* or 'bottomless') and held it – despite the growing might of the Latins and Etruscans who battled over central and southern Italy between the fifth and third centuries BC. There were periods of Etruscan rule (after they had spread from Tuscany) but these otherwise successful rulers ultimately fell to the Celtic tribes. The Celts began to create crude townships, which would in time become Milan, Como and the other towns and cities of the Lombardy region. The Po Valley's Celtic Boii clan were known as fierce fighters and their reputation largely protected them from attack. However, the Celtic tribes saw the success of the Latins and Etruscans in the south, and longed for expansion. Collectively named the Cisalpine Gaul ('Gaul on this side of the Alps') by the Latins, the trans-Alpine neighbours attempted a greed-driven attack on the Latin city of Rome. Unfortunately for the Celts, the fearful Roman forces had gathered an army to oppose them. Hopelessly disunited, the Celts gave battle until 233 BC and, with Milan as their last stronghold, the defeated tribes were ultimately driven back into the Alps.

The Romans triumphed in the north and became masters of the *Gallia Cisalpina* area, which is now Lombardy. Just as many regions asked themselves what the Romans had ever done for them, the answer in Lombardy was land-clearing, cultivation and roads – in short, modern civilization with advanced agriculture and trade.

Under the Romans, Milan was called *Mediolanum*, which referred to its position in the 'middle of the plain', and its centrality meant that Milan became an important city along the trade route to Rome. By AD 300, Milan was considered the commercial capital of the western Roman Empire.

In AD 313 Emperor Constantine signed the Edict of Milan, which granted religious freedom, and Christianity became the state religion. People's favourite St Ambrose became a leading Christian ecclesiastical figure in the late fourth century, giving away his inherited lands and possessions before becoming bishop of Milan. He quelled religious factions and soothed Church-State tensions. He was known as the honey-tongued doctor because of his oratorical abilities; imagery related to bees and bee-keeping naturally followed, and this type of decoration can be spotted throughout Milan.

The factious tendencies of the local area and the wider empire, however, couldn't be overcome by one man. Constantine had united the Roman Empire's western and eastern (Byzantine) parts, but at the end of the fourth century it was divided again. There were constant raids from northern countries and, in AD 476, Rome and the western empire fell to the Teutonic invader Odovacer.

The Dark Ages

During the sixth century, Byzantium tried to wrest back control of the former western empire and the region's towns and cities became battlegrounds. A sort of peace was restored only after the invasion of the Po Valley by Germanic Lombards, who swept down from the north in AD 568 and subsequently ruled much of northern and central Italy for around 200 years. While some of the Lombards were, at least initially, pagan, others were Christian and they built many churches – often over sites of pagan worship.

In the eighth century the Germanic Franks seized a proportion of Lombard territory – and granted a sizeable proportion of the land to the Pope, thus strengthening papal power. In AD 774 the Frankish king and militant Christian, Charlemagne conquered the Lombards and when northern Italy was safely in his grasp, he moved on to seize a vast swathe of southern Italy. In AD 800 he had the Pope crown him Holy Roman Emperor, a title that made him the assumed heir to the original western Roman Empire. Charlemagne was known as the 'father of Europe' until his death in AD 814. The wealth and power of the Church was evident in the extravagance of the buildings and monuments, and the Christian social structures that survived beyond Charlemagne's life.

The development of Lombardy now unravels into a bewildering tangle of historical threads. After Charlemagne's death, the major cities began to operate as independent, self-governing states, each ruled by a commune. This was an association of the great and the good (well, the rich and powerful) and generally included merchants and lawyers. The city state began to rise, able to shrug off traditional land-owning rural systems in favour of commerce, finance and banking. The enterprising class of the communes extended their activities into the rest of Europe: so much so that 'Lombard' is still a known term for bankers and money-changers.

The city states soon began to jostle for power and as they became increasingly wealthy, so each began to cast an acquisitive eye on its neighbour. The situation was already complicated enough – but now a religious element fired the cities' competitive fervour. Relations between the papacy and the empire had been strained for some time when a new Teutonic aggressor, Frederick I of the

Hohenstaufen dynasty, marched into Italy and seized as much of the northern and central lands as he could. Frederick, nicknamed Barbarossa ('red beard'), had himself crowned King of Italy and Holy Roman Emperor. He also appointed an imperial official, a *podestà*, to each commune to help wield his power.

Many communes resented this display of force, but the northern region took it particularly badly and banded together against Barbarossa. The Lombard League had the support of the Pope, who wished to see less imperial rule in Italy. The League fought under one flag, the Milanese red cross, hoisted from a *carroccio* – an oxen-driven war cart that served to rally the formerly disparate

Above: Charlemagne, 'father of Europe'.
Opposite page: Dante presides over Verona's piazza dei Signori.

groups. After a Lombard victory at Legnano in 1176, Barbarossa's family and supporters – thinking he was dead – began mourning their leader. He arrived home some days later, battered and red-faced. Unable to defeat the Lombard League, he signed a tentative peace agreement with the Pope.

Further conflict ensued later when Barbarossa's son and successor Henry VI died, and his child Frederick II was considered too young for the imperial role. Henry's brother, Philip, laid claim to the title of Holy Roman Emperor instead. His claim was heartily disputed by Otto of Brunswick and the Pope determinedly supported his claim. Frederick II eventually became Holy Roman Emperor in 1220, and fought against Otto for control of much of Italy. The death of Frederick II in 1250 was a turning point for the political health of the region's communes, as his threatened intervention in the politics of the north had kept the communes of the Lombard League united against a common foe. Faced once more with a power vacuum, the medieval communes fell to the rise of dynastic rule. When the new middle class of successful merchants grew in power, they ultimately developed political clout and the result was a tendency of one supreme family to effectively govern a city. This political system, called *signoria*, replaced the communes.

The Renaissance

Throughout Europe, the ways of the medieval 'dark ages' were eschewed, replaced by a brighter, enlightened era that focused on a finer appreciation of the arts and literature. Disunity between the northern city-states and their ruling *signori* spurred creative, rather than military, competition. This initiated an exciting period of prolific artistic production, the commissioning of extravagant state buildings, and the creation of wealth for individuals as well as for states. The spirit of individuality and creativity that developed during this period is still very much a part of the northern Italian psyche today.

The death of Frederick II in 1250 was a turning point for the political health of the region's communes, as his threatened intervention in the politics of the north had kept the communes of the Lombard League united against a common foe.

diminished and had virtually vanished by the mid-15th century. The Visconti name, though, still commands extraordinary respect to this day.

For the next three years the Ambrosian Republic, named after the earlier St Ambrose, was relatively peacefully self-ruled and battles, temporarily, became a thing of the past. But by 1450, another dynasty began to take shape, led by Francesco Sforza, who played a great part in enhancing the region's artistic wealth. He was a generous patron and under Sforza's benevolent rule Milan prospered. Work was restarted on the Visconti Castle, now renamed Castello Sforzesco, by which it is still known today.

Francesco's successor Lodovico Sforza was an even greater patron of the arts, and his support for creative endeavour resulted in what came to be known as the region's golden age. But it was not only art and architecture that benefited. Agriculture in the rich soil of the Po Plain developed through irrigation initiatives led by the ubiquitous Leonardo da Vinci – who also started to paint *The Last Supper* around this time. Rice cultivation, cheese and butter production all flourished, and continue to distinguish northern cuisine well into the 21st century.

Understandably, the *signoria* system had many flaws. There were ensuing rivalries between families, expansionist and defensive strategies, as well as familial conflicts. One such family was the Visconti dynasty of Milan, who succeeded in wresting control of the city from the ruling della Torre family, taking residence in the Palazzo Reale. Much of the Visconti dynasty's success came from Gian Galeazzo Visconti who, upon becoming Duke of Milan in 1395, greatly increased the family's expansionist efforts. Gian Galeazzo commenced work on a vast castle in Milan (which would later be named the Castello Sforzesco, after the next dynasty to reside there) and commissioned the building of the Gothic-themed Duomo, the heart of Milan even to this day. Galeazzo died in 1402, by which time much of the northern Italian regions were under Milanese rule. In his absence, however, the Visconti family's dominance

The Italian Wars & foreign occupation

The growing wealth of the region inevitably attracted foreign interest and when organized French armies defeated an unprepared and complacent Italian army at the Battle of Fornovo in 1495 and invaded the northern Lombardy region, they broke the Italian spirit for the next 300 years.

Thus followed the period dubbed The Italian Wars, during which the north was invaded first by the French, then by the Spanish, and finally by the Austrians. The Sforza dynasty's rule of Milan collapsed entirely in 1499, and the Italians' will to fight seemed at it lowest. The pressured circumstances brought on by occupation led to the Milanese government changing 11 times during the first 30 years of the 16th century.

The French army was eventually defeated by Spanish forces in the Battle of Pavia in 1525, and in the Treaty of Cambrai in 1529 French rule was ceded to Spain, with King Charles V crowned King of Italy. Fierce battles between the French, Spanish and Lombards continued, with France ultimately relinquishing the much-prized Lombardy region to Spain, which then governed the area for the next two centuries.

By the mid-17th century, the years of foreign occupation were beginning to take their toll on this once prosperous region. Lombardy was hit by economic recession mainly caused by the disruption to agriculture and textile production brought on by years of war. Plague then followed – described in Alessandro Manzoni's hugely influential book *I Promessi Sposi* (The Betrothed) – which devastated the region's crop production, leading to a decline in the population.

By the 18th century, however, shifts in the balance of power in western Europe began to take place, with a positive impact on Lombardy. The Treaty of Aix-la-Chapelle of 1748 left Austria in charge of the region, in place of the Spanish. The Austrians had a stabilizing effect, with the more progressive Habsburg dynasty heralding the the beginning of The Enlightenment. Debate began about the need for reform, with intellectuals such as Pietro Verri and Cesare Beccaria in Milan joining discussions with intellectuals from other parts of Italy and around Europe about the causes of underdevelopment in Italian states in comparison to the rest of Europe.

The Roman Catholic Church was identified as the most significant obstacle to progress, and radical economic and social reforms led to the development of a counter-clerical movement. By the 1790s the Church had lost much of its power, particularly in the Lombardy region. At the same time the impact of the French Revolution was felt particularly strongly in a country undergoing its own radical reforms, leaving Italy more susceptible to the tumultuous changes sweeping Europe.

Above: Milan's exquisitely detailed Duomo. Opposite page: Castello Sforzesco, dynastic home of the Sforza family.

About the region

The Risorgimento

When Napoleon invaded Italy in 1796, the people rose up against the ruling Austrians, forming several French-run republics, which were ultimately overthrown. The many Franco-Austrian battles of the French Revolution in northern Italy paved the way for the Italian revolt against foreign occupation and, finally, the emergence of a united Italy. During Napoleon's reign, France repeatedly occupied, and lost to Austria, the Lombardy region. Following his defeat in Russia in 1814, Napoleon abdicated and, in the same year, the Congress of Vienna made Austria the dominant power in Italy. This period is seen as a turning point in Italian political reform and the start of the Risorgimento – or 'Revival'.

Austria held a particularly fierce grip on the Lombardy region, one characterized by a large agricultural population, a declining and impoverished middle class, and a handful of intellectuals with revolutionary ideals for a unified Italy. Unrest spread throughout the region, making an uprising against the Austrians inevitable. The first occurred in 1820, following the Austrian repression of the pro-unity Lombardy publication *Il Conciliatore* (The Peacemaker) and the imprisonment of its publishers and writers.

As a result of Austria's reactionary control, nationalist unification ideas gained popularity. All the while, more and more radical ideas filtered through from a rapidly changing Europe, culminating in the continent-wide revolution of 1848. In Italy the First War of Italian Independence was fought on many fronts, initially in Sicily, then in Tuscany where constitutions were granted, and also in Milan where the *Cinque Giornate* (Five Days) revolt forced the Austrians out of the city during a siege which ended with a provisional government being set up. Just three months later the Austrians, led by septuagenarian Field Marshal Radetzky, returned and reclaimed Milan and nearby Brescia (which was nicknamed 'The Lioness' following its brave fighting during a 10-day anti-Austrian uprising).

The unification movement was not to be repressed for long. Several leading personalities emerged and gathered support from all classes across Italy's regions. Giuseppe Mazzini was an early leader in the Risorgimento movement, later exiled to England from where he orchestrated many revolts under the *Giovane Italia* (Young Italy) organization – a group dedicated to resisting Austrian rule.

In 1848 nationalists Camillo Benso di Cavour and Cesare Balbo together pursued a constitution and wrote and published the *Statuto* (Statute), which was to eventually become the basis of the constitution of the Kingdom of Italy in 1861. It was the charismatic Giuseppe Garibaldi, though, who proved to be the most popular hero of the unification movement, garnering huge support up and down the country.

Cavour was elected prime minister of the Piedmont kingdom, securing the support of its armed forces and, gradually, of the French army under Napoleon III. Together the armies gathered to fight Austria in Lombardy in the Second War of Italian Independence in 1859. The combined forces defeated the Austrians in battles at Magenta and Solferino, and Lombardy was ceded to the

Count Camillo Benso di Cavour.

Piedmontese. However, a quick peace treaty signed between the weary French and Austrians undid all the hard work, and Lombardy was once again in Austrian hands – this time as an Italian Republic. The fight for unification was on once more, with Cavour leading the way this time.

By 1861 Cavour had succeeded in bringing Milan and the Lombard states into the newly formed Kingdom of Italy. Italy was now unified under Piedometese leadership, with Cavour and Balbo's historic *Statuto* of 1848 forming the basis of a new constitution which established the three classic branches of government: the executive (the king); the legislative; and the judiciary (appointed by the king).

Fascism & the World Wars

The new Kingdom of Italy faced many challenges as agricultural production was in decline and farmers were increasingly impoverished. The textile industry, however, was growing, leading to the relatively fast return of Milan and the Lombard states to their former wealth. The southern states of Italy remained poor, with many southerners migrating north (and overseas) to pursue a better life.

The newly united Italy was under pressure to secure strategic foreign alliances and in 1882 an agreement was signed by the monarchy to secure a largely secret Triple Alliance with Germany and Austria-Hungary. The people's old ally France was notably excluded.

The monarchy set about enlarging the nation's armed forces, and military spending increased by 40%.

In Milan, splendid new state works commenced under Vittorio Emanuele II including the piazza del Duomo and Galleria Vittorio Emanuele II, railways were extended to link Milan with its northern industrial neighbours of Turin and Genoa, electric lighting was installed in the La Scala opera house, and in 1875 a free newspaper, *Corriere della Sera* (Evening Courier) was published for the masses.

In Milan and Turin major new industries grew, and by 1899 car production plants had been established. Such rapid industrialization led to the organization of factory workers into trade unions, leading in turn to the development of socialist ideas. In 1898 unrest amongst workers began to erupt and major protests occurred over the high price of bread. Reaction was swift and brutal and hundreds were killed in Milan when General Bava Beccaris opened fire on protesting crowds in the piazza del Duomo. One standout socialist who began to emerge in Milan in the early 1900s was the young Benito Mussolini, editor of socialist newspaper *Avanti!* (Forward!).

By 1910, a growing opposition force called the Nationalist Association had formed, comprised of those conservatives and imperialists who supported the Triple Alliance, the protectionist foreign policy, and strict state control of labour and production. By 1914, when the Great War broke out in neighbouring Austria-Hungary, Italy was in a state of flux, as few of its population would support a war in alliance with Austria against France.

Italy remained indecisively neutral until August 1915. The large body of socialists were content to stay out of the war, but a smaller group of nationalist interventionists, along with the militant Futurists (see page 42), were wealthier, more combative, and more passionate about Italy's place in the war. During this period, Mussolini resigned from his role at *Avanti!* and took up with the interventionists at *Popolo d'Italia* (People of Italy), the media vehicle for leading the masses to war and later the foundation for the Fascist movement. Italy would enter the First World War a divided and ill-prepared nation, fighting on two fronts, at home and away. Italy had fought alongside the Allies and expected just rewards from the Treaty of Versailles, but instead was at best overlooked and at worst humiliated. Italy had fought a very costly war and was left with high inflation and unemployment, the perfect ingredients for an emerging nationalist leader.

Following the First World War, Mussolini formed the nationalist Fascist Party in 1919, holding party meetings at Palazzo Castini in Milan. Its rise in popularity coincided with the rise of post-war trade unions formed by starving workers. In 1922, Mussolini came to power after the Fascist March on Rome, and the intimidated Vittorio Emanuele III handed him the reins of government. By 1924, Mussolini, now Prime Minister, was calling himself *Il Duce* (the Leader).

From the mid-1930s the Fascists, now clearly an expansionist party, invaded Libya and neighbouring Abyssinia (present-day Ethiopia). International protests were loud, with the exception of Hitler's Germany. The two leaders held similar beliefs and in 1939 signed the Pact of Steel, securing an alliance between Germany and Italy. When Hitler invaded Poland later in the year, Italy remained outwardly neutral, but as Germany's victories added up, Mussolini wanted a piece of the action and, in 1940, looked to Greece for his wartime coup. Italy suffered terrible losses, however, and Germany had to intervene to avoid a certain Italian defeat.

By the summer of 1943, it was clear that Italy, and, in turn, Mussolini's Fascist regime, were in deep trouble. When Mussolini was ousted, his standing was such that barely a protest was

By the summer of 1943, it was clear that Italy, and, in turn, Mussolini's Fascist regime, were in deep trouble.

Mussolini and Hitler.

heard and, after a period of unrest, Italy declared war against its former ally, Germany. Initially arrested but later freed, Mussolini went to face Hitler, who sent him back to Italy to set up the Italian Social Republic, which he established at German-controlled Salò on 23 September, 1943. This fragile puppet government was always in a tenuous situation, with the Allies taking more and more of Italy's territory, but it served Hitler well as a way of repressing the partisans fighting against the Germans in northern Italy. As the end of the war inevitably drew near, on 25 April, 1945, the Italian Social Republic disintegrated, with Mussolini and his mistress caught fleeing Italy. They were executed on Lake Como on 28 April, 1945.

The Italian Republic

The years immediately following the Second World War were difficult for Italy, which was forced to pay reparations. The country's economy was once again weak and fragmented and in 1946 a referendum saw the monarchy defeated. Italy officially became a republic and a new constitution came into effect on 1 January 1948.

In 1957, Italy became a founding member of the European Economic Community thus becoming part of a broader Europe – a positive step forward for both the nation's morale and economy. The north entered a period of industrialization, based on a new infrastructure funded by the USA under the Marshall Plan, and burgeoning industries in chemicals, iron, steel and cars helped to finally set the economy on track.

Milan continued to form one corner of the industrial triangle with neighbours Turin and Genoa. Large exhibition centres were constructed in the north to support trade and industry, and in 1965 the Mont Blanc tunnel opened, thus paving the way for tourism to flourish. The economic success of the industrial north , however, overshadowed the importance of agriculture, and once again poor southerners migrated north to find work and economic prosperity.

It's a fact...

Such was St Ambrose's dedication to Milan that he is now its patron saint, and his feast day (*Festa di Sant'Ambrogio* on 7 December) has been chosen as the date for the opening of La Scala's opera season.

By the end of the 1960s, the economic boom was over and political and industrial unrest began to appear, marked first by the student protests of 1968. There followed a period of anti-state terrorism by right- and left-wing extremist groups, the first instance of which was an explosion in a bank on piazza Fontana in Milan's city centre, killing hundreds. A neo-fascist terrorist movement called *Brigate Rosse* (Red Brigade) grew to prominence during the 1970s, formed from within the factories and universities of Milan and the other towns and cities of Lombardy. The Red Brigade would be held responsible for the assassination of former Prime Minister Aldo Moro in 1978, for which 32 Brigade members were imprisoned.

The 1980s and 1990s were marked by political scandals that rocked Italy, revealing extensive corruption in Milan, referred to as *Tangentopoli* (Bribesville). The national *mani pulite* (clean hands) investigation uncovered Milan's rotten core in 1992, sparking betrayals, despair, and suicides by some of the accused, marking the end of the First Republic and many of the political parties that had dominated the political landscape since the end of the Second World War. Mario Chiesa of the supposedly squeaky-clean Italian Socialist Party was the first to be arrested and tried. He had been quickly condemned by party leader Bettino Craxi who called him a *mariuolo* or 'villain', though Craxi himself was arrested a short time later. Betrayals led to a string of arrests in Milan and the north across the whole political spectrum and within industry and commerce.

In the political power vacuum that followed such widespread and devastating political change, the far-right Lega Nord (Northern League) rose to power.

Grand Touring
the grand lakes

The lakes of the north of Italy have been noted for their beauty since ancient Roman times and have always been a place of retreat and reflection. But it wasn't until the notion of the Grand Tour that writing about the lakes made them popular with these new travellers from England, other parts of Europe and America. These privileged travellers were also intrepid, for in the 18th century one could not know whether they would be attacked by bandits and robbed, or perhaps stuck for weeks due to bad weather. But by the mid-1800s, guidebooks began to appear, such as the brown-clothed *Murrays* in 1842, which described several itineraries for the Lombardy region, with visits to Villa Carlotta, Villa d'Este and Villa Serbelloni. The route over the Simplon to the Lakes was a rite of passage for Grand Tourists and by this time was in good enough shape, thanks to Napoleon, to be tackled by these travellers with their comfortable carriages. Lake Como, in particular, had become an artists' retreat and writers and musicians – themselves some of the first Grand Tourists – flocked to the lake for inspiration. By the time American novelist Edith Wharton's *Italian Villas and Their Gardens* was published in 1904, the secret of the beauty of the lakes had reached beyond the Grand Tourists. But the lakes have never shaken the romance of those days when author Henry James wrote to his sister, 'one can't describe the beauty of the Italian lakes, nor would one try if one could…'.

Organized crime continued its fearsome grip on Milan (see page 47) and welfare reforms were put in place in the 1990s to try to control this destabilizing situation. Wealthy Milanese businessman Silvio Berlusconi came to power in 1994 under the right-wing *Polo per la Libertà* (Freedom Alliance) and despite tumultuous times in the 1990s and 2000s – for a while, the average length of government was just 11 months – remains the one constant figure in Italian politics today.

Art & architecture

Medieval, Romanesque & Gothic

Milan and the smaller towns dotted around the Lombardy and lakes neighbourhood, such as Como, Brescia and Bergamo, offer a marvellous sample of the country's superb art and architecture from the medieval, Romanesque and Gothic movements, which span a period beginning around AD 400 and lasting until the 14th century. Lombardy was well heeled during the Middle Ages and the mighty Catholic Church invested extravagant sums to construct spectacular monuments that sometimes took centuries to finish. Fortunately, many of those have survived to this day.

Art

The best place in the region to see art from the Middle Ages is at the **Museo d'Arte Antica** (Museum of Ancient Art) at Milan's **Castello Sforzesco** (see page 96), although the castle's Pinacoteca (art gallery) and the **Pinacoteca di Brera** (see page 107), all boast art from the medieval period. The Museo d'Arte Antica hosts room after room of mosaics, sculptures, frescoes and even remnants of the city's architecture. There is an impressive display of Lombard (as well as Roman and Byzantine) sculptures from the Early Christian period through the early Middle Ages. Works include the *Testa di Teodora* (Head of Theodora, the Byzantine Empress), a stunning sixth

Above: A statue at the Pinacoteca di Brera.
Opposite page: Basilica di Sant'Ambrogio.

century marble sculpture, along with beautiful decorative floor mosaics and marble reliefs from Milan's ancient churches of Santa Tecla, San Protaso ai Monaci and Santa Maria d'Aurona.

Among the frescoes and sculptures on display at the museum from the Romanesque and Gothic periods are architectural pieces such as capitals and shelves crafted by local artisans. These have been found in churches in Milan and Pavia and feature intricate carvings of mermaids, dragons, lions and other beasts, real and mythical. There are also some fine examples of Romanesque sculpture and carved capitals from Como and Cremona.

Architecture

It may be the major city of the region, with a long, action-packed history, but apart from its monumental **Duomo** (see page 84), Milan's architectural delights are often overlooked by travellers, despite the city boasting some of the most impressive examples of medieval architecture in northern Italy. Piazza Mercanti, for instance, is an atmospheric marketplace that first took shape in 1228. Elsewhere, the Archi di Porta Nova is the only remaining part of the city's medieval walls and is adorned with sculptures of the Madonna and Child.

The **Basilica di Sant'Ambrogio** (see page 115) was built in honour of Milan's first bishop, St Ambrose. Considered to be a significant and fine example of Lombard Romanesque architecture, it became a model for many of the region's basilicas. It boasts a beautiful colonnaded quadrangle with columns carved with strange beasts, and a pulpit also adorned with wild animals. The building features Germanic influences that are the result of centuries of combative contact between the Lombards and neighbouring Germanic kingdoms. Artistic and architectural influences from the two groups during this period are so intertwined that it's difficult for all but avid architectural buffs to distinguish the features that identify their true origins.

About the region

The web-like layout of Milan has as its heart the colossal Duomo, the world's largest Gothic cathedral and Europe's second biggest cathedral after St Peter's in Rome. Started in 1386, it was constructed from rare Candoglia marble and boasts 135 spires, some 150 stained glass windows, countless intricate carvings and imposing buttresses, and a mind-boggling 3,400 statues. Leonardo da Vinci was integral to the cathedral's construction, creating a canal lock system which allowed the enormous stone slabs to be brought to the site. The gilded *Madonnina* (Little Madonna) sitting atop the Duomo's highest steeple is there to protect the city spread out before her.

Renaissance

When travellers think of Italian art they inevitably think of works from the Renaissance period. The Renaissance, or 're-birth' (*Rinascimento* in Italian), heralded a revolutionary movement away from the dark Middle Ages and towards a vibrant period of creative endeavour that saw the flourishing of art, architecture, literature and music.

Whilst much of the Renaissance action was centred on Florence and Venice, the movement quickly travelled to Milan and the wealthier northern regions, and later to Germany and northern Europe where it became known as the Northern Renaissance. One explanation for the impetus of the Italian Renaissance is the long-running series of wars and the intense rivalry between Milan and Florence, which had motivated Gian Galeazzo Visconti (Milan's ruler 1378-1402) to build a great empire in northern Italy.

When Francesco Sforza came to power in Milan in 1447 with similar ambitions to Visconti, he quickly transformed medieval Milan into an important centre for the arts, culture and learning. Sforza may have been ruthless but he was a generous patron and benevolent ruler. Sforza supported Renaissance greats such as as Leonardo da Vinci, the Milanese painters Ambrogio Bergognone, Andrea Solari and Vincenzo Foppa,

and the Lombard architects Giovanni Antonio Amadeo and Donato Bramante. As a result Milan now boasts some of the finest works of Italian Renaissance art and architecture.

Art

The art from this period in particular is now considered to be among some of the world's greatest, including Leonardo da Vinci's *Mona Lisa* (on display at The Louvre in Paris) and *Il Cenacolo* (The Last Supper, see page 102), both of which draw an astonishing number of visitors each day. Housed in the refectory of Milan's **Santa Maria delle Grazie** (see page 102), the painstakingly restored mural of *Il Cenacolo* is so precious it can only be viewed by small groups for a limited time. The Museo d'Arte Antica at Castello Sforzesco contains more da Vinci frescoes in the Sala delle Asse, along with Michelangelo's unfinished work, *Rondanini Pietà*, which he was working on when he died in 1564.

The **Pinacoteca Ambrosiana** (see page 87) is found within what was Europe's first public library and is home to Italy's first still life, Carravaggio's *Canestro di Frutta* (Basket of Fruit) and da Vinci's *Musico* (Musician), as well as works by Tiepolo, Titian and Raphael. The **Museo Poldi Pezzoli** (see page 92) is another great source of Renaissance treasures including the *Madonna della Loggia* (Mother and Child) by the Florentine School's master Botticelli.

Venturing further afield to the smaller town of Bergamo, visitors in search of a dedicated Renaissance collection will be rewarded at the **Accademia Carrara** (see page 223). A legacy of Count Giacomo Carrara, a wealthy collector and patron of the arts who left his extensive collection to the state at the end of the 18th century, the museum houses work by Renaissance artists such as Pisanello, Botticelli, Bellini, Carpaccio, Mantegna, Raphael and Moroni.

The art from the Renaissance is now considered to be among some of the world's greatest

Architecture

Notable architecture from the Renaissance includes Milan's striking red-brick **Castello Sforzesco**, which had been the Visconti castle. Leonardo da Vinci was a consulting engineer at the Sforza court and was responsible for some of its renovations, designing some of the castle's defence mechanisms, as well as the Navigli (the city's waterways). Another wonderful example of architecture from the period is the splendid Renaissance courtyard which united the city's hospitals into the great Ospedale Maggiore, better known these days as Ca' Granda. It was designed by Tuscan architect Filarete and encompassed work by Solari, Amadeo and Richini.

Five of the best

Art collections

❶ **Cenacolo Vinciano**, Milan Home to Leonardo da Vinci's *The Last Supper* (see page 102).

❷ **Civici Musei del Castello Sforzesco**, Milan Half a dozen superb museums in a splendid castle (see page 98).

❸ **Pinacoteca di Brera**, Milan One of the city's best art museums boasts a superlative collection (see page 107).

❹ **Pinacoteca Ambrosiana**, Milan Masterpieces by Caravaggio, Da Vinci and Raphael alone make a visit here worthwhile (see page 87).

❺ **Accademia Carrara**, Bergamo One of Lombardy's best art collections (see page 223).

Museo Poldi Pezzoli.

20th Century

Futurism and Fascism

At the end of the 19th century the late-starting Italy experienced the Second Industrial Revolution, and the prevailing social and economic conditions by the start of the 20th century ensured the timing was right for the birth of the Futurist movement (see page 35).

The founder of the Italian movement, writer Filippo Tommaso Marinetti, launched the *Manifesto del Futurismo* on 20 February 1909, in which he expressed a hatred of tradition, writing: "We want no part of it, the past, we the young and strong Futurists!" Instead, they desired a modern industrial city, technology over nature, urban living over country life, and preferred speed to the slower pace of the past.

The Futurist members were anarchists, nationalists and socialists initially, and while young socialist-nationalist leader Benito Mussolini had no personal interest in art, he supported their movement while funding a number of projects by artists and architects in order to buy their loyalty.

When the First World War came to an end, Mussolini announced his rather Futurist-inspired intention to speed up the reconstruction of Italy and dedicated funds to developing the railways and other public works. Initiated as far back as 1906 by Vittorio Emanuele III, the monumental **Stazione Centrale** was completed in 1931. The railway station's initial design by Milan-based architect Ulisse Stacchini had been simple, but under Mussolini's orders, it became increasingly grand as he wanted it to be a symbol of Fascist power. It's now recognized as one of the world's finest railway stations.

Under state patronage, art and architecture thrived during the period between the World Wars. A modern Rationalist-influenced architectural movement was born, pioneered largely by Giuseppe Terragni, a Milan-based architect who worked under Mussolini's regime. Terragni's most famous building was the innovative, contemporary-looking Casa del Fascio at Como,

When the First World War came to an end, Mussolini announced his rather Futurist-inspired intention to speed up the reconstruction of Italy

started in 1932 and finished in 1936, which was originally intended to function as a striking backdrop for mass Fascist rallies. During this period a series of art shows were launched, including **La Triennale** (see page 106) in Milan.

Brutalist Modernism

After the Second World War destroyed many of Milan's buildings, reconstruction and functionality took priority over form and style, and the practicalities of rebuilding shaped the architectural themes of the time. By 1950, a new architectural movement was born – Brutalist Modernism. The architects Banfi, Belgiojoso, Peressutti and Rogers, who became known as BBPR, designed the revolutionary **Torre Velasca**, completed in 1957. As space was at a premium in modern Milan, its base was built narrower than the rest of the building while protruding buttresses supported the upper, wider storeys. A modern interpretation of a medieval castle, the 20-storey tower draws on the medieval and Gothic architectural themes that are so much a part of Milan's makeup, such as the Duomo and the Castello Sforzesco, and still towers above other buildings in Milan.

Another towering landmark from the 1950s is the **Pirelli Tower**, built in 1950, which to this day is the tallest building in Milan. Designed by architect Giò Ponti, it was commissioned by Alberto Pirelli, director of the famous tyre company, to be built on the site of his tyre factory which had been bombed during the Second World War. Admired for its lofty proportions and design elegance, it remains a symbol of the economic prosperity of Milan and northern Italy.

The ground-breaking Pirelli Tower.

Italian Lakes today

Celebrated as a global design capital, Milan is a city where designers are nurtured and revered. The home of cutting edge fashion, furniture, lighting, interior, and product designers, the world's eyes are always on the region to see what will be produced and where future trends lie.

Milan and its surrounding provinces have been synonymous with great design for almost a century. Italians like to say that the region was built on the back of design, with so many sectors of the economy from Milan to Como to Bergamo contributing to, and flourishing from, the ever-evolving design industry. A region of unsurpassed imagination, innovative and intense creativity, its success is due to the fact that it has the industrial and manufacturing infrastructure to make radical ideas a reality.

Milan's world-famous design shows and fairs were founded in the early 20th century to showcase the most inspiring selection of designs and inventions. A selection of the region's most fêted works are on show at **La Triennale** (see page 106), Milan's main design museum. A turning point for design in the lakes was the end of the Second World War, after which followed a period that produced a new wave of Italian designers as the country was physically (and morally) rebuilt. Notably, Corradino released the Vespa scooter in 1946, which became the main form of transport for Italians. The Vespa was an ideal, affordable means of negotiating the congested streets and the mobility it provided revolutionized Italian society. The scooter's enduring design is a worldwide symbol of Italian youth, freedom and effortless chic.

During the 1960s and 1970s Italian designers experimented with plastics, glass and other materials in the Radical Design period, always with functionality and space as the springboard for their innovation. Carlo Bugatti designed his famous chairs, Joe Colombo released the *Tube Chair*, and Guzzini acrylic homeware took the world by storm.

The 1980s saw the Lake Orta-based Alessi plastic kitchenware brand emerge and grow as Alessi recruited different designers to work with the company, leading it to cult celebrity status with its fun and colourful range – most famously Philippe Starck's *Juicy Salif* three-legged juicer and Michael Graves' whistling bird kettle.

The 1990s saw Milanese plastic furniture designer Kartell gain a dedicated following – Ron Arad's curved *Bookworm Bookshelf* was its breakthrough release – and the company became famous for its chic transparent chairs. A string of prominent architects and interior designers incorporated Kartell's sleek Poliform furniture into projects, catapulting the company to global cool status by the end of the century.

Italian Prime Minister Silvio Berlusconi is Milan's most famous and most controversial figure, the man most Italians love to hate. He is also one of Italy's wealthiest men, a driven entrepreneur with a vast web of commercial interests – some overt, some subtle – across a broad spectrum of industries including property, construction, food, insurance, the media and sport. Berlusconi is a man with a finger in every pie.

Born in Milan in 1936, Berlusconi, now in his 70s, is renowned for his deep tan, hair transplants, and apparently frequent visits to the cosmetic surgeon. White-toothed and wrinkle-free, Berlusconi is not only the leader of the nation, but poster-boy for his right-wing political party, Forza Italia (meaning, 'Go Italy'). The party is named after the chant Berlusconi co-wrote for the football team AC Milan (which he owns).

Five of the best

Italian designs – something old, something new

❶ The 1948 *La Pavoni* coffee machine by Gio Ponti – everlasting cool.

❷ B&B Italia's *JJ Chair* by Antonio Citterio – the hippest rocking chair around.

❸ Porro's 2008 interpretation of Milanese designer Bruno Munari's (1907-1998) retro 1960s trolley – some things never go out of fashion.

❹ Milanese designer Ferruccio Laviani's polycarbonate baroque *Bourgie* table lamp for Kartell – proves classic can also be contemporary.

❺ Dada and Armani's jointly designed kitchen *The Bridge* – Armani needs to design an apron in keeping with the sleek style!

Milan's La Triennale showcases the region's design heritage.

About the region

Long shadows cast over Milan's piazza del Duomo.

Berlusconi started out from moderate beginnings, the son of a Milanese banker. Following his completion of a degree in law, he started a construction company called Elinord, funding the building of a residential complex of 4,000 flats on Milan's outskirts in the 1960s. A one-time nightclub singer, Berlusconi never lacked charisma or confidence, charming his way through negotiations and always looking to make powerful connections.

Berlusconi went on to buy half a dozen television and radio stations, Italy's largest publishing house Mondadori, and the daily newspaper *Il Giornale*, creating a media monopoly.

With uncontested control of much of Italy's media and public opinion, and with extensive commercial and social connections throughout Milan and Italy, Berlusconi entered politics representing his party Forza Italia in 1993. He ran for President of the Council of Ministers of Italy, the equivalent to Prime Minister of the Italian Republic, in 1994, and won decisively. With the party plagued by disorganisation, Berlusconi lost the 1996 elections. Unperturbed by the loss, or by the numerous fraud investigations into his affairs, Berlusconi was re-elected as Prime Minister in 2001 and 2005, lost in 2006 and was re-elected in 2008.

Milan's main man may be recognized by the Italian public as an aging controversial showman, infamous for his political incorrectness (he called US President Barack Obama suntanned, much to the embarrassment of the Italian population) – but he has also managed to maintain a fairly stable government for Italy in recent years, something unheard of before he came to power.

The Mafia web spreads to the north

The Mafia, Italy's much-feared organized crime network, conjures up images familiar to us from Hollywood of the underworld of powerful feuding families, petty crime, sawn-off shotguns, midnight murders and kidnappings.

The Mafia has had its home in the south dating to the 1800s, in Sicily and Calabria, with its web extending to the US in the post-war 1950s. But in recent years there's been concern over its spread to northern Italy, particularly Milan.

Like so many radical and violent political movements formed by a community to combat extreme economic hardship caused by centuries of war and occupation, the Mafia code is strict, and its terms deadly. Illegal drugs and weapons dealing, money laundering, black marketeering, and extortion for protection have made the Mafia an extremely wealthy entity.

Milan and the smaller wealthier northern cities have long been considered geographically and culturally far from the cities and towns of the south; however, the Mafia's wealth, and a membership with far-reaching social and commercial connections, meant that the area was a natural target. Elements first appeared in Milan during the Second World War; however, the bloodshed that had been previously confined to clan wars and internal skirmishes went public in the 1970s when an anti-Mafia taskforce was set up by parliament to tackle the fast-growing drug trade. This led to politicians being targeted and assassinated, and terrorist acts including bomb blasts rocked Milan and other northern cities, aimed at destabilizing the government and frightening the population into submission.

Milan and the smaller northern cities became infiltrated by Calabria's Mafia, the 'Ndrangheta, which formed an insidious network that infiltrated the city. Police blamed the 'Ndrangheta's for transforming Milan into the cocaine capital of Europe; in 2007 they seized a vast 1,400 kg in Lombardy. As well as controlling the ever-growing illicit drugs and arms trades, members now manage a vast array of 'ordinary' businesses in the area, from fruit shops to restaurants, shopping centres to construction companies. Milan is now considered to be a global centre for money laundering.

The value of the 'Ndrangheta business in the north is immense – estimated at around 4% of Italy's total GDP.

Nature & environment

The Italian Lakes boast sparkling expanses of water variously surrounded by softly undulating hills, serrated limestone cliffs, lofty mountains and lush agricultural plains, with the ever-present snow-clad Alps providing a dramatic backdrop. Dotted across Lombardy and straddling the borders with Piedmont and the Veneto, the lakes are where the northern Italians go to play, especially the Milanese and Veronese.

Alpine glaciers formed the glistening lakes of Como, Maggiore, Garda, Iseo, Orta and the others. Spanning 600 km from east to west and separating Italy from its northern neighbours, France and Switzerland (and further east Austria and Slovenia), the icy Alps are nearly always alluringly visible from the lakes. The Italian Alps provide a winter wonderland to escape to for skiing and snow sports during the cold months while their emerald slopes, blanketed in forest with limestone peaks poking through the clouds, provide ideal conditions for hiking, Nordic walking and climbing in the summertime.

The lakes may be lovely but they are also located in Italy's most highly populated and industrialized region. Travellers often forget that this complex natural landscape is home to scores of cities, hundreds of towns, and thousands of villages and hamlets, and the industry that has made the region so wealthy and given it such an

Above: All the locals take to the water in summer.
Opposite page: View of beautiful Isola di San Giulio.

outstanding quality of life is spread throughout. An agriculturally rich region, it has emerged as a major supplier of food to the rest of Italy, as well as establishing itself as a key exporter to the rest of the world.

So while there are plenty of opportunities to get out and enjoy the area's natural environment, unfortunately the air is not always as fresh as it could be and poor water quality occasionally means swimming in some of the lakes is not always advisable.

Heading for the hills
For those of you who want to experience nature in winter but don't want to fasten on skis, snow-shoeing is popular, while in summer the best way to experience the environment is to head for the hills, which in the warmer months are alive with hikers and Nordic walkers (more invigorating than your average stroll) enjoying the vibrant wildflowers that blanket the mountain meadows. All of the tourist offices in the region have information on organized hikes and hiring private guides or, at the very least, can provide good maps and itineraries for self-guided walks on sign-posted trails.

The area has dedicated areas to protect flora and fauna, including national parks, which are never more than a couple of hours' drive away. Northern Italy boasts dozens of national parks, the most popular and most accessible to Milan and the lakes being the *Parco Nazionale del Gran Paradiso* (Grand Paradise National Park) and *Parco Nazionale della Val Grande* (Great Valley National Park) in Piedmont. For details of a drive round the Great Valley National Park, see page 151.

Rivers, mountains, marshes & markets
The Po Basin, which makes up the rough boundaries of the northern Lombardy region, dictates the nature of this remarkable landscape. The basin,

flanks beech trees flourish, along with spruce and juniper. This is the main habitat of wildlife in this densely populated northern region, which is home to ibex and deer, and the rare brown bear. Alpine birds, including black grouse and the golden eagle, are spotted here.

The swampy marshland was considered ideal for rice production, so is home to rice paddies that produce one third of Italy's rice for risotto and other short grain rice dishes. Some of Italy's most prized risotto rice comes from the paddies surrounding Mantua in the region's east. Grapes are also grown in the region – where aren't they in Italy? – and the cool climate reds grown on the steep slopes of the Valtellina area are particularly delicious. Valtellina is the 'green' area along the north of Lombardy running along the foot of the Alps on the Swiss border. Agriculturally rich, fresh food markets are held in the market square of most towns and villages and there are annual produce festivals to herald rice, asparagus, wine and white truffle harvests. It's a pretty area, popular for skiing, cycling, hiking, and spa treatments in the thermal springs.

Milan's bowl v nature's fruit bowl

At around 120 m above sea level, and roughly halfway between the arid northern and swampy southern sections of the plain, Milan sits in the centre of the Po Basin with hills and mountains all around. The city's environment is marked by the pollution that accompanies any industrial city but the problem is compounded in Milan by the city's climate (characterised by damp, cold winters with occasional snow from December to February, and hot humid summers with temperatures rising to 30°C in summer) and bowl-like geography that means the pollution can't escape. This means Milan is sometimes covered in a light smog or fog, creating stunning photo opportunities when only the church spires are visible. Milan's residents cope by getting away to the lakes when it becomes too much!

The smaller towns and cities in the region each have very different environments and landscapes. The old city of Pavia to the south of Milan is a

Milan is sometimes covered in a light smog or fog, creating stunning photo opportunities when only the church spires are visible

at the foot of the mountains to the north, and Italy's longest river, the Po (645 km) to the south, is filled with silt from the mountains, forming the plain. The plain is less fertile in the far north and richer the closer it gets to the river, and industry and agriculture have developed accordingly.

The main forested areas of the region are at the base of the mountains, where oak, olive and cypress trees thrive, while higher up the alpine

Above: Enjoying the sunshine in Cannobio.
Below: Boating on Orta San Guilio.

significant agricultural centre and is encircled by crops (mainly rice) as much as industrial developments. The historic hilly city of Bergamo, to Milan's northeast, is set on the slopes of a lush hinterland on the lower flanks of the Alps and not far from pretty Lake Iseo. Further east, Verona and Brescia are each a hop, skip and jump from Lake Garda, which boasts natural thermal springs and the greenest environment of them all, despite the presence of industry and theme parks. The area has an unusual microclimate that is pleasingly temperate. Brescia itself was once one of the greatest producers of lemons, which still play an important role in the area's tourism and economy. Further east, medieval Cremona's principal agricultural industry is dairy farming (along with the production of agricultural machinery), while smaller and more tranquil Mantua sits to the east, on an open plain and the shores of a trio of less visited lakes, Lago Superiore, Lago di Mezzo and Lago Inferiore.

Tip...

The air is freshest and the light has the most clarity in spring and at the start of autumn, and throughout the year on Sundays and Mondays after a weekend of closed factories has allowed the air to breathe. Water quality levels are not as predictable and travellers should always check with the tourist offices or their hotels before venturing in for a swim or water sports.

Festivals & events

From food and wine, fashion and furniture to the Formula One, Milan and the lakes offer a diverse array of festivals and events sprinkled liberally throughout the year. Even if you're not into the reason for the celebration, you won't be able to resist joining in. You'll find the streets alive with people – even the hard-working northern Italians love an excuse to have a break and relax. Keep in mind though that accommodation around events such as the fashion weeks is reserved months in advance and restaurants can be fully booked.

January

Corteo dei Re Magi (6th)
Epiphany is a public holiday and is celebrated with the 'Wise Men Processional', a traditional Nativity procession, moving from Milan's Duomo to Sant'Eustagio. The children are happy because they get more festive presents – if they're good.

Carnevale di Verona
Dating back to the 1500s, this is one of the oldest celebrations in Italy. It recounts a local nobleman's gift of gnocchi (pasta dumplings made of flour and potato) to the people after the price of flour became exorbitant following the plague. Taking place in late January or early February, it features extravagant costumes, loud bands, lively parades and some unusually exuberant behaviour from the locals – said to be caused by the wind.

February

Carnevale Ambrosiano
Milan's Carnevale – the world's longest carnival – ends with a parade to piazza del Duomo. It's a great one for the kids, who roam the streets in fancy dress causing old-fashioned mischief (comune.milano.it).

Milano Moda Donna Autunno/Inverno
Held in late February, this is *the* fashion show of
the year, with the best designers draping their
autumn/winter collections over the skeletal frames
of girls just out of high school. Aperitivo bars and
restaurants are buzzing and celebrity spotting
becomes an addictive activity.

March

Milano Internazionale Antiquariato
This renowned international antique show, held
over four days at the Fiera di Milano, is one of the
highlights of the arts and antiquities calendar
worldwide. Held late March-early April, biennially
on even-numbered years.

April

Liberation Day (25th)
Celebrated all over Italy, it marks the liberation
of Italy by allied troops in the Second World War.

Above: The Navigli's antique market.
Opposite page: Busy Verona during the summer opera season.

Salone Internazionale del Mobile
Europe's massive furniture fair has a day for the
public (Sunday) where you can salivate over the
latest home furnishings and design. Milan has a
tangible buzz during the fair.

June

Festa del Naviglio
Milan's Navigli area comes to life for summer with
ten days of concerts and performances, cooking,
arts and the renowned antique market (also held
on the last Sunday of every month).

May

Le Piazze dei Sapori
Verona's 'Squares of Flavours' features several
days of celebrating local produce and wines,
with plenty of tastings, music and dance.

Festival Mix
The International Gay & Lesbian Milan Film Festival
(cinemagaylesbico.it) is an engaging week-long
celebration of gay and lesbian film and queer
culture – brush up on your Italian though, as
most of the films don't have English subtitles.

Mille Miglia
While it's no longer a serious car race as such,
Brescia's historic road race offers an opportunity to
witness the sights and sounds of some wonderful
Italian classic cars such as Alfa Romeos and Ferraris.

Garda Jazz Festival
This summer jazz festival, running over a couple of
weeks in Riva del Garda, features some great jazz by
Italy's often-underrated jazz players (gardajazz.com).

About the region

Milano d'Estate
Concerts in Parco Sempione and Castello Sforzesco over the summer months go some way in making up for Milan's muggy heat for those unable to escape to the beach.

Verona Opera Festival
The atmospheric Arena di Verona is home to this very popular outdoor summer opera series that sees the town filled to bursting point. Expect opera classics such as *Aïda*, massive sets, myriad extras, and plenty of noisy tour groups (arena.it).

Festa di San Giovanni (24th)
Fireworks are the highlight of a day of celebrations on Isola Comacina for St John.

July

Sognando Shakespeare
A celebration of the Bard and his infatuation with the city of fair Verona. During July and August, events include dance and jazz performances, and, of course, Shakespeare's plays (some in English).

Notturni in Villa
This series of free concerts in Milan's beautiful city villas feature an eclectic mix of genres, but mainly focuses on jazz and classical music.

Festival Latino Americando
Two months (July-August) of celebrating Latin American culture in Milan, with plenty of food, dancing and music at various venues around the city (latinoamericando.it).

August

Ferragosto (15th)
The Feast of the Assumption is celebrated all over the country with gusto – by doing as little as possible and eating as much as possible. For some it's the start of the summer holiday, for others it's the halfway mark.

Rustico Medioevo
Held in the second week of August, this is a charming medieval dance and folkloric festival at Canale di Tenno, Riva del Garda (rusticomedioevo.com).

A performance during the summer opera season at the Arena di Verona.

Festival Milano
A festival of contemporary music, dance and theatre, with events ongoing through to October.

Italian Formula One Grand Prix
This very popular round of the Formula One circus is beloved by the F1 drivers who enjoy the challenge of the high-speed track and the fanatical Italian Ferrari fans who make this an annual pilgrimage, complete with giant red flags (monzanet.it).

October

Milano International Film Festival
Featuring full-length features and documentaries, short films and retrospectives (milanofilmfestival.it).

Milano Marathon
Starting and ending at the imposing Castello Sforzesco, the flat course makes for fast times on the cobbled streets (milanocitymarathon.it).

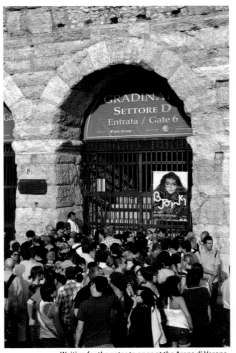

Waiting for the gates to open at the Arena di Verona.

November

Tutti Santi (1st)
All Saints' Day is a public holiday with numerous religious celebrations. Italians traditionally enjoy a harvest feast, give presents to their children, and attend a special mass.

December

Festa di Sant'Ambrogio (7th)
Throughout the region this is the public holiday to celebrate Milan's patron saint, St Ambrose. Piazza Sant'Ambrogio and the surrounding streets are the focus of attention, with stalls selling everything from chestnuts to cured meats.

La Scala Season Opening (7th)
Coinciding with the Feast of Sant'Ambrogio is the opening of Milan's famous opera season. Perhaps the biggest night on the Milanese social calendar, tickets to the opening opera are hard to come by.

Stalls of Santa Lucia (13th)
For several days before and after the Feast of Santa Lucia, Verona's piazza Bra is home to a lively Christmas fair with toys, gastronomic delights, and weird and wonderful bits and pieces.

Mezzanotte Di Fiaba (31st)
A spectacular fireworks display over the lake at Riva del Garda brings in the New Year.

Sleeping

The region offers a wide variety of accommodation, from stylish designer digs in Milan catering for the fashionistas, to romantic grand hotels on the lakes. While accommodation for budget travellers is patchy, mid-range and luxury travellers will have no problem finding accommodation that suits them in the destinations covered in this book.

Where to sleep

The best way to decide what kind of hotel to stay in is to align it with the theme of your visit. If you're in Milan for shopping in the Quadrilatero D'Oro (the shopping district), stick close to this exclusive quarter and stay in a place where your designer shopping bags will be lifted from your weary arms and magically appear in your room before you can order a glass of champagne. If you're design-focused, deconstruct one of the glossy, minimalist hotels. If you're after romance, nothing beats a grand old hotel or whimsical villa on a lake's shore or a charismatic *albergo* in the centre of an historic town such as Brescia or Mantua. If it's a family holiday, then you might want to consider renting an apartment or camping in one of the lakeside holiday parks.

Deciding on the location of a hotel is easy. In Milan, the centre or the shopping district is perfect to get a feel for the city sights and shopping, the Brera area is great if you're an art and antiques lover, and the Navigli is ideal if you want a more down-to-

Above: Park Hyatt Milano.
Opposite page: Near Lake Orta, Villa Crespi has grand rooms.

Tip...

Book accommodation for the Italian Lakes well in
advance. Milan has constant conventions and fairs
that not only fill all accommodation, but also launch
room prices into the stratosphere. At certain times
throughout the year, the region's towns brim for a
few days at a time, such as during Verona's summer
opera season. The lakes are jam-packed in summer –
seasoned visitors book months in advance.

earth feel and a great choice of local restaurants and bars – especially in summer. On the lakes, anything with a view is better than none, and the grander the hotel the better. And while there are certainly some swish hotels lining the lakes' shores, grand doesn't have to mean luxe. For those travelling with children or on a budget there are some wonderful old piles that fall into the two- or three-star category that ooze charm. In cities such as Bergamo and Verona, being right in the heart of the old towns – especially in atmospheric and historic lodgings – is the best way to make the most of your stay. There are also great value apartments in the centres of cities and towns for those self-catering, and cosy B&Bs and tranquil *agriturismo* options smattered throughout the region.

What to expect

On paper, Italy has a star classification system akin to other European countries, but the reality on the ground doesn't quite reflect the ratings. Amenities that have been listed often don't exist or don't work and sometimes you'll find staff more interested in looking good than looking after their guests. The hotels are graded from one- to five-star deluxe, but a well-run, well-positioned three-star can often offer a better experience than a five-star filled with self-absorbed staff or a position on the outskirts of the town centre.

In one- and two-star hotels (sometimes called *pensioni*) you often have to share bathrooms, but some of these properties can be full of atmosphere, with genial hosts. The three-star options almost always have an en suite bathroom and air conditioning – strongly recommended for the sticky summers. Many four-star options in Milan generally cater for business travellers and are quite anodyne, but there are a few boutique properties in this range that have unique decor, if not conscientious staff. The five-star hotels in Milan are generally excellent, with attentive service, flat-screen TVs and champagne waiting to be popped in a well-stocked minibar, while many of the five-stars on the lakes

offer faded charm, old-school glamour, and glorious views. If a place is described as an *albergo*, these days it simply means a hotel and it can have any star rating. Similarly with a *locanda*, which traditionally referred to an inn or a restaurant with rooms. A bed and breakfast can simply be a room in someone's residence (for better or worse) or can mean a charming stay in a lovely cottage or cabin where only breakfast is served.

While *agriturismi* – that is, rural accommodation or rooms on a working farm or vineyard – are hugely popular in regions such as Tuscany and Umbria, the trend has been slower to take off in the lakes area where the grand hotel experience dominates. If you're determined to seek out such experiences in this part of Italy, do your research carefully as many properties are based on a great idea but the experiences are poorly executed; see loveitaly.co.uk and agriturist.it for some of the best examples.

Above: Hotel Terminus is an elegant property in Como.
Opposite page: Hotel Piazza Vecchia is in the atmospheric Bergamo Alta.

generally a fairly simple affair of good coffee and tiny pastries – Italians are not big on hot breakfasts and it's unusual to find elaborate buffets anywhere but in the very best luxury hotels.

Whether or not a hotel has parking is worth considering if your trip involves driving around the lakes. Don't even think about hiring a car for Milan, as parking is a challenge. If you're staying in Milan before heading off to the lakes, as many travellers do, then pick the car up on your way out and drop it off on your way back. Outside of Milan, hotels that have parking (especially if they are located in the centre of the city or town) are advantageous, as many towns don't have street parking in the historic centre. Always check parking arrangements and pricing with the hotel when you book your accommodation, as the hotel garages can often be tricky to locate and some close early and on Sundays.

Something else to consider if you need to work or simply stay in touch with family and friends while you travel is the availability of the internet in hotels. Regardless of whether it's advertised or not, in-room Wi-Fi can be expected to be delivered about as often as it snows in Milan (hint: not often); broadband is the better option if available. Unfortunately, the hotels that deliver the most reliable internet are generally the bland four- and five-star business hotels, for obvious reasons. Most other hotels rely on outside providers to deploy and run the internet services in the hotel and the lack of a connection is often treated with a shrug that would do the French proud. For those who need to do business while travelling, your best bets are the upmarket chains that will have a functioning business centre and reasonably good internet access. Elsewhere access is sporadic at the best of times, and expensive.

If you are intending to spend more than a week in one place and you're not planning on bugging the concierge every 15 minutes for directions or restaurant bookings, seriously consider renting an apartment for your stay. Not only will you save money if you're looking at anything from mid-range or above, but shopping for groceries at the local markets and living like a local in a city that you want to get to know better can be just as enjoyable and rewarding as seeing a major attraction you've always dreamt of visiting.

What you get for your euros

While some of the hotels mentioned in this book have great restaurants (and a couple are worth staying at for the cuisine alone), you'll find that breakfasts in all but the five-star hotels are

Eating & drinking

Dining and imbibing in the Italian Lakes is an absolute joy, with interesting local dishes dotted throughout the region, and wonderfully distinctive wines. Just like the rest of Italy, you don't have to haunt haute cuisine restaurants to have a satisfying meal – often the simplest dish at the most basic *enoteca* (wine bar) can be something special. The wines of northern Italy stand tall in any company with the big standout red, Barolo, appearing on most wine lists in the region.

Local specialities

Lombardy – and also Piedmont and the Veneto, which the lakes area falls within – have an interesting gastronomic pedigree, with mountains, valleys and sweeping plains offering diverse terrain for cultivation, providing a wide range of recipes. Dishes tend to be heavier in the north, with more use of butter and cream rather than just olive oil. One of the dishes that defines the region is the Milanese dish *ossobuco* (slow-braised veal shanks) served with *risotto alla milanese* (rice with saffron threads). While breaded veal cutlets (*cotoletta alla milanese*) might appear to be influenced by the Austrians, with its apparent connection to *wiener schnitzel*, but was in fact created much earlier.

Above: An absolute must of foodies is Milanese gastro deli Peck.
Opposite page: L'Antica Riva, Como, serves up fresh seafood.

della Valpolicella (made with air-dried grapes). The Piedmont region is home to Italy's superstar wine, Barolo, and the wineries of the region are more 'boutique' affairs. Barolo is a big red made from the local Nebbiolo grapes and it's one that is best left to age for a few years, and it can drink well for twenty years and beyond. Barbaresco is the less famous, and more affordable, brother of Barolo and drinks well at an earlier age.

Given that Milan is the largest centre, it's not surprising that regional specialities from all over the north (not just Milan and the lakes) appear widely on menus. You'll typically see dishes from Genoa, which gives us *pesto alla genovese* (classic basil pesto), Modena, which exports its wonderful *aceto balsamico* (balsamic vinegar), Parma, which kindly lets the rest of us try its brilliant hams and Parmigiano-Reggiano cheese, and arguably most famous of all, Bologna, which gives us its *ragù alla bolognese* (Bolognese sauce). Specialities also include *bresaola di Valtellina* (air-cured, thinly sliced beef from the Valtellina area near Switzerland) and *polenta*, a cornmeal peasant staple that has found favour again in the best restaurants of the world.

Local wines

Just as in France, the region from which wine comes provides one of the most important characteristics of the tipple, and the Italians have a wine categorisation system comparable to that of France. In the Lombardy region, much of the production goes to making table wines; however, the sparkling wines of Franciacorta are arguably the best in Italy, along with the Nebbiolo grape's reds, grown on the steep slopes of the Valtellina region.

The Veneto region produces the most wine in Italy and is notable for Soave (a popular dry white), Bardolino (a red) and Valpolicella (a light, easy-going red) wines, as well as Prosecco, sparkling wine. An interesting wine from here is Amarone

Types of eateries

The demarcation of eateries in Italy is quite complex, but as you'll see from the recommendations in this book, an *enoteca* (wine bar) can offer just as satisfying a meal as a restaurant. A *ristorante* is an establishment with linen tablecloths, formal waiters, and no prices on the menus for the women, and hefty prices on the menu for the gentlemen. A *trattoria* is more casual than a *ristorante* and usually has a seasonal menu

Tip…

While a cover charge (*coperto*) may be included on the bill (*il conto*), this is not a tip calculated into the bill. It is supposedly for water and bread included with the meal. If you see *servizio* on the bill, this is for service and a tip isn't necessary. If you wish to leave a tip for good service, a couple of euros or up to 10% of the bill is a good amount.

Time to eat?

Colazione (breakfast) for the locals is generally a light meal of a pastry such as a *cornetto* (croissant) and a short coffee, eaten standing at a bar or on the run. It's generally taken between 0700 and 1030. *Pranzo* (lunch) generally runs from noon until 1400-1500 and can often be the biggest meal of the day. *Cena* (dinner) runs from 1930 until 2230 and is often preceded by aperitivo, which usually involves snacks to tide people over until a late dinner date. Cafés and bars usually have some panini if you're caught in between meals.

Five of the best

Regional specialities

❶ *Ossobuco with risotto alla milanese*
Veal shanks and slow-cooked rice.

❷ *Cotoletta alla milanese* Breaded veal cutlets.

❸ *Tortelli di zucca* Mantua's pumpkin and crushed
biscuit-filled pasta.

❹ *Pastissada de caval* Verona's horse meat stew,
often served with polenta.

❺ *Panettone* Milan's own Christmas 'cake'.

with local specialities and often pan-Italian favourites. Both are generally open for lunch (approx 1200-1500) and dinner (1900-2200), closing in between. An *osteria* is a small eatery with a short, focused menu and wine list, generally featuring local specialities and is usually only open in the evening. An *enoteca* is a wine bar that will have a few dishes or just great local cheeses and cold meats served on platters – an excellent substitute for dinner if you're still struggling after a big lunch. A café serves coffee, drinks and sandwiches, as does the more pared-back, unpretentious bar, and these usually stay open all day and night, opening early and closing late. A pizzeria, of course, sells pizza, but a guide to the good ones will be the words *forno a legna* (wood-fired oven) somewhere near its name.

Shopping & markets

Stalls laden with freshly picked fruit and vegetables, specialist vans selling cheeses and meats, cases of table wines sold off the back of a truck … market shopping in the Italian Lakes is truly first class. With fruit and vegetables, if it's in season it's in stock, if it's not then you're out of luck. Salamies, most cheeses, and breads are never out of season. The same goes for wonderful wines and preserves – all perfect for a picnic (see box opposite). When shopping for food, keep in mind that some items may not be allowed through customs when you return home, so enjoy it while you're here!

Vegetarian options

Vegetarians are in luck anywhere in Italy, with plenty of wonderful pasta dishes and pizzas on menus that do not contain meat, as well as brilliant grilled vegetables. Salads, polenta, beans and risottos are excellent without *carne* (meat) as well.

Below: Aperitivo at El Brellin, Milan. Opposite page: Michelin-starred 'natural haute cuisine' restaurant of Pietro Leemann.

The €10 picnic

1 x *pane*	€1
50 g Bresaola (salted air-dried beef from Valtellina)	€1.30
50 g *Salame di Varzi* (pork salami from Pavia)	€1.20
100 g Gorgonzola (blue veined cheese from Gorgonzola, village near Milan)	€2.10
100 g Taleggio (typical cow's milk cheese of Lombardy)	€1.90
2 x *pere Mantovane* (pears from Mantua)	€0.80
1 bottle San Pellegrino (mineral water from Lombardy)	€1.70
Total	**€10**

Menu reader

General

affumicato smoked
al sangue rare
alla griglia grilled
antipasto starter/appetizer
aperto/chiuso open/closed
arrosto roasted
ben cotto well done
bollito boiled
caldo hot
cameriere/cameriera waiter/waitress
conto the bill
contorni side dishes
coperto cover charge
coppa/cono cone/cup
cotto cooked
cottura media medium
crudo raw
degustazione tasting menu of several dishes
dolce dessert
fatto in casa homemade
forno a legna wood-fired oven
freddo cold
fresco fresh, uncooked
fritto fried
menu turistico tourist menu
piccante spicy
prenotazione reservation
primo first course
ripieno a stuffing or something that is stuffed
secondo second course

Drinks (bevande)

acqua naturale/gassata/frizzante still/sparkling water
aperitivo drinks taken before dinner, often served with free snacks
bicchiere glass
birra beer
birra alla spina draught beer
bottiglia bottle
caffè coffee (ie espresso)
caffè macchiato/ristretto espresso with a dash of foamed milk/strong
spremuta freshly squeezed fruit juice
succo juice
vino bianco/rosato/rosso white/rosé/red wine

Fruit (frutta) & vegetables (legumi)

agrumi citrus fruits
amarena sour cherry
arancia orange
carciofio globe artichoke
castagne chestnuts
cipolle onions
cocomero water melon
contorno side dish, usually grilled vegetables or oven-baked potatoes
fichi figs
finocchio fennel
fragole strawberries
friarelli strong flavoured leaves of the broccoli family eaten with sausages
frutta fresca fresh fruit
funghi mushroom
lamponi raspberries
melagrana pomegranate
melanzana eggplant/aubergine
melone light coloured melon
mele apples
noci/nocciole walnuts/hazelnuts
patate potatoes, which can be *arroste* (roast), *fritte* (fried), *novelle* (new), *pure' di* (mashed)
patatine fritte chips
peperoncino chilli pepper
peperone peppers
pesche peaches
piselli peas
pomodoro tomato
rucola rocket
scarola leafy green vegetable used in torta di scarola pie.
sciurilli or *fiorilli* tempura courgette flowers
spinaci spinach
verdure vegetables
zucca pumpkin

Meat (carne)

affettati misti mixed cured meat
agnello lamb
bistecca beef steak
bresaola thinly-sliced, air-cured beef from Valtellina
carpaccio finely sliced raw meat (usually beef)
cinghiale boar
coda alla vaccinara oxtail
coniglio rabbit
involtini thinly sliced meat, rolled and stuffed
manzo beef

pollo chicken
polpette meatballs
polpettone meat loaf
porchetta roasted whole suckling pig
prosciutto ham – *cotto* cooked, *crudo* cured
salsicce pork sausage
salumi cured meats, usually served mixed (*salumi misto*) on a wooden platter
speck a type of cured, smoked ham
spiedini meat pieces grilled on a skewer
stufato meat stew
trippa tripe
vitello veal

Fish (*pesce*) & seafood (*frutti di mare*)
acciughe anchovies
aragosta lobster
baccalà salt cod
bottarga mullet-roe
branzino sea bass
calamari squid
cozze mussels
frittura di mare/frittura di paranza small fish, squid and shellfish lightly covered with flour and fried
frutti di mare seafood
gamberi shrimps/prawns
grigliata mista di pesce mixed grilled fish
orata gilt-head/sea bream
ostriche oysters
pesce spada swordfish
polpo octopus
sarde, sardine sardines
seppia cuttlefish
sogliola sole
spigola bass
stoccafisso stockfish
tonno tuna
triglia red mullet
trota trout
vongole clams

Dessert (*dolce*)
cornetto sweet croissant
crema custard
dolce dessert
gelato ice cream
granita flavoured crushed ice
macedonia (di frutta) fruit cocktail dessert with white wine
panettone type of fruit bread eaten at Christmas

semifreddo a partially frozen dessert
sorbetto sorbet
tiramisù rich 'pick-me-up' dessert
torta cake
zabaglione whipped egg yolks flavoured with Marsala wine
zuppa inglese English-style trifle

Other
aceto balsamico balsamic vinegar, usually from Modena
arborio type of rice used to make risotto
burro butter
calzone pizza dough rolled with the chef's choice of filling and then baked
casatiello lard bread
fagioli white beans
formaggi misti mixed cheese plate
formaggio cheese
frittata omelette
insalata salad
insalata Caprese salad of tomatoes, mozzarella and basil
latte milk
lenticchie lentils
mandorla almond
miele honey
olio oil
polenta cornmeal
pane bread
pane-integrale brown bread
pinoli pine nuts
provola cheese, sometimes with a smoky flavour
ragù a meaty sauce or ragout
riso rice
salsa sauce
sugo sauce or gravy
zuppa soup

Entertainment

Despite the hard-working reputation of the Milanese and other Italians in the northern regions, the locals love to socialize and everything from aperitivo hour to the opera is treated as a team event. Music, from classical to jazz to contemporary pop, is treated with the same respect, while any festival without live music is not a festival at all. Clubbing is elevated to an art form and bar-hopping is executed with military precision long into the night. When they actually do take time off in the north, they well and truly make the most of it!

Bars & clubs

While the Navigli area of Milan (see page 130) is the centre of the action, the aperitivo scene at bars, such as the one at the Sheraton Diana Majestic (see page 122), draws a stylish fashion crowd. The club scene is at its best in winter when places like the exclusive Hollywood and the more democratic Alcatraz attract an eclectic crowd until the early hours. While there are buzzing bars and clubs in towns such as Como, Verona and Bergamo, none have a scene to match Milan's.

Children

Child-friendly Italy is a great place for families, but Milan's relative lack of green spaces presents some planning challenges for parents with restless children. **Museo Nazionale della Scienza e della Tecnica Leonardo da Vinci,** which boasts life-size trains they can climb all over, and the **Museo Civico di Storia Naturale** with its model dinosaurs will keep the kids entertained – as will **Castello Sforzesco** (see page 96). On the lakes during summer, water-based activities are ideal for kids in the calm waters, as is a visit to any gelateria when parents need a break.

Cinema

Despite long-standing ties between Milan and the cinema, unless you speak Italian, Milan's cinema scene won't be of much interest to you. While the city screens plenty of first-run movies, most are dubbed into Italian and Italians generally don't have English subtitles. While this rules out much of Milan's cinemas for entertainment, the Italian DVD collections in multimedia stores such as FNAC and Messaggerie Musicali (see page 135) make excellent souvenirs if you like arthouse cinema.

Festivals and events

There are plenty of festivals and events that slip under the radar in Milan, due to the prevalence of design and fashion inked into the calendar. The International Gay & Lesbian Milan Film Festival (cinemagaylesbico.it) held in June draws the crowds. In July-August, the Milan Jazz Festival

The Navigli is the centre of aperitivo action.

Museo Teatrale alla Scala.

(milanojazzinfestival.it) attracts the best local and international players. During the summer months there are all kinds of small festivals and events around the lakes. Visit the tourist offices when you are in town for times and locations, and see page 52 for a pick of the best.

Gay & lesbian

Gay and lesbian Milan has a notoriously unpredictable bar and club scene. Many venues are straight six nights of the week and have one great gay-friendly night on the other, but the nights and the clubs change often. The best thing to do when you get to town is to contact Arcigay di Milano (arcigaymilano.org) which can distribute membership cards to most gay venues. Despite the fickle nature, Afterline (see page 133) is a good choice for men, while Sottomarino Giallo (see page 133) is a dependable choice for women.

Music

Italians have very eclectic taste when it comes to contemporary music. Rock, pop (both good and cheesy), jazz, hip-hop, and world music all have strong followings. Local acts that are popular in rock and pop tend to be quite generic, but international touring acts nearly always have

Milan on the tour schedule playing in places such as Alcatraz (see page 133) or Rolling Stone (see page 133), while in Verona, large acts take over the Arena di Verona (see page 243) in summer. Jazz thrives in Milan, with the most reliable venue being a branch of the Blue Note (see page 133) franchise.

Opera & classical

Milan has a box-seat in the history of opera thanks to the renowned opera house **Teatro alla Scala** (see page 90), celebrated composer Giuseppe Verdi who premiered works there, and the legendary performer Maria Callas whose artistic legacy is tied to La Scala. The exquisitely restored La Scala is a must-do for anyone with an interest in music. There is also a symphony season at La Scala as well as many classical performances around the city. Maria Callas also performed at the breathtaking outdoor Arena di Verona and Verona's summer operas are sell-outs – some would say in more ways than one.

Shopping

Whether you're a fashionista heading to Milan to shop in the fashion district or a foodie making the pilgrimage to gastro deli Peck (see page 137), Milan has something for everyone and more than lives up to its reputation as a global shopping capital. Lombardy is Italy's economic powerhouse and its affluent residents boast high disposable incomes. Every city and town, from the lakes to the hills, seems to have streets crammed with equally enticing shops – from Como with its elegant stores displaying the fine silk products the city is famous for, to Bellagio with charming shops lining its cobblestone lanes selling local crafts, such as carved wooden objects.

Italians prefer to shop at small specialist stores and lively markets rather than shopping malls, supermarkets and department stores. If you're keen to do as the locals do, in most towns you can reliably start browsing on the main square, which is where most shopping streets converge. Make sure you take time to explore the pedestrian lanes and tiny side streets where you'll find the most fascinating shops.

Most cities and towns hold weekly and monthly markets, where you can buy everything from fresh local produce (ideal for filling the picnic hamper) to vintage clothes, arts and crafts, and antiques and bric-a-brac (all of which make original souvenirs). Check market days with the local tourist offices as schedules can change depending on the season.

If you can't resist a good department store, you'll be pleased to know that most cities and big towns are home to a branch of La Rinascente, Italy's largest chain of very elegant department stores, and Coin, a more down-to-earth and budget-conscious franchise. The service may not be nearly as personal, and the staff not as attentive or knowledgeable as they can be in the smaller specialist stores, but sales staff are generally professional and helpful. The branches in Milan are naturally the best stocked and Milan's La

Above: Via Montenapoleone, a street in the fashionable Quadrilatero d'Oro. Opposite page: Milan is great for window-shopping.

Rinascente likes to boast that Giorgio Armani himself dressed their windows when he was starting out in the 1960s.

Shopping malls are rarely found in the historic centres, and are much more likely to be situated in the outer suburbs. While you'll find small supermarkets in the centre, the outskirts are where you'll generally locate large European supermarket chains such as Carrefour. These can be handy if you're driving and staying in self-catering accommodation and want to stock up on groceries. They're also a great source for memory cards and batteries for your digital cameras and the lower prices make the trip worth it.

Fashion

As Milan is the world's fashion capital, it makes sense to buy a chic piece from one of the famous Italian fashion houses in the glamorous Quadrilatero d'Oro (Golden Quarter), also known as the Quadrilatero della Moda (Fashion Quarter). Look out for stylish Milanese labels such as Missoni, Moschino and

Prada, as well as Valentino (originally from a town just north of Milan) and Gianfranco Ferre (Genoan-born but lives on Lake Maggiore), along with Italian fashion-heavyweights Armani, Dolce and Gabbana, Gucci, Versace, Trussardi, Pucci, and Mariella Burani. If you only visit one designer boutique, make it Georgio Armani (see page 105), a mini department store selling fashionable home interiors, glossy books, heavenly scents and decadent chocolates, as well as Armani's impeccable clothes.

The prices of the most exclusive Italian labels are high, as you'd expect, but they are lower in Italy than they are elsewhere. Bargains can be found during the end-of-season sales and at factory outlets, most of which are found between Milan and the lakes (Milan Tours and Activities for shopping tours, see page 139). Many of the most exclusive designer stores have branches in other cities in the region, such as Verona and Como, while towns like Brescia and Cremona will have independent boutiques which stock a handful of labels they'll often list in elegant print on their shop front.

Italy also gave birth to some of the hippest global high street fashion companies around, including Miss Sixty, Diesel, Benetton, Sisley and Replay. You'll find the biggest and best branches in Milan, but there are also outlets in Verona, Como, Brescia, Cremona and Bergamo (in the lower town). The ranges tend to be wider and available for longer in Italy, and the prices are slightly lower.

Hats, gloves & accessories

Milan led the way in the production of bonnets, hat straw, gloves and ribbons in 16th century Europe, which is why the English called Milanese haberdashers 'milliners'. Today, Milan still creates some of the most exquisitely handcrafted hats, gloves, shoes, handbags and belts, so it's a wonderful place to invest in something special. Borsalino (see page 136), established in 1857, remains one of the most respected hat-makers, celebrated for their fedoras and panama hats. Their most elegant (and most crowded!) store is at Milan's Galleria Vittorio Emanuele II, but there is also a shop in Como (see page 190). One of Italy's most renowned glove-makers, Sermoneta (see page 136) also has a store in Milan with an enormous range of fine quality leather and suede gloves in an array of colours. Like the staff at Borsalino, here they take time to ensure your purchase fits properly. Como and Bellagio are the places to shop for silk scarves, shawls and ties, the most famous of which is Pierangelo Masciadri (see page 190) whose Bellagio store displays photos of world leaders, royalty and movie stars who have bought his products.

Design

After fashion, Milan and the lakes are most celebrated for their cutting-edge contemporary furniture, lighting, interior and industrial design. Milan is where you'll find most of the sleek flagship stores belonging to the biggest names in design (see page 135), while most of the manufacturers and factory outlets are located around the lakes area, such as Alessi, which has its headquarters and factory on Lake Orta. Cities and towns such as

Tip...

Non-EU residents should check the Global Refund website (globalrefund.com) to find out if they are eligible to receive a tax refund if taking expensive items out of Italy. The tax can be 20%, 10% or 4%, so it's worth looking for shops which display the 'Tax Free Shopping' logo.

Como, Bergamo and Verona all have a handful of shops selling several brands under one roof. Names to look for include Artemide, B&B Italia, Boffi, Cappellini, Kartell, Matteograssi, Minotti, and Zanotta. While Kartell's Ron Arad-designed *Bookworm Bookshelf* might be a tad tricky to get home on the plane (although you can arrange shipping), a cool motorcycle helmet from Momo or a playful kitchen accessory from Alessi is sure to fit in the carry-on.

Food & wine
While you'll find delicious cheeses and cold cuts, olive oils and wines all over the region, especially in Como and Bergamo, Milan is undoubtedly the area's gastronomic centre, and Peck (see page 137) is the temple at which connoisseurs of fine cuisine worship. While Milan and the other cities and towns of the region, from Brescia to Mantua, all boast wonderful delicatessens, along with mouth-watering fresh food markets, none match the variety and quality of Peck. Whether it's a jar of the finest truffles or simply a decent bottle of pressed olive oil for the picnic basket, Peck will have it. A warning: even the Milanese admit that it's expensive, but it's a fantastic one-stop shop and they also gift-wrap.

Books, music & movies
Italian books, CDs and DVDs make attractive souvenirs; see page 22 for some ideas. Italy's biggest and best media franchises are Messaggerie Musicali and Ricordi Media Stores, both of which you'll find in most cities and towns in the region, with colossal branches in Milan. The larger stores also stock translated foreign literature, travel guidebooks, dictionaries and phrase books, which you'll also find at the Italian Touring Club bookshops.

Tip...
Provided your country's customs authority permits you to take food products home (check your local customs website), some of the region's best souvenirs are those you can eat and vacuum-packed cheeses, sausages and cured meats are cheaper in Italy than outside the country.

Above: Hand-painted wares in Bellagio.
Opposite page: Sermoneta Gloves.

Activities & tours

Dinner on the water at Bellagio.

The hard-working people in the north take leisure just as seriously as they do work. Summer sees them hiking and biking in the mountains, and practising their favourite sports under sail and wind power, while in winter they're busy planning their *settimana bianca* (white week) in the tiny ski resorts nearby, or the iconic ones further north. Join them, or sign up instead for a cultural activity, language course, or guided tour. Many of the region's leisure sports are lake-based and undertaken during the warmer months; however, golf is also a popular pastime, especially on the courses that line lakes Como, Garda and Iseo. Another popular activity is horse-riding with the fresh mountain air and gorgeous lake vistas offering an excellent back-to-nature experience.

Cultural

As the grand hotels, lakeside villas and luxuriant gardens sprawling on the shores attest, the Italian Lakes have been a popular getaway spot for European nobility and Grand Tourists for centuries. Many of the hotels and villas are open to the public and their interiors are filled with antique furnishings and hung with stunning art, while their gardens boast beautiful sculptures, fountains and, in some cases, intriguing oddities (see page 202). Many villas, such as **Villa Serbelloni** (bellagiolakecomo.it) and **Villa Carlotta** (villacarlotta.it), offer guided tours. If you fancy the idea of wandering the gardens with a book of Italian poetry or a copy of *I Promessi Sposi* (see page 24) in hand, you had better sign up for an Italian language course first. A range of language courses are available in Milan with Istituto Dante Alighieri (dantealighieri.org) amongst others offering classic 'Italian for Foreigners' courses, while Inlingua (inlingua.it) has Italian classes in Como.

Cycling

Italians are huge cycling fans and the sport is particularly popular in northern Italy. While you can hire bikes in Milan, you'd better make it a mountain bike with shock absorbers due to the cobbled streets and tram tracks! The lakes make for a more relaxing ride, but you can make it taxing by heading up into the mountains where there are some famously punishing hill climbs. The lakes – which you can circumnavigate – have comparatively little traffic (and local drivers are bicycle aware) and fantastic scenery. It's not uncommon to see lycra-clad lads sipping an espresso in the local cafés after a long ride in the hills. Bikes, tours and self-guided tour routes are all available from local tourist offices.

Food & wine

While Milan and the rest of northern Italy love their food and wine, creating awareness of their wonderful cuisine and wine for foreigners is not high on their list of priorities. If you're expecting Tuscan-style cooking schools aimed at gourmet travellers and expats, to Tuscany you should go! However, during summer in Verona, for instance, there are Wine, Art and Tasting excursions which include tours that combine visits to castles and museums with trips to vineyards and wine-tastings (anteprimaopera.it).

Football

Italy has had a long love affair with soccer – they won the 2006 World Cup – and the northern region of Italy is home to many of the teams competing in *Serie A* (Italy's premiere league and one of the most highly regarded in the world). Two of these teams are supported in Milan – Inter Milan and AC Milan – and both are stellar clubs in *Serie A*. The matches between these two teams are dubbed the *Derby della Madonnina* and the

north of Milan, is home to one of motor sports' most legendary events, the Italian Formula One Grand Prix. This annual race on *La Pista Magica* (the magic track) is for many Italians the highlight of the sporting calendar. In the winter months, the track is often open for general driving where you can take street cars onto the circuit and do a lap (monzanet.it).

Walking

Walking and hiking are extremely popular around the lakes, especially in summer, and almost every town and village tourist office has information on walking trails with maps and itineraries. You can organize a local guide or sign up at a local tourist office for an organized hike, or embark on self-guided walks on sign-posted walking routes using the good maps that are available from tourist offices. All of the lakes have circular walking paths as well as hiking trails and rock climbing in the mountains. It's best to combine the activity with a landmark that you want to visit, such as the Castle of Vezio in Varenna, or the medieval castle ruins at St Marta near Menaggio or the many other castles or churches that are in abundance in the region.

matches between Inter Milan and Juventus (from Turin) are called the *Derby d'Italia*. The premiere place to witness a match is unequivocally Milan's legendary Stadio San Siro – don't miss the opportunity if it's there!

Motor racing

Car lovers tend to gravitate to Modena, the home of sports car manufacturer Ferrari, and Bologna, the address of Ducati motorcycles, but Milan and the lakes are a Mecca for the motor sports fan. One of Europe's oldest motorcycle manufacturers, Moto Guzzi, has its home on Lake Como, and Monza, located just

Water sports & boating

In the warmer months, water sports are very popular on the lakes, as are all forms of boating. Sailing, windsurfing and kitesurfing take place mainly on the northern ends of the lakes where the wind is the most consistent, especially in the early morning and late afternoon. Como and Iseo are popular, but Lake Garda is the best spot to head to because of the excellent facilities and availability of lessons on offer for all types of activities that use a sail. Catamarans and sailboats can be hired (with or without instructors) and motorboats can be hired as well. Those wanting to get a little more hands-on can hire canoes to explore the lake. There are also boat cruises worth taking on every lake.

Well-being

The Italian Lakes are home to a number of thermal spring spas (*terme*) offering an array of therapeutic massages and pampering treatments from hydromassage to shiatsu, aromatherapy to reflexology, and beauty rituals and detoxifying treatments. Spas such as Villa Paradiso (villaparadiso.com) are destinations in themselves, while there are also excellent day spas such as La Dolce Acqua (ladolceacqua.it). Back in Milan both The Chedi Milan (thechedimilan.com) and the Bulgari Hotel (bulgarihotels.com) have notable well-being facilities.

Winter sports

Going away for a *settimana bianca* (white week) in the mountains is a very popular pastime for those living in the region. There are some small ski resorts such as Montecampione (monticolo.it) near Lago d'Iseo and Mottarone (mottaroneski.it), which is the mountain between Lago Maggiore and Lago d'Orta. Visitors, however, are usually better off heading for resorts with higher altitude, more terrain, longer seasons and more snow-sure conditions. The best resort is at Cervinia (cervinia.it), up near Switzerland, where you can ski across the border to the famous ski resort of Zermatt. You can either drive (great if you're exploring the lakes) or catch the train to the resort from Milan.

Top: Sailing near Cannobio.
Above: Nordic walking in the mountains.
Opposite page: Milan and the lakes are a Mecca for petrolheads.

Contents

79 Introduction
80 *Map: Milan Metro*
82 *Map: Milan*
84 Sights
88 *Map: Central Milan*
94 Great days out:
A walk through the *centro storico*
104 Great days out:
Milan fashion walk
118 Great days out: Certosa di Pavia
120 Listings:
120 Sleeping
124 Eating
128 Entertainment
130 Great nights out: The Navigli
135 Shopping
138 Activities & tours

Milan

Style swarms in the streets of Milan.

Introduction

When people talk about Italian style, they're really talking about Milanese style – an effortless sense of chic. And while many think of Milan as simply the engine that drives the Italian economy, they're mistaking the city's industrious nature for a lack of Italian flair, which couldn't be further from the truth. Milan might be short of the romance of Venice or Florence, but for those who have even a fleeting interest in fashion, art, design or food, Milan easily sets the heart aflutter.

The Milanese do everything with gusto, from work to play to weekends away. Shopping in Milan – as you would expect – is remarkable, with everything from couture to cutlery displayed with exquisite care. The cuisine is unrepentantly and distinctly northern Italian, with the city showing the best of the region's produce in restaurants that really have to work hard to earn the respect of the discerning locals who obsess over food as much as fashion. Even aperitivi, pre-dinner drinks, are treated as an important undertaking, just as opera and live music are.

And while Milan may be the home of modern multidisciplinary design, creating everything from furniture to furniture factories, the past is always treated with the respect it deserves, as the daily crowds (including Milanese) to Milan's magnificent Duomo and da Vinci's iconic *The Last Supper* attest. But don't expect the Milanese to boast about this, they're too busy being effortlessly cool.

Galleria Vittorio Emanuele II.

What to see in…

…one day
Saunter through Milan's *centro storico* (see page 94), which takes in the main city sights, including the splendid **Duomo**, **Galleria Vittorio Emanuele II**, **Teatro alla Scala**, and **Castello Sforzesco**. Don't miss *The Last Supper*, for which you'll need to book well ahead, and try to see an opera at **La Scala**.

…a weekend or more
Spend a morning at one of Milan's world-class museums, (**Civici Musei del Castello Sforzesco** or **Pinacoteca di Brera**) and the afternoon browsing the glam boutiques of the **Quadrilatero d'Oro**. In the evening, enjoy a gastronomic meal at one of Milan's many superlative restaurants.
A longer visit will allow you to take in more of the city's dazzling architecture, design stores and squeeze in more shopping. You could visit more of Milan's outstanding museums, galleries and churches, enjoy a picnic in leafy **Parco Sempione**, or spend an evening testing out the best aperitivo spots on the **Naviglio** area.

Essentials

❶ Getting around Milan is a great city to walk around, except at the height of summer; however, there is a good public transport system if you need it. The public transport system is run by **ATM** (Azienda Trasporti Milanesi, T800-808181, atm-mi.it) and you can use the same ticket for the buses and trams that crisscross the city. The underground metro system is also effective, if a little tiresome unless you're going at least a few stops. There is an ATM Info Point in the Duomo underground station where you can pick up free route maps. Multi-day passes are available as well. While motor scooters are the most popular way to get around, it's not advisable unless you're used to big city riding,

while bicycle riding in Milan is difficult with the tram tracks and cobbled streets.

❻ Train stations Stazione Centrale (services all major Italian cities), piazza Duca d'Aosta, T892021, trenitalia.it; **Milano Nord Cardona** (for Lake Como), piazza Luigi Cadorna, T892021, trenitalia.it; **Stazione Porta Garibaldi** (For Malpensa Airport Express & regional towns), piazza Sigmund Freud, T892021, trenitalia.it.

❺ Bus station Stazione Porta Garibaldi (international, long-distance, some regional buses), piazza Sigmund Freud, T02-3391 0794.

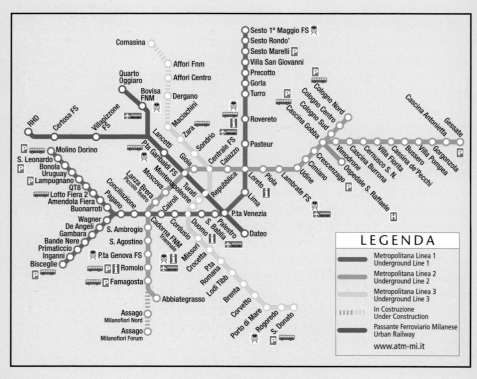

ATMs Cash machines are prevalent, but you can count on: corso Vittorio Emanuele II, via Dante, corso Venezia, via Torino.

Hospital Ospedale Maggiore 'Policlinico', via F Sforza 35, T02-55031.

Pharmacy Carlo Erba, piazza Duomo, T02-8646 4832.

Post office Via Cordusio 4, piazza Cordusio, Mon-Fri 0800-1900, Sat 0830-1200.

Tourist information office Piazza Duomo 19a, T02-7740 4343, visitamilano.it, Mon-Sat 0845-1300 & 1400-1800 Sun 0900-1300 & 1400-1700.

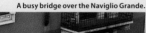

What the locals say

The best way to see Milan is to walk – especially around the old centre. You always discover things here best by foot. I walk everywhere and I always see new and unexpected things.

Pietro Leemann,
Michelin-starred Chef at Joia.

A busy bridge over the Naviglio Grande.

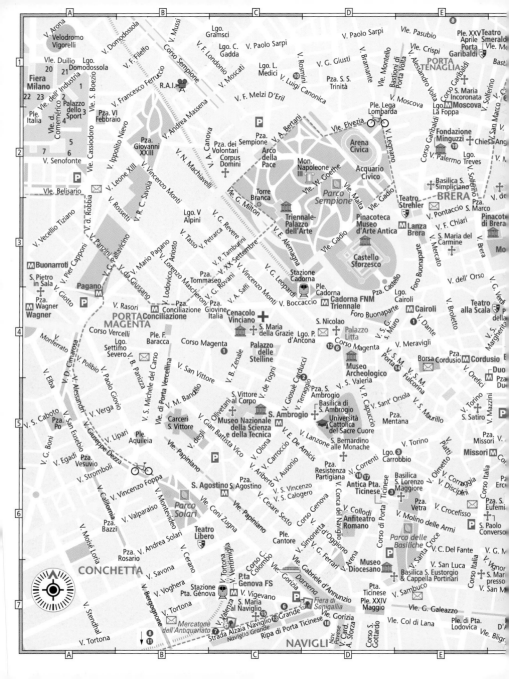

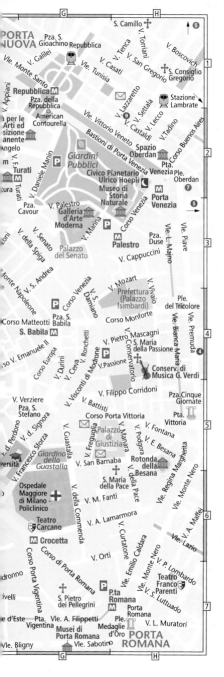

Milan listings

Sleeping

1 Antica Locanda Leonardo *corso Magenta 78* **C4**
2 Antica Locanda Solferino *via Castelfidardo 2* **F1**
3 Ariston *largo Carrobbio 2* **E5**
4 Bulgari *via Privata Fratelli Gabba 7/b* **F3**
5 Chedi, The *via Villapizzone 24* **H1**
6 King *corso Magenta 19* **D4**
7 Sheraton Diana Majestic *viale Piave 42* **H2**
8 Una Hotel Tocq *via A De Tocqueville 7d* **E1**

Eating

1 Artidoro *via Camperio 15* **E4**
2 Boccondivino *via Giosué Carducci 17* **D5**
3 Cantina Della Vetra *Papa Pio IV* **D6**
4 Da Giacomo *via Sottocorno 6* **H4**
5 Da Giannino L'Angolo d'Abruzzo *via Rosolino Pilo 20* **H3**
6 El Brellin *vicolo Dei Lavandai & Alzaia Naviglio Grande 14* **C7**
7 Fabbrica *via Alzaia Naviglio Grande 70* **C7**
8 Gnocco Fritto *via Pasquale Paoli 2* **B7**
9 Joia *via Panfilo Castaldi 18* **H2**
10 L'Altra Pharmacia *via Rosmini 3* **C1**
11 Le Vigne *Ripa di Porta Ticinese 61* **B7**
12 Litta *corso Magenta 25* **D4**
13 Luca & Andrea *Alzaia Naviglio Grande 34* **C7**
14 Marchesi *via S M alla Porta 11a* **E4**
15 Officina 12 *Alzaia Naviglio Grande 12* **C7**
16 Pizzeria Naturale *via Edmondo de Amicis 24* **D6**
17 Pizzeria Traditionale *Ripa di Porta Ticinese 7* **D6**
18 Rinomata Gelateria *Ripa di Porta Ticinese & viale Glorizia* **D7**
19 Solferino 35 *via Solferino 35* **E2**
20 Viel *via Manzoni 3e* **F5**

Duomo & centre

Duomo

Piazza del Duomo 18, T02-463456, duomomilano.it.
Metro: Duomo
Map: Central Milan, F5, p88.

Milan's main attraction, the monumental Duomo, is indeed something to marvel – dominating piazza del Duomo, it's one of the world's largest cathedrals. But up close it's clear that size isn't all that matters – the fine marble, intricate carvings and exquisite attention to detail are even more impressive. Built on the site of an ancient temple, and facing the public forum, the Duomo remains to this day the city's social and geographical hub, as well as Milan's spiritual centre.

A basilica dedicated to Milan's patron saint, St Ambrose, once stood on the site of the current Duomo as early as the fifth century, but was

damaged by fire in 1075. It wasn't until 1386 that Gian Galeazzo Visconti commissioned the current late-Gothic building. More than 300 workers had exclusive use of Candoglia marble, and canals were dredged to bring the stone from Lake Maggiore's quarries. Architects, engineers and artisans came and went and the cathedral was only half-complete when Visconti died in 1402 and construction stalled. Work started and stopped for another four centuries until Napoleon Bonaparte, crowned King of Italy in 1805, ordered that the project be finished, hence the Milanese expression *Fabbrica del Duomo* (meaning 'like the building of the Duomo') to describe a job that takes forever to complete.

Start your tour at the front of the handsome Duomo, facing the mottled pinkish-grey marble façade from the piazza's centre. Here you can best admire its symmetry, elegance and ornamentation: from the beautifully-balanced

Duomo essentials

Duomo Daily 0830-1845, free.

Treasury Mon-Fri 0900-1300 & 1400-1600, Sat 0930-1330 & 1400-1700, Sun & holidays 1330-1600, €1, tickets at bookshop.

Rooftop terrace Oct-Mar 0900-1645 (last ticket at 1620), extended hours for sunset viewings available Apr-Sep; €5 by stairs, €8 by lift, €10 family ticket (2 parents and up to 2 children under 14, additional children €5, by stairs); tickets at lift entrance, can also be booked online, booking fee €1.50.

Museum Closed indefinitely for extensive renovations.

Information Daily 0900-1200 & 1300-1800. Group bookings, audio guides, books and information are available from Duomo Info Point, located in the Archbishop's Palace which is to the south of the cathedral (via Arcivescovado 1, T02-7202 3375).

Note A modest dress code applies, which means covered back, chest and shoulders for women and no shorts for anyone. It's easy to forget in summer, so girls should carry a pashmina with them and guys wear travel pants with zip-on/off legs. Wear shoes with grip for the sloped rooftop.

Above: Statues stand atop the many Gothic spires.
Opposite page: Cherubs outside the Duomo.

arched windows and towering rows of spires and pinnacles crowned with curlicues, to the 192 statues and 47 bas-reliefs adorning the 3,500 sq m façade. Do a circuit of the Duomo's exterior to more fully appreciate its size and look closely at the thousands of statues decorating the porticoes and set within niches, each a work of art in itself: note the way that material falls and the folds of baby fat on the cherubs. Facing the cathedral, before you enter, admire the bronze panels on the huge doors; started in the mid-1800s they weren't completed until 1966.

Once inside, allow your eyes to adjust to the dimness before exploring these 12,000 sumptuous sq m. Sit awhile to take it all in: the splendid 15th-century stained-glass windows, the 52 columns, and the immense vaulted ceiling. Stroll around, noting the 14th-century tombs of archbishops Ottone Visconti and Giovanni Visconti, and the grisly sarcophagus of St Bartholomew being flayed alive, three splendid altars by Pellegrino Pellegrini, and a Renaissance marble altar embellished with gold statues. Look high above the apse to the dome and the red light bulb: it apparently points to the spot where a nail from Christ's cross was placed. Don't miss the stairs down to the early-Christian baptistery.

Return outside to the rear of the Duomo and take the stairs or elevator to the 70-m high, 8,000 sq m roof terrace. Make your way around the roof's perimeter, stopping here and there to better appreciate the wonderful web of flying buttresses, the forest of 135 intricately decorated pinnacles, scores of splendidly carved statues, and enchanting towers with delicate embellishments. Here, the Duomo appears in all its splendour, like something out of a fairytale. Take the stairs to the very top of the roof for marvellous views of Milan framed by Moorish-style arches and soaring steeples. Here you're as close as you're going to get to the gold baroque *Madonnina*, sculpted by Guiseppe Bini, which stands atop the soaring central spire. From her giddy height of 108 m, the little Madonna is said to protect the city.

Tip…

Summer sunsets from the Duomo's rooftop are sublime, so save your visit until late afternoon then head upstairs to savour the spectacular views.

Work started and stopped for another four centuries … hence the Milanese expression Fabbrica del Duomo (meaning 'like the building of the cathedral') to describe a job that takes forever.

Galleria Vittorio Emanuele II

Piazza del Duomo.
Metro: Duomo
Map: Central Milan, E9, p88.

Once widely known as 'Milan's drawing room', this colossal covered shopping gallery was named after Vittorio Emanuele II, the first king of united Italy,

and designed by Giuseppe Mengoni. Built between 1864 and 1878, the splendid double arcade design is in a cruciform shape leading off piazza del Duomo and ending at piazza della Scala some 196 m away and travelling 105 m on its east-west axis. It was one of the first buildings in Europe to employ iron and glass as structural elements, with its central octagonal space topped with a glass dome 47 m in height. The four floor mosaics around the octagon at the building's centre represent Europe, Africa, Asia and America. You'll see visitors spinning around on one heel under the dome – they're looking for luck by placing their heel on the testicles of a mosaic bull. Luck did not befriend the buildings designer, however… poor Giuseppe Mengoni died from a fall off the roof before the building was completed.

Tip…

While you're shopping at Galleria Vittorio Emanuele II or simply taking in the atmosphere of piazza del Duomo, a coffee at **Zucca in Galleria** is a must. But don't sit down at the tables inside the Galleria (you could be anywhere). Order an espresso and pay the cashier and drink your coffee standing up at the bar inside, just like the locals.

Palazzo Reale

Piazza del Duomo, T02-4391 1119.
Mon 1430-1930, Tue-Sun 0930-1930,
Thu 0930-2230, free entry
(temporary exhibition fees vary).
Metro: Duomo
Map: Central Milan, E6, p88.

The elegant neoclassical Royal Palace served as the seat of the Milan city council in the 11th century, and as the private residence of the Visconti family from the 12th century. That was until the murder of one of the Viscontis saw the ducal seat moved to the safer address of Castello Sforzesco. The present appearance of the palace is dated to 1778 when it was remodelled as part of a redevelopment of the cathedral square. After extensive restoration in the beginning of this century, the palace is fit for royalty once again, but it essentially serves as a museum and frequently exhibits some highly commended contemporary art, visual design and, occasionally, fashion exhibitions (artpalazzoreale.it).

Left: The ceiling of Galleria Vittorio Emanuele II was a feat of engineering. Opposite page: Francesco Hayez' *The Kiss*.

Pinacoteca Ambrosiana

Piazza Pio XI 2, T02-806921, ambrosiana.it.
Tue-Sun 1000-1730, €8/5.
Metro: Duomo or Cordusio
Map: Central Milan, C6, p88.

One of Milan's best galleries, the Pinacoteca Ambrosiana's building dates back to 1609 when Cardinal Federico Borromeo introduced it as a public library. The Cardinal's interest in art eventually began to seep into the library and eventually, in 1618, he set up an art gallery here, starting with his own collection of 172 pieces including Titian's *Adoration of the Magi* and Caravaggio's *Canestra di Frutta* (Basket of Fruit) which are both on display. Today there are over 35,000 manuscripts, over 700,000 printed works, some of Leonardo da Vinci's manuscripts, and some excellent paintings in the collection. Notable in the Renaissance collection is Leonardo da Vinci's *Musico* (Musician), while other outstanding painters represented are Botticelli (with the wonderful *Madonna del Padiglione*), Tiepolo and Raphael. There are plenty of curios in the biblioteca but the most interesting are not available for the public to see, including Leonardo da Vinci's twelve-volume, bound set of drawings and writings, *Codex Atlanticus*.

Casa del Manzoni

Via Morone 1, T02-8646 0403, casadelmanzoni.mi.it.
Tue-Fri 0900-1200 & 1400-1600, free.
Metro: Montenapoleone
Map: Central Milan, F3, p88.

One of the most stunning things about the home of the great Milanese writer Alessandro Manzoni (1785-1873) is just how perfectly preserved the house is. Manzoni, whose most famous work – *I Promessi Sposi* (The Betrothed) – is an Italian language classic, lived here from 1814 until his death in 1873. The study where he worked features a wonderful painted ceiling.

Five of the best

Works of art in Milan

❶ Leonardo da Vinci's *The Last Supper*: one of the world's most iconic paintings hardly needs an introduction, at Cenacolo Vinciano (see page 102).

❷ Caravaggio's *Canestra di Frutta* (Basket of Fruit): regarded as Italy's first still life subject, at Pinacoteca Ambrosiana (see page 87).

❸ Botticelli's *Madonna del Padiglione*: an outstanding painting by this Italian Renaissance master, also at Pinacoteca Ambrosiana (see page 87).

❹ Michelangelo's *Rondanini Pietà*: this unfinished work (the sculptor was working on it only 100 days before he died) still manages to be one of his most compelling and most personal works, at Pinacoteca, Castello Sforzesco (see page 98).

❺ Francesco Hayez' *The Kiss*: this painter's finest work is a lovely example of Italian Romanticism, at Pinacoteca di Brera (see page 107).

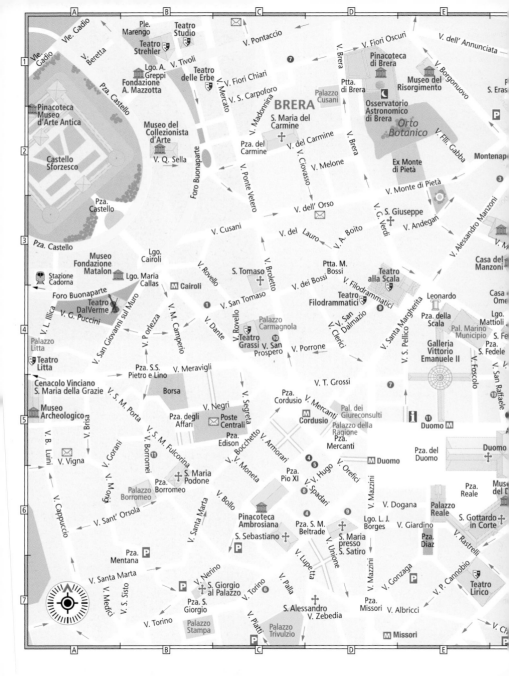

Central Milan listings

Sleeping

1 Alle Meraviglie *via San Tomaso 8* B4
2 Four Seasons Hotel *via Gesù 81* G3
3 Grand Hotel et de Milan *via Alessandro Manzoni 29* F2
4 Gritti *piazza Santa Maria Beltrade 4* D6
5 Manzoni *via Santo Spirito 20* G2
6 Milano Duomo *via Torino 46* C7
7 Park Hyatt Milano *via Tommaso Grossi 1* D5
8 Spadari al Duomo *via Spadari 11* C6
9 Speronari *via Speronari 4* D6
10 Straf Hotel *via San Raffaele 3* F5
11 Vecchia Milano *via Borromei 4* B5

Eating

1 Antico Ristorante Boeucc *piazza Belgioioso 2* F3
2 Bistrot Duomo *via San Raffaele 2* F5
3 Cova *via Montenapoleone 8* G3
4 Italian Bar *via Cesare Cantù 3* D5
5 Il Ristorante Cracco *via Victor Hugo 4* D5
6 Il Salumaio di Montenapoleone *via Montenapoleone* G3
7 Nabucco *via Fiori Chiari 10* C1
8 Trattoria Bagutta *via Bagutta 14-16* G3
9 Trussardi alla Scala & Caffè Trussardi *piazza della Scala 5* D4
10 Victoria Caffè *via Clerici 1* C4
11 Zucca in Galleria *Galleria Vittorio Emanuele II 21* E5

Teatro alla Scala

Piazza della Scala, T02-88791, teatroallascala.org.
Metro: Duomo
Map: Central Milan, D3, p88.

La Scala is one of the most famous opera houses in the world, both for the beauty of the theatre itself and for the history of famous (and infamous) performances and opera debuts – with this elegant theatre the big dramas are not always reserved for the stage! It remains one of the best venues in the world to witness opera and the season-opener is one of the most anticipated events in Milan's, if not Europe's, arts and social calendars.

Milan's lavish opera house was inaugurated on 3 August 1778 with Antonio Salieri's opera *L'Europa Riconosciuta*. The name of the theatre came from the church of Santa Maria della Scala which was deconsecrated and demolished to make way for the theatre, now generally just known as 'La Scala'.

While the privileged sat comfortably in their private boxes to enjoy the opera, the main floor of the theatre had no seats (and no orchestra pit) so the less fortunate stood to watch performances.

La Scala tickets

After the major expansions to the theatre, the programme of events runs throughout the year except in Aug, when most of the city takes a break. The spectacular season opening is on 7 Dec.

Information For seating availability and guidelines for purchasing subscriptions and tickets, call **Infotel** (daily 0900-1800, T02-7200 3744).

In advance Make use of Infotel (see above), book via the website for authorized advance sales, or buy from Central Box Office (Galleria del Sagrato, Duomo metro underpass, beneath piazza del Duomo, performance days 1200-1800).

On the day Buy tickets from Central Box office (see above). Or try for one of 140 cheap tickets sold by L'Accordo musical association (one ticket per person present) at Evening Box Office (via Filodrammatici, La Scala) 2 hrs before performances; only sold to people queuing: for opera/ballet get yourself on the list at 1300 (queue at Central Box office), for symphony/choir get on the list at 1700 (queue at Evening Box Office), for 7 Dec Opening (queue at 1800 6 Dec at Evening Box Office). If you don't make the list, try your luck by showing up – and queuing! – for the leftovers.

Aficionados who didn't have the connections to score a box seat stood above the boxes in an area called the *loggione*, and the diehard opera fans who still take pride of place here are called the *loggionisti*.

Over the years, countless celebrated performances and premieres have been held at the theatre – alongside many contentious ones. Puccini's 1904 premiere of *Madama Butterfly* was jeered, but the posthumous premiere of his unfinished *Turandot* was moving, the famed conductor Arturo Toscanini putting down the baton and ending the performance where Puccini's notation of the score ended. Even Giuseppe Verdi, the composer whose name is synonymous with La Scala, had his failed openings here. He was at opening night to witness the failure of *Un Giorno di Regno* (1940) whose run was quickly cancelled before success finally came with *Nabucco* (1842). Even Verdi's greatest works were at the mercy of those performing them – *Aïda*, one of the most popular operas in the world, opened the season in 2006 only to have the tenor Roberto Alagna flee the stage during the second night after being booed by the *loggionisti*. His stand-in had to sing the rest of the act in his jeans.

After having just about survived bombing during the Second World War and various renovations, the opera house moved to a new theatre in 2001 while an extensive – and controversial – renovation began. As well as concern over the sensitivity of the planned work on the main opera house, there was concern over the addition of a 'fly tower' – a structure that enables the storage of multiple sets: one of the problems of the old theatre had always been insufficient storage. Despite the controversy, the renovation of the interior was greeted with relief when the theatre and its new museum reopened in 2004.

Tip...

Get into the spirit of the opera and dress for the occasion – girls should wear a cocktail dress (not a ball gown) and men a suit or at least a smart jacket. Avoid the crush at the bar between acts and head over to **Trussardi alla Scala** (see page 124) for some bubbly.

Museo Teatrale alla Scala

Inside Teatro alla Scala.
Daily 0900-1230 and 1330-1730 (closed public holidays), €5 museum only, €10 guided tour with booklet (organize directly with official guide Francine Gardino garino@fondazionelascala.it).

Located inside the opera house, the fabulous museum, restored and reopened in 2004, offers visitors a marvellous insight into La Scala's melodramatic history. While the first floor exhibitions feature lots of fascinating memorabilia and paraphernalia in display cases spread across several rooms, from exquisite antique musical instruments to old opera programmes and photos, the highlight of the exhibition is upstairs in a dramatically lit room of theatrical costumes, many worn by the legendary Maria Callas. Suitable for aficionados and amateurs alike.

Above: Museo Teatrale alla Scala.
Opposite page: Teatro alla Scala during rehearsals.

Museo Poldi Pezzoli

Via Manzoni 12, T02-796334, museopoldipezzoli.it.
Tue-Sun 1000-1800, €7/5.
Metro: Montenapoleone.
Map: Central Milan, F3, p88.

Art collector Gian Giacomo Poldi Pezzoli was born into an art-loving family and after inheriting the family palace, he began scouring Europe to find elaborate pieces to decorate each room in a different style. On his death, Gian Giacomo, who had no children, stated that he wanted the house and its contents to become a museum, and in 1881 his dying wish was fulfilled. The result is a stunning collection of paintings, tapestries, glass, ceramics, jewellery, clocks, and statues. One of the finest house-museums you'll see anywhere in the world, it's like an antique shop on steroids.

To many art lovers, the key works are the paintings. Gian Giacomo's treasure-trove was never intended to be broadly inclusive, but was meant to be part of a greater collection, helping to illustrate the progress of art in the region, from the Renaissance onwards. Early works in the collection include the painted wooden icon *Madonna dell'Umiltà* by Vitale da Bologna, while the Renaissance period sees plenty of religious paintings. Botticelli is represented by the wonderful Virgin with Child and *The Dead Christ Mourned*. Of the 17th and 18th century artists, Giovanni Battista Tiepolo's *Allegory of Strength and Wisdom* is a highlight. From the 19th century, paintings of interest include a portrait of Gian Giacomo Poldi Pezzoli by Francesco Hayez, and a portrait of Giuseppe Poldi Pezzoli by Giuseppe Molteni.

Murano glass fans will love the room dedicated to antique examples of the craft. Armoury was an

Tip...

If you're a fan of decorative arts, leave plenty of time to see the collection and leave friends or family who aren't fans of decorative arts in a café nearby – the collection is that good!

early collecting favourite of Gian Giacomo Poldi Pezzoli and the results can be seen in the Gallery of Arms. The appropriately named Treasure Chamber is the home of some wonderful jewellery, including ancient Etruscan, Greek and Roman pieces, as well as hoards from the latter centuries of the last millennium. Ancient works are also represented by the archaeological collection, with some beautiful, if not significant, pieces. The collection of timepieces is significant, on the other hand, with some rare sundials, clocks and watches. The extensive porcelain collection also has some priceless pieces, while the sculptures, fabrics and furniture scattered throughout are worth your while inspecting.

Gian Giacomo Poldi Pezzoli (1822-1879)

Gian Giacomo Poldi Pezzoli's father, Giuseppe, had inherited a fortune from his uncle, including the palace where the museum is now housed. His mother's family, the Trivulzios, had one of the most splendid art collections in Milan, so Gian Giacomo was born into a family where art and beauty were heavily prized.

Following his father's death, when Poldi Pezzoli was only 11, his mother Rosina Trivulzio took charge of his education and continued to nurture his interest in the arts. When he turned 24 in 1846, Poldi Pezzoli was granted access to a considerable fortune, along with the palace. Austrian repression in Lombardy, however, forced Gian Giacomo to take voluntary exile in Europe.

In exile, Gian Giacomo was accumulating knowledge about art collecting, and after being repatriated in 1849, started plans to decorate his personal apartment within the family palace. He methodically collected pieces to suit every room while two of the most noted interior designers of the time, Luigi Scrosati (1815-1869) and Giuseppe Bertini (1825-1898), went to work on the decor. By 1870 the apartment had become famous in art circles. Gian Giacomo Poldi Pezzoli died in 1879, at only 57; in a secretly penned will, he expressed a wish for the house and art to become a museum, and in 1881 his wishes were fulfilled with the museum's opening.

Museo Poldi Pezzoli is housed in the family's grand palace.

A walk through the *centro storico*

Milan may be a sprawling metropolis but its historic centre is reasonably compact compared to that of Rome or Venice. It's easily explored in 24 hours, although you could add days to visit Milan's world-class museums, see an opera or shop in the fashion quarter. While there are few signs left of ancient Roman *Mediolanum*, there are some marvellous monuments from the Middle Ages and Renaissance, when Milan flourished under the Visconti and Sforza dynasties, like the Duomo and Castello Sforzesco. The periods of French, Spanish and Austrian rule, the Risorgimento and Italian Unification are evident in much of the centre's architecture. This leisurely saunter takes you on a loop from Milan's central square via most of the city's main sights. Do-able in an hour, you could stretch it out to a full day if visiting museums on the way.

Begin your promenade on **piazza del Duomo**, Milan's main square, home to the magnificent **Duomo** (see page 84) and sumptuous shopping arcade **Galleria Vittorio Emanuele II** (see page 86). A public meeting place since Roman times, the piazza is where Milan gathers to celebrate and where tourists and locals alike meet up with friends. To the south are the grand **Palazzo Arcivescovile** (Archbishop's Palace) and the neoclassical **Palazzo Reale** (see page 86), a museum and venue for contemporary art exhibitions.

Head towards **Galleria Vittorio Emanuele II** (see page 86) to kick-start your walk with a stand-up

espresso at the elegant art deco bar at **Zucca in Galleria** (see page 125) with the locals (only tourists sit down) then wander through the galleria, browsing the beautiful window displays before stopping under the central dome to appreciate the mosaics beneath the glass dome, representing each

of the continents, and the floor mosaics of the zodiac. Stand in line to stand on Taurus's testicles for good luck, as local custom demands, and watch people get creative with their approaches!

Leave the Galleria by the opposite exit to get to **piazza della Scala**, where you'll find a statue of Leonardo da Vinci. On your right is **Palazzo Marino**, a fine 16th-century residence that has housed Milan's council since 1860. Generally closed to the public, you might be lucky to see an orchestra performing in the interior courtyard, which is used for official functions. To your left is elegant **Teatro alla Scala** (see page 90) where you can pick up an opera programme and visit the museum to see the lavish collection of theatre costumes, exquisitely crafted musical instruments, and other opera paraphernalia.

Cross the piazza and veer right – the splendid **Chiesa di San Fedele** will be on your right – and take the tiny lane now to your left, via degli Omenoni, to admire the extraordinary edifice of **Casa degli Omenoni**. Built in 1565, its impressive façade is comprised of colossal carvings of *omenoni* (great men).

At the lane's end, turn left onto via Morone at **Palazzo Belgioioso** where a little further along on your left you'll see **Casa del Manzoni** (see page 87), the restored home of Italy's celebrated author Alessandro Manzoni. At via Alessandro Manzoni, head right to visit the sumptuous **Museo Poldi Pezzoli** (see page 92) or cross Manzoni toward Teatro alla Scala, turning right onto via Giuseppe Verdi for the arty neighbourhood of **Brera** and **via Brera**, lined with contemporary art galleries, design stores, and all kinds of interesting little shops.

When you arrive at the baroque palazzo housing **Pinacoteca di Brera** (see page 107), head inside for a look or turn left onto via Fiori Chiari (and some of Milan's most testing cobblestones!) to explore more of the delightful Brera and its antique stores and coffee shops. Halfway down via Fiori Chiari turn left (where you'll come across a tarot card reader and fortune teller or two) for **piazza del Carmine** and the wonderful **Santa Maria del Carmine** church.

Above: Naviglio Grande.
Opposite page: Casa degli Omenoni.

Cross via Mercato, taking another tiny street to busy Foro Bonaparte for the striking **Castello Sforzesco** (see page 96), home to the **Civici Musei** (see page 98) and behind it tranquil **Parco Sempione** (see page 100). Alternatively, turn left to largo Cairoli, then left again on via Dante, a busy commuter corridor and tourist eat street. Once at piazza Cordusio, turn around to admire the Castello views before continuing along this busy pedestrian thoroughfare to the medieval square **piazza Mercanti**, home to the vaulted, red-brick 13th century **Palazzo della Ragione**.

Cross via Mazzini and you're back at piazza del Duomo. If it's late afternoon, amble along via Torino and corso di Porta Ticinese to **Naviglio Grande** for an aperitivo at one of the canalside bars and try the **Navigli Great Night Out** (see page 130).

Around the city

Castello Sforzesco

*Piazza Castello, T02-8846 3651/3700,
milanocastello.it.*
Daily 0700-1800 (winter) & 0700-1900 (summer).
Admission free for castle grounds.
Metro: Cadorna Triennale, Caroli or Lanza.
Map: Milan, D3, p82.

Spend a few days in Milan and the majestic red-brick towers of this stately castle, one of Italy's most striking fortifications, will quickly begin to serve as a helpful landmark. If you find yourself approaching the castle from behind, through leafy Parco Sempione, then linger here, or rest up on the manicured lawns of piazza delle Armi within the castle walls – there's a castle to explore and six superb museums to work your way through! But let's start with the castle…

Like the Duomo, Castello Sforzesco has undergone extensive remodelling and renovations over the centuries. Galeazzo II Visconti initiated construction of the first (considerably smaller) defence fortress here on Milan's medieval walls in 1360. The ruins you see to the left of the Filarete Tower are the Porta Vercellina fortifications. His successor Gian Galeazzo strengthened the fortress, while his heir, Filippo Maria, transformed the castle into his own private residence, adding towers to the corners and establishing a big back yard for himself – Parco Sempione. With Filippo Maria's death in 1447, and no direct descendents, Milan was proclaimed a republic and the castle was demolished, its bricks used to rebuild the city walls.

Francesco Sforza married Filippo Maria's illegitimate daughter, Bianca Maria Visconti, three years later and became Duke of Milan. Sforza had a new castle built on the old fortress' foundations with the Filarete tower and round towers. Next in line, Galeazzo Maria built a luxurious residence within the courtyard, the Corte Ducale, and the adjoining fortress within a fortress, the Rocchetta, with the high Torre di Bona. At the end of the late 15th century, Leonardo da Vinci and architect

Donato Bramante built a bridge over the outer moat and da Vinci painted the frescoes that are in the Sala delle Asse.

Throughout the sporadic French occupations that spanned nearly 300 years, the castle survived various battles and sackings, until the Filarete tower, being used as ammunition storage at the time, was hit by lightning and exploded. Under Spanish rule in 1526 a star-shaped fortification was constructed around the castle; you'll see this on a number of beautiful illustrations in the museum. Milan's Austrian rulers, who used the castle solely as a military base, strengthened the fortifications over the course of the 18th century, until 1796 when Napoleon's troops arrived to do some damage. Sadly, Napoleon demolished the striking star-shaped structure to better accommodate his troops; the Corte Ducale and da Vinci's beautifully painted Sala stabled the horses!

Following the Unification of Italy in 1861, architect Luca Beltrami reconstructed what was left of the bruised and battered old building so it could be given to the city. In 1905 the splendid new Filarete tower was unveiled and a wonderfully restored fortress was presented to the city for the purpose of housing civic museums.

If you're into museums, you could easily spend a day exploring the castle interiors as you stroll through its many fine exhibitions. If you're simply a fan of castles, then approach the fortress from via Dante, taking in the moats, watchtowers and bulwarks before entering under the stunning Filarete tower. Sprawl out on the grass of the piazza delle Armi with a picnic so you can take in the impressive structures, especially the striking Rochetta, then saunter around the perimeter before resting once again in the shade of a tree in Parco Sempione.

Napoleon demolished the striking star-shaped structure to better accommodate his troops … da Vinci's beautifully painted Sala stabled the horses!

Tip...

The castle is splendidly lit –
especially the Filarete tower – so
make an effort to see it at night.
If you're here in winter, visit the
museum in the afternoon, and
you'll see the lights coming on
at sunset. If you're here during
summer when it doesn't get dark
until much later, then plan to
take a stroll along via Dante, the
best place to savour the view.
Very romantic!

Civici Musei del Castello Sforzesco

Castello Sforzesco, piazza Castello, T02-8846 3651/3700, milanocastello.it.
Tue-Sun 0900-1730 (last admission 1700), €3/1.50. Prices for temporary exhibitions vary. Free admission on Fri 1400-1730, Tue-Thu & Sat-Sun 1630-1730.
Metro: Cadorna Triennale, Caroli or Lanza.
Map: Milan, D3, p82.

If exploring the interiors and taking in the architecture of the Castello Sforzesco weren't reason enough to visit these impressive fortifications, inside are half a dozen museums,
some of Milan's best, boasting rich collections of archaeology, art, decorative objects and musical instruments. If you're a fan of these, you might want to allocate a couple of days. If you merely want to get an overall impression and focus on the castle itself, you can probably walk through in an hour or so.

Museo Della Preistoria e Protostoria & Museo Egizio
Perhaps start with the Castello's Archaeological Museum, located beneath the Ducal Courtyard. It actually comprises two museums: the Museum of Prehistory and Protohistory and the Egyptian Museum. The former has displays on the Neolithic Age, Bronze Age and Iron Age, while the latter has an admirable collection of ancient Egyptian artefacts, from exhibits on Egyptian writing in the basement rooms to a fascinating collection of mummies, busts of pharaohs and everyday items in the Visconti rooms.

Museo d'Arte Antica
On the ground floor of the Ducal Apartments, the Museum of Ancient Art is one of the castle's most impressive museums, with a first-rate collection of sculptures, frescoes, mosaics, stone and terracotta objects, from early Christian times to the 11th century. A highlight is the richly-frescoed, wood-panelled Sala delle Asse (room 8), dating to 1498 and decorated by Leonardo da Vinci. Also worth noting is Michelangelo's unfinished final piece *Rondanini Pietà*, and *Funerary Monument of Gaston de Foix* by Agostino Busti (better known as *Il Bambaja*), both in the Sala degli Scarlioni (room 15).

Upon entering the Sala della Cancelleria (room 1), you'll see the imposing 12th-century marble *Arco della Pusterla dei Fabbri*, a city arch named after the 'posterula', a small back door within one of the medieval city gates. There's a vast collection of Lombard, Roman and Byzantine sculptures from the Early Christian to Middle Ages (from seventh to ninth centuries), including the *Testa di Teodora* (Head of Theodora, the Byzantine Empress) along with splendid fourth century floor

---

Five of the best

Things to see in the Civici Musei del Castello Sforzesco

❶ *Rondanini Pietà* (Museo d'Arte Antica, room 15) Michelangelo died at the age of 89 in 1564, before completing this splendid marble sculpture of the Virgin Mary and Jesus.

❷ *Sala delle Asse* (Museo d'Arte Antica, room 8) The vaulted ceilings of the 'Hall of Wooden Panels' boast wonderful frescoes by Leonardo da Vinci; unfortunately they've been retouched so many times there's little left of the original trompe l'œil vines first painted by da Vinci's hand in 1498.

❸ *Madonna in Glory with Saints* (Museo delle Arti Decorative, room 23) One of Mantegna's final pieces, this impressive altarpiece, painted in 1497 for a Veronese church, was one of his last works.

❹ *Trivulzio Tapestries* (Museo delle Arti Decorative, Sala della Balla) Named after General Gian Giacomo Trivulzio who commissioned the stunning *Tapestries of the Twelve Months*, designed by Bramantino in 1503.

❺ *Portale del Banco Mediceo* (Museo d'Arte Antica, room 14) This impressive marble portal, dating to 1463, features the portraits of Francesco Sforza and Bianca Maria Visconti; built to seal the Sforza-Visconti alliance, it once stood on via dei Bossi.

mosaics and marble reliefs. Room 2 is crammed with sculptures from Lombardy, particularly Milan, from the Romanesque and Gothic ages, and a huge array of architectural pieces by Lombard artisans such as capitals and decorative shelves found in 12th-century churches in Milan and Pavia, and the Duomo in Cremona. Notable also are Romanesque sculptures from Como and Cremona, and Bonino da Campione's arresting marble *Sepulchral Monument of Bernabò Visconti* on horseback, dating to 1363.

The beautifully-lit Sala del Gonfalone (room 7) is worth some time for the room itself and its decorated ceiling; however, the highlights here are rich tapestries, particularly the colourful embroidered silk gonfalon (a banner hung from a crossbar) that depicts the life and miracles of St Ambrose and was consecrated by Milanese cardinal Carlo Borromeo in 1566.

Pinacoteca Upstairs, on the first floor of the Ducal Courtyard in rooms 20 to 26, you'll find Milan's most important 'picture gallery'. The Pinacoteca, reopened in recent years after extensive renovations, boasts a brilliant collection of some 1,500 paintings, of which 230 are on display, with a wealth of art from the medieval period through to the 18th century, including masterpieces by Mantegna, Canaletto, Antonello da Messina, Tintoretto, Bellotto, Tiepolo, Foppa, Cesare da Sesto, Procaccini, Cerano, and others, along with some important 20th-century pieces by Picasso, Fontana and Sironi. Highlights include several old Milanese collections, such as that of the Trivulzio family. The work is displayed thematically within chronological sequence, with occasional contrasts of genre and period to illustrate the development of different artists and schools of painting. Alongside the paintings are exquisite sculptures, ceramics, terracotta and wooden bas-reliefs.

Museo delle Arti Decorative To get to the Museum of Decorative Arts, follow the stairs leading up from the Ducal Courtyards museums to Ducal Apartments, where the ladies and knights

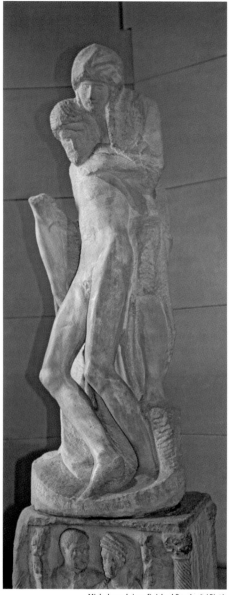

Michelangelo's unfinished *Rondanini Pietà*.

Around the city

of the Sforza Court once gathered in rooms such as the Sala della Balla. The apartments hold two fabulous museums, the Museum of Musical Instruments (see below), and a museum showcasing a comprehensive collection of furniture, ceramics, majolica tiles, art, precious objects, textiles, jewellery, costumes, armour, and weapons, mostly from Milan and Lombardy, covering the evolution of applied arts from the 15th to the 20th centuries. The pieces are displayed thematically in authentic environments that wonderfully evoke the mood of particular periods, so you can appreciate how fashion has affected taste and lifestyles in Italy, and how different ideas and styles have permeated through various art forms, genres, and even ages. The museum also makes excellent use of multimedia, lighting and interpretative displays to enrich the experience.

The exhibition starts with a display on the 19th-century origins of applied arts and the evolution of 19th and 20th century decorative arts, before returning to the 15th-16th century with 'The Court and the Church' (room 17), the 17th century Chamber of Wonders (room 18), 17th-18th century baroque (room 19), 18th century Collections of the Milanese Nobility (room 16), and the 18th-21st century Masters of Style, from Maggiolini to Sottsass (also in room 16). Don't miss the 14th-16th century frescoes that decorate many of the walls and ceilings, some of which have come from Milanese homes and deconsecrated churches. In room 17, the Chamber of Griselda is a full-scale replica of a room of 15th-century frescoes from Parma's Castello di Roccabianca. A real highlight is the furniture, which features pieces by celebrated designers Ferdinando Bologna, Mario Praz, Alvar Gonzales-Palacios, Peter Thornton and Enrico Colle, and the Masters of Style which illustrates how traditional craftsmanship has evolved in Italy, particularly Milan, through the passing down of skills to an unbroken line of successors, and how this familiarity with historical styles and techniques has resulted in the superlative design that Italians are celebrated for.

Museo degli Strumenti Musicali Remaining upstairs in the Ducal Courtyard museums, you'll find, in what was once a ballroom, one of the finest and largest collections of musical instruments in Europe. A highlight in the Museum of Musical Instruments is the collection of rare violins by Stradivarius, in rooms 36 and 37, and 16th- and 17th-century lutes, guitars, and stringed instruments by the other famous instrument-making families of Cremona: the Amati and the Guarneri. There's also a vast array of wind instruments, including old hunting horns. Gems for the music buffs to seek out include a 16th century Venetian harpsichord, Pietro Verri's rare glass harmonica, Johannes Maria Anciuti's oboe dating to 1722, and Mango Longo's prettily-decorated ten-string guitar.

Parco Sempione

Daily 0630-2000 Nov-Feb, till 2100 Mar, Apr & Oct, till 2200 May, till 2300 Jun-Sep.
Metro: Cairoli, Cadorna or Lanza.
Map: Milan, D2, p82.

This massive park, sprawling behind Castello Sforzesco, is Milan's loveliest green retreat. While the space was only landscaped in its current form in 1894, it was used as a garden and hunting reserve for centuries before. There is lots of shade here, plus waterways, ducks and other birdlife, and plenty of activity in summer when the rest of the city is very quiet – although it's advisable outside of summer to vacate the park before dusk turns to night.

Parco Sempione hosts a casual game in football-mad Milan.

Il Cenacolo (The Last Supper) & Santa Maria delle Grazie

*Corso Magenta, T02-8942 1146,
cenacolovinciano.org.*
Tue-Sun 0815-1845, closed 1 Jan, 1 May, 25 Dec.
Bookings essential. Tickets can be booked online, €6.50 with €1.50 reservation fee.
Visits last 15 mins.
Metro: Cadorna or Conciliazione.
Map: Milan, C4, p82.

Leonardo da Vinci's massive mural that decorates a wall of the Cenacolo Vinciano, the refectory of the Chiesa di Santa Maria delle Grazie, is truly an iconic painting. Much copied, parodied and theorised

Da Vinci's much-hyped mural, *The Last Supper*, adorns the refectory wall.

over, the mural represents the moment when Jesus announces that one of the Twelve Apostles would betray him. Painted between 1495 and 1498, the mural, measuring 880 x 460 cm, has a rich history that almost overshadows seeing the painting in the flesh. Almost.

The church is built in Late Gothic Lombard genre and the nave and two-aisle interior remained traditional in style until 1490, when Ludovico Sforza, a member of Milan's Sforza dynasty, decided to turn the church into his family mausoleum. Ludovico Sforza was an important

Tip...

While the painting is significant, don't go with over-inflated expectations about its condition – while it has been well-restored, it's clearly a shadow of what it would have looked like after the master stood back and admired his own work for the first time.

patron of the arts, and while the artist Donato Montorfano was watching the paint dry on his *Crucifixion* for the refectory in 1494-95, Leonardo da Vinci was being commissioned by Sforza to adorn the facing wall. Da Vinci decided that the traditional fresco technique – which required that the painting be completed quickly before the wall plaster dried – was unsuited to his style, which involved working in short spurts of inspiration followed by reflection and further embellishment of the work. While Sforza fretted over the time taken, da Vinci was unperturbed, creating sketches and studies, as well as researching painting techniques to fulfil his vision.

Just like the Madonna and Child, the Last Supper was a recurring religious theme for painters. However, da Vinci presented the final gathering of Jesus and his followers in a new style. The Renaissance saw an increasingly realistic portrayal of scenery and people in paintings and da Vinci was an expert at depicting figures in a naturalistic fashion. For instance, while other Last Supper paintings portrayed Judas (the disciple who betrayed Jesus) overtly singled out either with a 'missing' halo or seated apart from Jesus and the other eleven disciples, da Vinci depicts him slightly in the shadows, with an elbow on the table and a small money bag (presumably holding his fee for betraying Jesus) in his hand. Also notable is da Vinci's use of perspective, a relatively new concept at the time, which has the viewer seeing the painting as part of the space of the refectory. Tickets to see the painting are limited to a certain number a day and entry is carefully controlled, so if you plan to see the painting you must book well in advance. This doesn't mean that you might not get in if you arrive in Milan and spontaneously decide to see it – there's always a chance. But it's best to make sure you don't miss out. You can book online or by phone, but regardless of how you have booked you need to be there at least 20 minutes beforehand to collect the actual tickets – otherwise they may be re-sold. Note that if you've paid by credit card, the cardholder must be present and show identification to collect the tickets.

Deterioration & restoration

Leonardo's technique and materials saw the painting deteriorate even in his lifetime. Centuries of poor attempts at restoration, floods and a bombing during the Second World War have all conspired to rob the painting of its impact. The most recent attempt at restoration, which began in 1978 and was completed in 1999, has restored some of the lustre to one of the world's great art treasures.

Santa Maria delle Grazie.

What the locals say

Don't be afraid to speak Italian, even if it's just a few words. Italians don't make a big deal if it's not correct, and they will try to understand what you mean – with plenty of gestures!

Eleonora Corona
Manager, Sermoneta Gloves.

Milan fashion walk

Fashionistas will want to start early for this spree through Milan's famous Quadrilatero d'Oro (Golden Quarter), the city's fashion district, home to glamorous headquarters and flagship stores of exclusive fashion houses. The quadrangle of streets between pedestrianized via della Spiga, via Sant'Andrea, via Montenapoleone and via Manzoni are not only the centre of fashion in Milan, but also a major global fashion hub alongside Paris, New York and London.

Those not so keen on maxing the credit card might consider an evening amble when the streets are quiet and the window displays are even more dramatic; the experience is akin to browsing an illuminated fashion museum. But stroll these smart streets by day and you'll find yourself sharing the cobblestones with brand-obsessed fashion-tourists, stick-thin catwalk models, unflappable fashion designers and their frazzled assistants, and if you're in town during the seasonal fashion weeks, nip'n'tucked celebrities accessorising with bodyguards. The people-watching is half the fun!

Start this walk at **via Manzoni 31**: Emporio Armani. One of Milan's most striking edifices, the statues on the façade of the Assicurazioni Generali building are the patron saints of Milan, Venice and Trieste. Kickstart your stroll with an espresso from **Armani Caffè** on nearby via Croce Rossa.

Continue along via Manzoni, passing design stores Da Driade and Flou, turning right into **via della Spiga**. This cobblestone lane is the quarter's most attractive, boasting some of Milan's best stores, including Sermoneta Gloves, Roberto Cavalli, Moschino, Dolce & Gabbana, Tiffany, Miu Miu, Hermès, Prada, and Bulgari.

Best-dressed foot forward on via Montenapoleone.

Milan's most exclusive designers

Armani
Via Manzoni 31, T02-7231 8600.
Armani heaven with Emporio Armani, Armani Jeans, Armani Casa, and Armani Caffè all under one roof.

Dolce and Gabbana
Via della Spiga 2 & 26 & corso Venezia 7, T02-7600 1155.
D&G boast some of the sexiest men's and women's ranges, and seductive window displays.

Gianfranco Ferre
Via Sant'Andrea 15, T02-780406.
These smart tailored designs took this northern Italian from a job at a Genoan raincoat factory to the luxurious Lake Maggiore villa he now owns.

Gucci
Via Montenapoleone 5/7, T02-771271.
Maurizio Gucci may have been shot outside his via Palestro office in 1995 (his wife hired an assassin), but sophistication lives on in his elegant stores.

Missoni
Via Sant'Andrea 2, T02-7600 3555.
The Milanese Missoni family's vibrant textured knitwear has made a comeback, extending the brand to home décor, beach towels and bikinis.

Moschino
Via della Spiga 30, T02-7600 4320 & via Sant'Andrea 12, T02-7600 0832.
Don't miss the whimsical windows of this audacious label started by Milan's wild child and former Brera Academy art student, Franco Moschino (1950-1994), who began his career in the 1970s as an illustrator for Versace.

Prada
Via Montenapoleone 8, T02-777 1771 & via Spiga 18, T02-780465.
Miuccia Prada, granddaughter of Prada's founder, operates the company that began life in 1913 as a leathergoods shop before evolving into this prestigious fashion house; she also runs playful label Miu Miu (her nickname).

Pucci
Via Montenapoleone 14, T02-7631 8356.
Pucci's psychedelic fashions, big in the 1960s and 1970s are still funky and fashionable. Make sure you browse this swinging store.

Valentino
Via Montenapoleone 20, T02-7602 0285.
Born just outside of Milan in 1932, Valentino's tailored suits and evening gowns are popular with movie stars.

Versace
Via Montenapoleone 11 & via San Pietro all'Orto 10-11, T02-7600 8528.
Milan's most famous fashion store. Donatella Versace has headed design since her brother, Gianni, was murdered in 1997 in Miami; his funeral was held at his Lake Como villa.

At the end, turn right on busy **corso Venezia**, then right onto **via Montenapoleone**, home to Louis Vuitton, La Perla, Ralph Lauren and Gucci. At the corner of **via Sant'Andrea**, stop for refreshments at charming **Cova** (see page 126), a restored tearoom; you might be surprised who you see dropping in for takeaway pastries.

Continue along via Montenapoleone, browsing the alluring windows of Versace, Dior, Pucci, Cartier, Frette, Valentino, Yves Saint Laurent, Ermenegildo Zegna, and Bruno Magli. When you reach **via Manzoni**, backtrack three short blocks and turn left into via Gesù. Call into perfume house Acqua di Parma (see page 137) to inhale their seductive scents and take a look at the lobby of the sumptuous Four Seasons Hotel, accommodation of choice for supermodels and celebrities during Fashion Week.

Turn right onto **via della Spiga**, then right into **via Sant'Andrea**, where you'll find more jaw-dropping window displays at Gianfranco Ferre, Viktor & Rolf, Costume National, Chanel, Kenzo and Trussardi. Turn left into via Bagutta for a meal at one of Milan's most atmospheric eateries, **Trattoria Bagutta** (see page 125).

La Triennale

Viale Alemagna 6, T02-724341, triennale.it.
Tue-Sun 1030-2030, €11.
Map: Milan, C3, p82.

It's surprising that Milan didn't really have a design museum until recently, considering the output of cool, contemporary, cutting-edge Italian design over the past century. Fittingly, La Triennale building where the design museum is now housed was originally the Palazzo dell'Arte, built from 1931-1933 for the specific purpose of holding decorative art exhibitions every three years. After the expos fizzled out, and many hiccups later, the doors to Milan's design museum were finally opened in 2006. Today the museum hosts major semi-permanent exhibitions which are installed every 12-18 months, as well as smaller temporary exhibitions, changed every few months.

The striking Palazzo dell'Arte was designed by Giovanni Muzio, who created a massive building that carefully balanced the relationship between external and internal spaces and took advantage of natural light. The architect envisioned the structure as a container in which the interior spaces were flexible – essential for housing exhibitions; however, this was a groundbreaking notion, which made it even more in tune with the purpose of the space.

In 2002, architect Michele De Lucchi overhauled the building, and restored the structure as close as possible to its initial form. In 2006 the building was unveiled to much anticipation, and the Milanese quietly breathed an elegant sigh of relief. The Palazzo dell'Arte had been reinvented in a stunning manner, giving fresh life to the old space while emphasising the innovative qualities of the early design.

Aptly, the first major exhibition held at the new museum was entitled 'What is Italian Design?' The show highlighted the obsessions of Italian designers, with a special contribution by Welsh film director Peter Greenaway that told the stories of Olivetti (who made business equipment sexy long before Apple) and Vespa (those beloved little motor scooters the Italians ride) amongst others. The inaugural exhibition

Fib design at La Triennale.

Antonio Citterio

While there are many designers of note in Milan, Antonio Citterio, born in 1950, epitomizes what makes Italians so prolific and prominent in the world of design. A graduate of the architecture programme at the Politecnico di Milano in 1972, Citterio has designed everything from lamps to lounge chairs and beds to buildings (such as the Bulgari Hotel, see page 121), and his designs are in the permanent collection of both MoMa (Museum of Modern Art, New York) and the Centre de Pompidou (Paris).

Citterio's work for B&B Italia, Vitra and Kartell furniture companies are wonderful testaments to his skills – and those of Italian designers more generally – combining high-tech research into materials, with comfort, form, and that legendary Milanese style that's understated but still sexy.

As far back as the 1970s Citterio's designs reveal an aesthetic that has continued though to his work in 2008 – indeed B&B Italia have a sofa created in 1979 still in production alongside his more recent designs. One of Citterio's greatest skills as a designer is to be able to 'fit' into the style of the firm he has been commissioned by, while still producing distinctive pieces that have his unique mark on them.

The architect's other enviable skill is his ability to design across different disciplines – his studio now handles everything from engineering corporate buildings to creating the graphic identity to go with them. But Citterio's not alone. Many multidisciplinary designers hail from or have worked in Milan, such as the late great Giò Ponte (see box, page 114). Must be something in the *acqua*…

served to explain how the designs came to be more than purely functional – they became a vital part of Italy's cultural identity. The second major exhibition (as of early 2009) was on the relationship between art and design – another fitting theme for an outstanding design museum's exploration of Italian innovation.

When you visit, start with the semi-permanent exhibition on at the time, then see the temporary shows, but make sure you leave time to explore the excellent bookshop. Indeed, design junkies might even want a spare hour or two. The hip design café has an open kitchen and, of course, designer chairs and excellent coffee.

Pinacoteca di Brera

Via Brera 28, T02-722631, info line: T02-8942 1146, brera.beniculturali.it.
Tue-Sun 0830-1930, €10, €3.50 audio guide.
Metro: Lanza or Montenapoleone.
Map: Central Milan, D1, p88.

Located in the lavish 17th-century Palazzo di Brera in the former bohemian quarter, once the atelier of the city's artisans, the sprawling Pinacoteca di Brera boasts one of the most significant collections of Lombard art and a most outstanding collection of Italian and European art from the 13th to 20th centuries – with works by Bellini, Caravaggio, Raphael, Goya, El Greco, Rembrandt and Picasso. Many would argue that if you only see one art museum in Milan, this should be it.

When you visit the pinacoteca one of the first things you'll notice are the art students sketching in front of paintings and hanging out in the courtyards. Most are enrolled at the Accademia di Brera. Established in 1776 it was innovative in its time and remains a prestigious international art school. In 1803, courses were established in architecture, painting, sculpture, engraving, perspective, anatomy and the figure, and in 1805 annual exhibitions of student work were launched which toured Italy and Europe. When the academy's success demanded further expansions, the 14th-century Church of Santa Maria di Brera was demolished. The beautiful sculptures, bas-reliefs, portal and other fragments from the church's façade are in the Museo d'Arte Antica (see page 98) while some of the church's frescoes and paintings are at the pinacoteca itself.

During the Romantic era, under artist Francesco Hayez, the academy led the way in academic

Tip…

While the Brera still has a little of its former bohemian flavour in its cafés, bars and pubs, it's now a fairly affluent neighbourhood and its cobbled lanes are lined with elegant art galleries and antique stores. Allow time to explore the area after your gallery visit.

Above: Students sketching in the courtyard at the Pinacoteca di Brera. Opposite page: Museo Bagatti Valsecchi.

painting. The school became highly respected for its art history teaching and, to this day, a place at the academy remains highly prestigious. You'll hear a variety of languages as you pass students chatting in the stairwells – the academy takes 25% of its students from over 50 countries. As a result of the diverse academy, the pinacoteca has a tangible energy and vibrancy about it.

The pinacoteca and collection were established as part of the academy, giving students access to exemplary works of art and sculpture that they could copy and from which they could make plaster casts. The first paintings were acquired during the 'reassignment' of works of art from churches and monasteries under Napoleon Bonaparte's rule, including Raphael's splendid *Sposalizio* (Marriage of the Virgin). Napoleon also sent paintings to the gallery from territories the French army conquered. In 1805, a series of annual art exhibitions was established as a counterpart to the Parisian Salon, and art prizes were introduced, which led Milan to become a centre for fine art throughout the 19th

century. After Napoleon III's visit in 1859, a bronze statue of Napoleon I as peacemaker was erected in the courtyard to honour his contribution to the gallery and academy.

The pinacoteca's collection is extensive and exquisite. There are masterpieces from Boccioni, Botticelli, Hayez, Leonardo da Vinci, Tintoretto, Titian, Raphael, Rubens and Modigliani. Highlights include Andrea Mantegna's *The Dead Christ*, which, oddly enough, he painted for his own tomb in Mantua; Mantegna's application of perspective and use of light are exemplary. Gentile Bellini's *St Mark Preaching in Alexandria* is another extraordinary artwork which impresses particularly for its size. At an enormous 347 x 770 cm, it's one of the museum's biggest pieces. The Venetian painter began the painting in 1504, but following his death it was finished by his brother Giovanni Bellini who, in 1510, painted another masterpiece on show, the *Madonna and Child*. Also look out for Lombard artist Giovanni di Milano, from Caversaccio near Como, and Milanese Gaudenzio Ferrari.

Museo Bagatti Valsecchi

Via Gesù 5, T02-7600 6132,
museobagattivalsecchi.org.
Tue-Sun 1300-1800, €8.
Metro: San Babila or Montenapoleone.
Map: Central Milan, G3, p88.

Housed in Palazzo Bagatti Valsecchi, this museum was the home of brothers Fausto and Giuseppe Bagatti Valsecchi who filled – and we mean filled – this 19th-century mansion with exquisite art, furniture and other beautiful objects dating back to the Renaissance era. It's a sumptuous dwelling that's every bit as intriguing as the two brothers intended to make it.

Museo di Milano

Palazzo Morando Attendolo Bolognini,
via Sant'Andrea 6, T02-8846 5933,
museodimilano.mi.it.
Tue-Sun 1400-1730, free.
Metro San Babila or Montenapoleone.
Map: Central Milan, G3, p88.

One for the museum buffs and scholars of art, this compelling museum is home to a fastidious collection of documents and paintings related to the history of Milan, particularly from Napoleonic times through Austrian rule. Exquisitely renovated, the 18th-century Palazzo Morando Attendolo Bolognini is also a living museum showing the apartments of Countess Bolognini and their beautiful objects. The building also houses the Museo di Storia Contemporanea (see below).

Museo di Storia Contemporanea

Palazzo Morando Attendolo Bolognini,
via Sant'Andrea 6, T02-8846 5933,
museodistoriacontemporanea.it.
Tue-Sun 1400-1730, free.
Metro: San Babila or Montenapoleone.
Map: Central Milan, H3, p88.

Housed in the same lovely, restored palazzo as the Museo di Milano (see above), the fascinating Museum of Contemporary History looks at the more recent development of the city, and in particular how it has culturally and geographically expanded, with an emphasis on changes following unification, and particularly around the two World Wars.

Museo del Risorgimento

Via Borgonuovo 23, T02-8846 4176,
museodelrisorgimento.mi.it.
Tue-Sun 0900-1300 & 1400-1730, free.
Metro: San Babila or Montenapoleone.
Map: Central Milan, E1, p88.

The Risorgimento ('Revival') was the political and social movement that led to unification of Italy after Napoleonic rule. The museum, housed in the

Museo dell'Ottocento, formerly known as the Galleria d'Arte Moderna.

distinguished Palazzo Moriggia in Brera, has a wealth of Napoleonic memorabilia – including the crown used by Napoleon at his 1805 coronation as King of Italy in Milan. Those with a real bent for history will enjoy the immense collection of Risorgimento manuscripts and documents in the library.

Museo dell'Ottocento

Villa Barbiano di Belgiojoso (formerly known as Villa Reale), via Palestro 16, T02-7600 2819.
Tue-Sun 0900-1300 & 1400-1730, free.
Metro: Palestro.
Map: Milan, G3, p82.

The 'Museum of the 1800s' is appropriately located in the elegant, neoclassical Villa Barbiano di Belgiojoso (known until recently as Villa Reale), built in 1790 for Count Ludovico Barbiano di Belgiojoso, but better known as the residence of the King of Naples Gioacchino Murat and his wife (Napoleon's sister) Carolina Bonaparte, during the early 1800s.

The collection of the renovated and re-focused former Galleria d'Arte Moderna (Gallery of Modern Art) is spread throughout 35 rooms and features Italian and European neoclassical art (ground floor), art from the Romantic period, the Milanese Scapigliatura movement, Post-Impressionist Divisionism and Futurism (first floor), and the Grassi and Vismara collections of Italian and international modern art, which include work by masters such as Gaugin, Matisse and Picasso (second floor). Even after renovation, it seems there still isn't enough room to show all 2,700 paintings and sculptures from the Gallery of Modern Art, and part of the collection will move to another new museum, the Museo dell'Arengario, currently undergoing renovation on piazza del Duomo and scheduled to open in December 2009.

The villa's romantic English-style gardens boast beautiful bas-reliefs and statues of mythological subjects and are worth a wander; guided tours are also offered.

Padiglione d'Arte Contemporanea

Via Palestro 14, T02-7600 9085, comune.milano.it/pac/.
Fri-Sun 0930-1900, Tue & Wed 0930-2000 (opening hours can vary according to exhibitions), €5.
Metro: Palestro.
Map: Milan, G3, p83.

Adjoining the Galleria d'Arte Moderna, this cutting-edge contemporary art gallery hosts temporary exhibitions that are almost always engaging and often provocative. The building's history is equally compelling. Built in 1947 as a symbolic post-war gesture to replace the Villa Belgiojoso, which had been destroyed by bombing, it was closed in the 1970s and renovated and reopened a decade later with new aims, only to be bombed again by the mafia in 1993! On re-opening, the museum was each time determined to become significantly more pro-active. This guiding principle persists today, particularly through its art education programme and artistic teaching laboratory for the visually impaired. The building itself is used to teach art, enabling students to interact with the building's structure and surfaces as well as the art. There's a good bookshop, cafeteria and video room.

Giardini Pubblici

0630-dusk.
Metro: Palestro.
Map: Milan, G2, p82.

These elaborate public gardens were built in the mannered English style. Designed in 1784 by Giuseppe Piermarini, they are the largest gardens in the city centre, providing relief from the inner city and the suburbs of Milan. Piermarini also designed Teatro alla Scala (see page 90) and corso di Porta Romana, the first paved street of modern Europe. Museums and galleries ring the park and it's a good one for joggers – just watch the dogs! Children who aren't obsessed with portable video games will get a kick out of the old-fashioned

Five of the best

Milanese monuments

❶ **Arco della Pace** Neoclassical Arch of Peace in Parco Sempione features decorative sculptures.

❷ **Archi di Porta Nuova** The Arch of the New Gate on via Alessandro Manzoni, built in 1171 and restored in 1861, is on the old medieval city boundaries.

❸ **Tempio della Vittoria** The marble Temple of Victory north of Sant'Ambrogio honours 10,000 Milanese killed during the First World War. There's an eternal flame to the unknown soldier.

❹ **Porta Ticinese** The red-brick Ticinese Gate south of San Lorenzo alle Colonne (see page 116) was the southernmost gate to Milan's medieval city.

❺ **Porta Venezia** On the northeastern corner of the Public Gardens the Venice Gate, built between 1826 and 1828, replaced Porta Orientale (Oriental Gate), one of six city entrances.

amusements at the park's western end. The natural history museum, planetarium and film museum are all located in the Giardini Pubblici.

Museo Civico di Storia Naturale

Corso Venezia 55, Giardini Pubblici, T02-8846 3280.
Tue-Fri 0900-1730, Sat-Sun 0900-1800, €3/free.
Metro: Porta Venezia or Palestro.
Map: Milan, H3, p82.

The Museum of Natural History is housed in a handsome terracotta neoclassical building dating to 1838. It was constructed mainly to house the collection left to the city by Giuseppe de Cristoforis and the exhibits cover botany, geology, mineralogy, palaeontology and zoology, which essentially translates to plenty of old-fashioned fun, stuffed animals and strange rocks. The dioramas of animal habitats are a treat as are the life-size dinosaur skeletons.

Planetario Ulrico Hoepli

Corso Venezia 57, Giardini Pubblici, T02-8846 3340.
Public viewing sessions Tue & Thu 2100, €3/1.50.
Metro: Porta Venezia or Palestro.
Map: Milan, H2, p82.

Donated to the city by the publisher Ulrico Hoepli, the Planetario was designed by Pietro Portaluppi in 1930 and is still the biggest public planetarium in Italy. During viewing sessions, a film of the celestial seasonal positions is projected onto the dome of the planetarium.

Museo del Cinema

Palazzo Dugnani, via Daniele Manin 2, Giardini Pubblici, T02-655 4977, cinetecamilano.it.
Thu-Sun 1500-1900, €3.
Metro: Turati, Porta Venezia or Palestro.
Map: Milan, G2, p82.

Located on the west side of the park, this cinema museum, housed in the restored 17th-century Palazzo Dugnani, is an intimate one. Film geeks will love the equipment from the early years of cinema, such as hand-wound cameras and sound equipment, as well as some wonderful retro film posters. The museum has screenings of Italian film classics as well; see the website for screening details.

Stazione Centrale

Piazza Duca d'Aosta.
Metro: Centrale.

While most people are too focussed on getting out of the station as quickly as possible with their purse or wallet still in their possession (the station is a long-standing pick-pocket paradise), Stazione Centrale is a remarkable and muscular structure. Commissioned in 1912, it wasn't completed until 1931, hence the mix of predominately art nouveau (*stile Liberty* as it was called in Italy) style, smatterings of art deco, and the flamboyant trappings of Fascist-era architecture. Its size is epic, with a 207-m long façade and a height of

70 m, while its enormous glass and iron roof is a thing of beauty. Over 300,000 people pass through the station every day, most of whom would be unaware that *binario* (platform) 21 has the dubious distinction of being the platform where 600 Jews started their chilling trip to Auschwitz in 1944. A thorough renovation of the station started in 2006 and was still going strong at the time of writing.

Torre Velasca

Piazza Velasca.
Metro: Missori.
Map: Central Milan, F5, p88.

This mischievous medieval-influenced 106-metre tower (*torre* is tower in Spanish, as well as Italian, and the square on which it stands was named after Spanish Governor de Velasca) is a fascinating example of post-war Italian engineering and ingenuity. Built by the firm BBPR, named after the founding architects – Gianluigi Banfi (who was deceased before this building was designed), Lodovico Belgiojoso, Enrico Peressutti, and Ernesto Nathan Rogers – the tower was built between 1956 and 1958. It's unique because of the top nine floors, which are larger and protrude from the floors below, and are supported by buttresses, just like a medieval fortress. One doesn't have to look far to find inspiration for the building – the famous Castello Sforzesco (see page 96) has a very similar form. The mixed-utility building (both residential and office use) was controversial upon its

Above: Inside the Stazione Centrale. Opposite page: Torre Velasca.

completion, not just because it exploited a loophole in town planning laws, but because of the apparently backward-looking design for the times. Ernesto Nathan Rogers, a well-respected professor of architecture, argued that the shape came organically, once the architects explored what the needs of the building were – and refused to acknowledge that it was based on a medieval tower at all. You can't tour the inside – it's residential and commercial – but it's the exterior architecture that's important.

Pirelli Tower

Piazza Duca d'Aosta.
Metro: Centrale.

When the president of the Pirelli Company (famous for its vehicle tyres, cable manufacturing and girlie calendars) wanted a new skyscraper to be built on

the land where their first factory was located, few would have known that he had commissioned what was to be one of the most influential buildings of the second half of the 20th century. Architect Giò Ponti, with the assistance of Pier Luigi Nervi (a master in structures made of reinforced concrete) and Arturo Danusso, designed the building to be a different expression of what a skyscraper could be. Topping out at 127.1 m it is the tallest building in Milan – and the only building standing higher than the *Madonnina* of Milan's Duomo. An all-concrete construction (most skyscrapers have a skeleton of steel), work started on the building in July 1956, was completed in August 1958, and it opened in 1960. Ponti saw the unusual diamond shape as a 'graphic slogan', being somewhat obsessed with the diamond form during the 1950s. Also known as 'Pirellione' (or Big Pirelli), today it's home to the Lombardy regional government – which had an unexpected tragedy on 18 April 2002 when a light plane unintentionally crashed into the building, killing the pilot and two office workers. The building structure remained intact and was repaired and still stands as testament to the prosperous and creative post-war era of Italy. Although you can only enter the lobby, one of the best uninterrupted views of the tower is from the piazza just in front of Stazione Centrale – just watch out for pickpockets…

Giò Ponte

Giò Ponte (1891–1979) was one of the most influential and important Italian architects of the 20th century, known not just for his creations in cement and steel, but also for his work as a publisher. Ponte studied at the Politechnico di Milano, graduating in 1921, and first earned his reputation working with ceramics. In 1928 he founded the magazine *Domus*, which was to be one of the most influential design magazines in the world, which he edited (apart from a break between 1941-48) until his death. In addition, Ponte was also an academic and was a professor in the Faculty of Architecture at the Politechnico di Milano from 1936 to 1961.

Throughout his career, this leading light of modern Italian design created many objects that are seen as classics today. Chairs and sofas, for instance, were one area where he left his modernist mark. Ponti had a light touch, best demonstrated by his famous *Superleggera* chair (1957), which he spent ten years perfecting in an attempt to find the right balance between lightness and strength – hence the name 'superlight'. The chair – able to be lifted with one finger by a child – is still manufactured by Cassina furniture in Italy today. Another example of his great multidisciplinary work is the La Cornuta Mod 47 espresso machine designed in 1948 for La Pavoni (inventors of the first espresso machine in 1905), which appears more on museum shelves than in cafés these days. However, it is the hexagonal-based Pirelli Tower in Milan that Ponti is mostly remembered for, although those with only a passing interest in architecture would be hard-pressed to see the significance of it. But this is exactly what *is* significant about architects such as Ponti – until the Pirelli Tower, most skyscrapers were simply boring rectangular blocks.

Museo Nazionale della Scienza e della Tecnica Leonardo da Vinci

Via San Vittore 21, T02-485551, museoscienza.org. Tue-Fri 0930-1700, Sat & Sun 0930-1830, €8/6. Metro: Sant'Ambrogio.
Map: Milan, C5, p82.

Housed in a former 16th-century monastery, the Leonardo da Vinci National Museum of Science and Technology is a must for fans of da Vinci and science geeks. Tracing the history of technology and science in an engaging fashion is the aim of this educational museum and while it will expand your mind, the drawings coming from the mind of one of the most talented human beings ever to walk the earth – Leonardo da Vinci – are quite extraordinary.

There are six different easy-to-navigate areas of the museum, dedicated to the history of science and technology – Materials, Energy, Transport, Communication, New Frontiers, and Leonardo, Art and Science – but prepare yourself for an overwhelming 10,000 objects in the collection.

Da Vinci's sketch of a perpetual motion device.

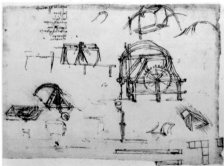

Tip…

While there is all this technology and science to admire at the Leonardo da Vinci National Museum of Science and Technology, don't forget to check out the gardens and the cloisters, along with the Sala del Cenacolo with frescoes by Pietro Gilardi.

Fortunately, there are interactive guides and stations to explain many of them, and one of the highlights for children (of all ages!) is the iLabs – 15 interactive laboratories.

In the Materials area you can learn how paper, metal and plastic are processed for use, and look at the techniques used to manufacture them in the 'iLab'. The Energies area looks at how energy is harvested and distributed, and includes the wonderful Regina Margherita, an elegant thermoelectric power plant that still functions. The Transport section is one of the most visual of the museum, with a full-size submarine that you can board, the *Enrico Toti*, built in 1967, and put out of service in 1999. Other exhibits include trains, ships, aeroplanes and helicopters. In the Communication section everything is covered from Gutenberg's movable type machine to mobile phones, with a look at graphic art and sound as well. The New Frontiers section explores the worlds of biotechnologies, genetics and robotics, and takes a peek into the future. Looking back to one of the greatest minds of history is the Leonardo Gallery, where outstanding models have been made of the great thinker's sketches, vividly bringing them to life, while the Art and Science section (something that da Vinci had no problem combining) looks at how art and technology have a symbiotic relationship.

Weekends and public holidays might be crowded at the museum, but there are more activities scheduled, including guided tours and plenty of interactive learning experiences taking place. This is definitely one place where children will have a great time, so allow for at least a couple of hours – even more if they're scientifically inquisitive.

Basilica di Sant'Ambrogio

Piazza Sant'Ambrogio 15, T02-8645 0895.
Mon-Sat 0715-1200 & 1430-1900,
Sun 0715-1315 & 1500-1945, free.
Metro: Sant'Ambrogio.
Map: Milan, D5, p82.

Bishop Ambrogio (Ambrose is the anglicised form), the patron saint of Milan, commissioned this

Leonardo da Vinci

When you stand in front of one of the most significant paintings in the world, *The Last Supper* (see page 102), it's hard to believe that the same man who painted it was also the first known person to conceptualise the helicopter.

Leonardo da Vinci (1452-1519) might not have built a prototype of the flying machine, but he was the prototype of what was to be named a 'Renaissance man', with an unquenchable thirst for knowledge of science, nature and the arts. This quest for knowledge was complemented by his abilities as an inventor. However, many of his sketches would only come to life hundreds of years after his death.

While alive, Leonardo da Vinci had his mysteries. An illegitimate child, he was never married nor had children. Instead, he devoted himself to mentoring others. While his extraordinary talents in such diverse fields have seen him labelled perhaps the greatest genius of mankind, it was his talent as a painter that has earned him his place amongst the greatest artists to ever live.

Both *The Last Supper* and the *Mona Lisa* are more than just paintings – their iconic status has seen these works of art widely copied and parodied. Ironically, it was da Vinci's own experimentation and restlessness that led us to have so few of his works surviving today. Painted in 1498, *The Last Supper* was already showing serious signs of deterioration by the mid 1500s, due to da Vinci's experiment with the technique of tempera – mixing pigment with egg. See also page 103.

fascinating basilica which was constructed between AD 379-386, and built over a cemetery that held the bodies of two Christian martyrs. Since then it has been rebuilt several times, resulting in the assortment of styles that is present today, which explains the mismatched bell towers – the shorter being built in the ninth century, the taller in 1124. Inside, the ciborium (the freestanding canopy over the altar) is notable, as is the golden altar housing the remains of St Ambrose, and dating to the ninth century. It features reliefs of the life of Jesus on the front and the life of the saint on the back.

Chiesa di San Lorenzo Maggiore

Piazza Vetra, corso di Porta Ticinese 39.
Daily 0730-1230 & 1430-1830, free.
Metro: Missori.
Map: Milan, E6, p82.

This church is one of the first Christian churches built, dating to AD 355-372. It was commissioned by Bishop Ambrose and renovated in the 13th century, its large dome rebuilt in 1573. Outside the church, the statue in the piazza is a copy of one of Emperor Constantine, who allowed Christianity to be practised with the Edict of Milan in AD 313. Also here are Milan's most beloved Roman remnants – a row of 9-metre tall columns that were part of a third century temple moved here in the fifth century. The piazza remains one of Milan's favourite meeting spots and locals like to sit at the base of the columns and enjoy a cold beer on balmy summer evenings.

> **The piazza remains one of Milan's favourite meeting spots and locals like to sit at the base of the columns and enjoy a cold beer on balmy summer evenings.**

Five of the best

Churches in Milan

❶ San Sepolcro (1030), *piazza San Sepolcro*
Dedicated to the Holy Sepulchre during the Second Crusade, this imposing red-brick church has a Romanesque crypt and a neo-Romanesque façade courtesy of 1879 renovations.

❷ Rotonda di via Besana (1254), *piazza San Marco*
Rebuilt in 1871 in a neo-Gothic style, it boasts a splendid stone portico with a relief of Christ as a child; Verdi premiered his Requiem here.

❸ San Babila (1575), *corso Venezia* A splendid campanile was added in 1820, and Romanesque revisions made in 1853 and 1906.

❹ San Maurizio (1503), *corso Magenta* Notable for 16th-century frescoes by Bernardino Luini, including impressive ones on the Life of St Catherine.

❺ Santa Maria presso San Celso (1493), *corso Italia*
Originally built to house an icon of the Madonna, the church features excellent Renaissance and baroque art.

Sant'Eustorgio

Piazza Sant'Eustorgio.
Daily 0730-1200 & 1530-1830, free.
Metro: Missori or Porta Genova.
Map: Milan, E7, p82.

Another one of Milan's churches featuring a medley of styles, the origins of this one date back to the seventh century. It was updated in the ninth century, and once again altered in the 11th, with more modifications up to the 15th before it was topped by a neo-Romanesque façade in 1865. The highlights of the church are the *Cappella Portinari* (Chapel of St Peter Martyr) built between 1462 and 1466, and the frescoes by Renaissance painter Vincenzo Foppa.

Above left: Sant'Eustorgio.
Opposite page: Detail of Sant'Eustorgio.

Architectural glossary

aedicule frame around a doorway or window comprised of columns or pilasters and an entablature on top, typical of Classical and Gothic architecture; could be a mini decorative structure housing a statue.

arcade row of columns that support arches.

architrave lower part of an entablature, which meets the capitals of the columns.

baldachin canopy over a tomb, supported by columns.

campanile bell tower.

capital top or 'crown' of a column, often adorned with scrolls (Ionic) or acanthus leaves (Corinthian).

cloister open covered passage around a courtyard (usually part of a church or monastery), supported by columns or arches.

columns the Greek order of columns include **Doric**, plain with vertical grooves called fluting; **Ionic**, characterized by scrolls; and **Corinthian**, with a bell-shaped capital, often adorned with acanthus leaves and volutes. The Roman's **Tuscan** order are without decoration, while the **Composite** order was a mishmash of the three Grecian orders.

choir chancel of a church, used by the clergy and choir, occasionally separated from the nave by a screen.

colonnade series of columns.

cornice horizontal ledge or moulding. For practical purposes it's a gutter, draining water off the building, or a decorative feature if purely aesthetic.

cupola dome on a roof.

entablature held up by columns, the entablature includes the architrave, frieze and cornice.

frieze centre of an entablature; often decorated.

loggia open ground floor gallery, recessed gallery, or corridor on the façade of a building.

nave central body of the church, between the aisles.

narthex long porch along the entrance of a church, before the nave.

pilaster rectangular column that only slightly protrudes from a wall.

pinnacle small, often ornate, turret, popular in Gothic architecture.

plinth lower part or base of a column.

portico doorway, often roofed, serving as an entrance (real or decorative) to a building.

sacristy room off the main or side altars in a church or a separate building housing sacred vessels, vestments and records.

tracery ornamental stonework that supports the glass in Gothic windows.

Certosa di Pavia

An easy half-hour ride from Milan, the exuberant Certosa di Pavia (Charterhouse of Pavia) is an enchanting place to while away a day. Built between 1396 and 1465, this splendid Carthusian monastery complex has a fairytale Gothic church with an extravagant façade and elaborate interior. The elegant palace has graceful gardens to stroll through as you contemplate (in silence of course!) the stark contrast between the monks' simple life of confinement and the lavish riches on show within the church.

Located at the end of a shaded lane and set in velvety parkland that was once the Visconti dynasty's hunting park, the place is perfect for a picnic. You'll have to bring your own hamper as there's nowhere to purchase anything nearby, though you can buy dessert here – the monk's homemade chocolate from the monastery shop.

Home to the Carthusian monastic order, Certosa di Pavia is the finest Carthusian monastery in Italy: there is no match when it comes to sheer architectural grandeur, opulent detail and the extraordinary riches on display inside. Commissioned by Gian Galeazzo Visconti, the magnificent church and monastery were principally built to house the Visconti dynasty mausoleum. Indeed, the location was a strategic choice – part way between Milan and the duchy's second city, Pavia, where the Duke kept his court.

Inspired by Milan's Duomo (see page 84), the richly ornamented church façade is a model of symmetrical perfection. Adorned with inlaid marble, intricately carved statues, buttresses, and bas-reliefs that tell the history of the *certosa*, it boasts a beautiful classical arched portal with Corinthian columns, a large central window, and elegant rows of shallow arched balconies. What makes the church so impressive, though, is its truly monumental interior, which is modelled on the Latin cross plan, with a colossal nave, two aisles and transept. The glorious vaulted ceiling is supported by Gothic arches and decorated with a starry sky. Throughout the main chapel and its adjoining enormous chapels are marble altars, wooden choir stalls, beautiful bronze candelabra and ivory triptychs.

If that wasn't enough, the whole church is decorated with a wealth of art. Required to spend revenue from the lands to improve the building, the monks gradually amassed enormous collections of riches with particularly impressive artworks from the 15th and 18th centuries. Expect to see wonderful frescoes, paintings and panels by Bergognone, Giovanni Battista Crespi and Guercino, sculptures by Giovanni Antonio Amadeo and the Mantegazza brothers, and stained glass windows by some of Lombard's finest 15th-century artists, including Bergognone, as well as Zanetto Bugatto and Vincenzo Foppa. The tomb of Gian Galeazzo Visconti is in the southern transept while that of dynastic rival Ludovico Sforza and his wife Beatrice d'Este (see page 238) is in the northern transept.

After you've lingered in the church awhile, exit through the elegant portal at the rear (a monk is usually there to show you the way), which leads to the Small Cloister with a pretty garden at its centre and arcades decorated with frescoes. From here you can peek into the Grand Cloister, where the monks' cells open onto the main garden. In this cloister the columned arcades are prettily decorated in pink and white marble with saints, prophets and angels. Take a leisurely amble around the perimeter of the small cloister; from the southern side you can enjoy a lovely vista across the gardens to the church, which is the real highlight for some.

Time spent at the *certosa* is really a wonderful assault upon the senses, so allow lots of it. Before you leave, drop by the shop where you can buy Chartreuse liqueur and chocolate made by the monks alongside herbs grown in the gardens and aromatic soaps.

If you have your own wheels, then Pavia is worth a quick look. Once one of northern Italy's most powerful cities, the town has a pleasant medieval *centro storico*, and the Università degli Studi di Pavia is one of Europe's oldest.

Essentials

Viale Certosa, Pavia, certosadipavia.com.
Church & grounds daily 0900-1700; *certosa* (including cloister & shop) Tue-Sun 0900-1130 & 1430-1730, free.

Certosa di Pavia is 30 km south of Milan and 10 km north of Pavia. If driving from Milan, take the SS35 to Pavia, then turn left at viale Certosa. Buses from Milan leave from Milan Famogasta metro station (€3), dropping you a 15-min walk from the *certosa*; tell the driver where you are going so they can alert you when to hop off. Remember to dress modestly.

Sleeping

Self-catering

Friendly Home €
T02-8691 0453,
friendly-home.org.
An organization offering a range of B&Bs and studios (suitable for self-catering) for short stays in Milan. Some are situated in historic houses, while others are of the modern Milanese style. As they have properties all over, make sure you choose according to your itinerary.

Milan Apartment Rental €-€€
T02-950 5689,
milanapartmentrental.it.
While amenities vary, generally these apartments are elegant and stylish, fully furnished, and fully equipped for self-catering. All have Wi-Fi, satellite TV and DVD player, and bed linen and towels. As with any of these kinds of properties, location is king, so make sure the apartment is in a good area for living like a local.

RentXpress €-€€€
T02-583490, rentxpress.com.
RentXpress offers a virtual phonebook full of apartments across Milan that are fantastic value if you're staying more than a few nights. Many of them boast chic decor and most are fully equipped for self-catering. Some are in superb locations, such as the waterfront apartments in the Navigli; however, some are inconveniently located for sightseeing.

Duomo & Centre

Park Hyatt Milano €€€
Via Tommaso Grossi 1, T02-8821 1234, milan.park.hyatt.com.
Map: Central Milan, D5, p88.
The unbeatable position (Duomo, Galleria and La Scala just steps away) would be enough to make this hotel popular, but the service and attention to detail are what really sets it apart. The rooms are sizeable, with plush carpets, every imaginable amenity, and large Italian marble-clad bathrooms. The hotel's restaurant is excellent.

Hotel Spadari al Duomo €€€
Via Spadari 11, T02-7200 2371, spadarihotel.com.
Map: Central Milan, C6, p88.
A small design hotel that has oodles of real personality is rare, but the Spadari has it in spades. Each room is well-appointed and cosy, personalized by Italian artists, but it's the staff and service that really make this small hotel something quite special. A fantastic location just one block from the Duomo and right next door to the best delicatessen in Italy, Peck (see page 137), makes it a tempting option.

Straf Hotel €€-€€€
Via San Raffaele 3, T02-8909 5294, straf.it.
Map: Central Milan, F5, p88.
Since the Straf's opening, guests' responses to it have been mixed to say the least. Some love the design (cement walls, black stone, burnished brass and low-key lighting) while others appear to have been distressed by the experience of the womb-like rooms. We've only been slightly traumatised by the service, which is hit and miss, but we love the aperitivo scene, the good breakfast and the great location.

Hotel Gritti €
Piazza Santa Maria Beltrade 4, T02-801056, hotelgritti.com.
Map: Central Milan, D6, p88.
A three-star hotel on quiet piazza Beltrade, the location just off busy shopping street via Torino, with the Duomo just down the road, makes Gritti a decent option. While it's a little worn around the edges, the rooms are clean and comfortable.

Hotel Speronari €
Via Speronari 4, T02-8646 1125.
Map: Central Milan, D6, p88.
The best of the budget picks has an unbeatable location in an atmospheric area near the Duomo. Basic rooms can be booked with or without bathroom (the former are much better) and rooms facing the courtyard are quieter than street-facing rooms. The hotel might not be as interesting as the streets around it, but in this category in this fantastic location, it's slim pickings.

Park Hyatt Milano.

Bulgari €€€
*Via Privata Fratelli Gabba 7/b,
T02-805 8051, bulgarihotels.com.*
Map: Milan, F3, p82.
Exclusive and exquisite with lovely gardens, this hotel designed by renowned Antonio Citterio is quite the oasis of cool. Unlike other 'boutique' style properties in Milan, the staff are helpful and the fantastic spa is worthy of a serious set of treatments. Rooms are generous in size and the bar and restaurant exemplary, so it's actually hard to leave the premises and face the 'real' Milan outside.

Four Seasons Hotel €€€
*Via Gesù 81, T02-77088,
fourseasons.com.*
Map: Central Milan, G3, p88.
There's nothing austere about this elegant former 15th century monastery right in the heart of the shopping district. Unapologetically lavish and with service that lifts this Four Seasons above the pack, it's *the* address to put your bags down in after a serious shopping excursion. Unless you're in one of the spacious suites, you might find the rooms a tight squeeze.

Grand Hotel et de Milan €€€
*Via Alessandro Manzoni 29,
T02-723141,
grandhoteletdemilan.it.*
Map: Central Milan, F2, p88.
This is Milan's opera-lovers' hotel of choice, not only for the proximity to the famous La Scala, but for the fact that it was once home to composer Giuseppe Verdi. Originally opened in 1863, the opulent furnishings in the rooms reflect the different eras of the hotel's life. Staying in the Verdi suite and eating at the fabulous Don Carlos restaurant makes for a memorable night in.

Una Hotel Tocq €€
*Via A De Tocqueville 7d,
T02-62071, unahotels.it.*
Map: Milan, E1, p82.
The Italian Una group has a
number of hotels in the city,
but this one is best positioned
(in the heart of corso Como) if
you're in town for shopping, bars
and clubs. While the design isn't
as fashionable as it once might
have been, the rooms are a
decent size and have a good
level of amenities.

Hotel Manzoni €€€
*Via Santo Spirito 20, T02-7600
5700, hotelmanzoni.com.*
Map: Central Milan, G2, p88.
The Manzoni's enviable
shopping district location
(between the two best shopping
streets in the city) has recently
been matched with an enviable
revamp. It's now a sumptuous
property, with plenty of marble
and fancy furnishings. With LCD
TVs, Wi-Fi and all other mod
cons, it's an excellent value
four-star, so upgrade to a suite
before the prices inevitably rise.

Antica Locanda Solferino €€
*Via Castelfidardo 2, T02-657
0129, anticalocandasolferino.it.*
Map: Milan, F1, p82.
This comfortable, personal
locanda has 11 individually
decorated rooms with lovely
engravings and fascinating
antique pieces. Its charm lies in
its idiosyncratic and arty nature,
so those wanting to tick off

Aperitivo time at the Sherton Diana Majestic.

amenities lists should look
elsewhere. The Brera is a great
area to stay in, with plenty of
restaurants and shopping.

East

Sheraton Diana Majestic €€€
*Viale Piave 42, T02-20581,
starwoodhotels.com.*
Map: Milan, H2, p82.
This wonderful *stile Liberty*
building is home to a hotel
with a dual personality – the
charming and welcoming set
of 107 rooms and suites with
original furniture (and wonderful
beds) is offset by the chic
aperitivo scene that is unrivalled
in Milan. A great address in a city
where guests can otherwise be
treated a little offhandedly.
There's a fine restaurant too,
if you can't be bothered with
leaving the hotel after aperitivo.

The Chedi €€€

Via Villapizzone 24, T02-3631 8011, thechedimilan.com.
Map: Milan, H1, p82.
The cool Chedi style is a good fit for Milan – the Asian-warmth-meets-Milanese-minimalism of this 'urban resort' is an excellent idea. The large club rooms with the access to the Chedi Club are worth the extra outlay. The only problem is that the hotel is not as 'urban' as one would like – on the edge of the city it's better situated for the fairs than sightseeing.

South

Hotel Ariston €€

Largo Carrobbio 2, T02-7200 0556, aristonhotel.com.
Map: Milan, E5, p82.
The Ariston is a decent three-star hotel that's well positioned for the sights, shopping and nightlife. Room sizes vary; there are some spacious doubles (the deluxe rooms on the eighth floor are recommended), but some singles are only fit for a monk. The hotel has pretensions to being an ecological hotel with 'bioarchitecture', but there's little evidence of it. There is, however, very handy on-site parking.

Hotel Vecchia Milano €

Via Borromei 4, T02-875042, hotelvecchiamilano.it.
Map: Central Milan, B5, p88.
A small and very modest 27-room hotel, it has the feel of a B&B rather than a fully-fledged hotel. All rooms have A/C (sometimes they don't in this price range) and are simply decorated. Friendly staff and handily placed for shopping and local restaurants.

Bed & Breakfast Milano Duomo €

Via Torino 46, T347-779 6170, bbmilanoduomo.it.
Map: Central Milan, C7, p88.
A welcome addition to the property-starved B&B scene, the location (right near the Duomo on a busy shopping street) and fresh renovation make it a good choice. Bright and comfortable, the rooms are relatively generous in size and spotlessly clean. The staff take pride in knowing where to send guests to dine. No credit cards.

West

Antica Locanda Leonardo €€

Corso Magenta 78, T02-4801 4197, anticalocandaleonardo.com.
Map: Milan, C4, p82.
This small, family-run hotel is for those who dislike the anodyne experience of a chain hotel. Room styles vary, but all have a/c, Wi-Fi and satellite TV. The bonus comes with the service, with the staff happy to make bookings for you at recommended restaurants and get tickets for the must-do *Il Cenacolo* (The Last Supper).

Alle Meraviglie €

Via San Tomaso 8, T02-805 1023, allemeraviglie.it.
Map: Central Milan, B4, p88.
A small B&B done up in a style your grandmother would probably like, it's a simple, charming place that provides respite from the busy streets of Milan. Everything here is fresh, light and floral, and while amenities are thin on the ground it's all about the atmosphere – for better or worse, depending on your needs.

Hotel King €

Corso Magenta 19, T02-874432, hotelkingmilano.com.
Map: Milan, D4, p82.
Recently renovated, the 'King Mokinba', as it's fondly known, offers up decent and endearingly old-fashioned digs. The rooms do vary in size (so be persistent in asking for a larger room), all are spotless, and the amenities level is good. Good location, with bars close by and the convenience of Cadorna and the Malpensa Express (for the airport) a short distance away.

Eating

Duomo & Centre

Antico Ristorante Boeucc €€€
Piazza Belgioioso 2,
T02-7602 0224.
Closed Sun & Mon lunch & Aug.
Map: Central Milan, F3, p88.
This timeless restaurant, elegantly housed in an 18th-century palazzo, reflects the clientele of bankers and businesspeople – they want reliable, unsurprising food offering a good return for their investment. Boeucc delivers with refined versions of Milanese classics such as ossobucco.

Trussardi alla Scala €€€
Piazza della Scala 5,
T02-8068 8201.
Closed Sat & Sun lunch.
Map: Central Milan, D4, p88.
Chef Andrea Berton's dishes are a delight, with comforting classics such as risotto uplifted with sweetbreads. There's a brilliant cellar and a surprisingly relaxed atmosphere considering it's now sporting two Michelin stars.

Il Ristorante Cracco €€€
Via Victor Hugo 4, T02-876774.
Closed Sat & Sun lunch & Aug.
Map: Central Milan, D5, p88.
Carlo Cracco is Milan's mad-scientist chef, his experimentation has earned him a place amongst the best chefs in the world and the elegant confines of his restaurant belie the wildness of his vivid imagination. While foodies

flock here, less adventurous or informed diners might baulk at some of the creations.

Bistrot Duomo €€
Via San Raffaele 2, T02-877120.
Closed Sun & Mon lunch & Aug.
Map: Central Milan, F5, p88.
If you can take your attention away from the dramatic views of the Duomo from the top floor of La Rinascente department store building, this refined restaurant serves up regional classics. You can't go wrong with this good mix of views, cuisine, service and a decent wine list.

Italian Bar €€,
Via Cesare Cantù 3, T02-869 3017.
Closed Sun.
Map: Central Milan, D5, p88.
This smart, no-nonsense restaurant (part of the Peck delicatessen empire) has locals so loyal the waiters can punch in their order from memory. While others might struggle to actually get a waiter's attention, it's worth persevering for the quality and simplicity of the cuisine. Good short wine list.

Il Salumaio di Montenapoleone €€
Via Montenapoleone,
T02-7600 1123.
Closed Sat & Sun lunch.
Map: Central Milan, G3, p89.
Along with Trattoria Bagutta (below), this small, enticing courtyard restaurant, fronting their excellent delicatessen,

Eating in Milan

Milan is great for foodies, boasting some of Italy's finest gastronomic experiences at the best restaurants. It can also be a really fun city to eat in, with countless casual trattorias, osterias and enotecas offering an easy and quick no-nonsense meal – or a slow one if you prefer it! Always check in advance to make sure your restaurant of choice is open, as owners have been known to close on a whim – if there's a big football match on, for instance, or the weather is particularly bad. Generally, most restaurants and trattorias open for lunch (1200-1500) and dinner (1900-2300) at least six days and nights a week, although some of the finest restaurants might only open for dinner. Osterias and enotecas won't often open until late afternoon, but will stay open serving food later than restaurants. The best restaurants close for August, when the locals head to the beaches and Milan becomes a ghost town; they might also close for a couple of weeks in January, after Christmas and New Year, so it's best to book your Michelin-starred restaurants well in advance.

Pizzeria Tradizionale.

knows how to refuel patrons in the middle of a shopping expedition. If you think the filled tortellini might see you go up a size, don't dare peruse the dessert menu.

Trattoria Bagutta €€
Via Bagutta 14-16, T02-7600 2767.
Closed Sun.
Map: Central Milan, G3, p89.
Don't be put off by the dark entrance – seating out the back, in or adjoining the courtyard, are *primo* positions for lunch. Calorie-counters pick at the first-rate antipasto bar while everyone else lets the old-school atmosphere take over and orders staples such as *ossobucco*.

Cafés
Café Trussardi
Piazza della Scala 5, T02-8068 8295.
Map: Central Milan, D4, p88.
This stylish café and bar opposite La Scala is a local favourite because you can get everything here from panini in the morning or an excellent quick lunch to aperitivo hour drinks and prosecco during the opera's intermission.

Zucca in Galleria
Galleria Vittorio Emanuele II 21, T02-8646 4435.
Map: Central Milan, E5, p88.
Milan's must-do café is a stand-up caffeine-shot-stop for the locals, while visitors

dominate the outside seating. Check out the lovely art deco interior.

Victoria Caffè
Via Clerici 1, T02-805 3598.
Map: Central Milan, C4, p88.
This sumptuous café hosts a parade of Milan's financiers who re-energize with coffee during the day and something stronger after the markets close. Great aperitivo snacks.

North

Joia €€€
Via Panfilo Castaldi 18, T02-2952 2124.
Closed Sat & Sun lunch.
Map: Milan, H2, p82.
A vegetarian restaurant with a Michelin star is no mean feat, but one in meat-loving Milan is quite extraordinary. Chef Pietro Leemann sees this as an opportunity rather than a drawback and his dishes dazzle with creativity, flavour and beautiful presentation.

Nabucco €€
Via Fiori Chiari 10, T02-860663.
Map: Central Milan, C1, p88.
For years Nabucco has been the pick of via Fiori Chiari. A creative menu working on the popular premise of tradition with a twist, the light meat and fish dishes are outstanding. A notable wine list, elegant interior, and, during the warmer months, outdoor seating.

L'Altra Pharmacia €€
Via Rosmini 3, T02-345 1300.
Map: Milan, C1, p82.
While it's a little off the tourist trail, this is an honest eatery serving up good sized portions of cooking that cures your ills. Ask for a recommendation from their interesting wine list to wash down their signature creamy risotto served in a round of Parmesan – just what the doctor ordered.

Artidoro €€
Via Camperio 15, T02-805 7386.
Closed Sun.
Map: Milan, E4, p82.
A neighbourhood favourite, this *osteria* is busy at night when the candle-lit interior makes up for the romance that's absent during lunch with the clock-watching crowd. The food is good at anytime, though platters of aged cheese, mixed salami plates and homemade pastas are the attraction.

Solferino 35 €€
Via Solferino 35, T02-2900 3345.
Closed Sat & Sun lunch.
Map: Milan, E2, p82.
This cosy local restaurant is a firm favourite, with an excellent short menu and well-matched wine list. A tasty starter selection followed by anything cooked in the wood-fired oven (ask for the specials) is the way to graze the menu.

Cafés

Cova
Via Montenapoleone 8,
T02-7600 5578.
Map: Central Milan, G3, p88.
This restored tearoom is a classic destination on a shopping excursion, either for an espresso hit to help maintain the shopping pace or for a glass of prosecco to celebrate scoring a bargain designer get-up.

Viel
Via Manzoni 3e, corso Buenos Aires 15, T02-2951 6123.
Map: Milan, F5, p82.
One of Milan's best-known producers of *frullati di frutta* (fruit shakes) and ice cream sorbets, Viel have been making their huge range of flavours since the 1940s.

What the locals say

I wake up early and go to Giardini Pubblici – the park is fantastic in the morning with so many birds around. I have breakfast in a café on piazza Tre Colori, Café Cici, that's off-the-beaten-track, which I love; owned by a North African who makes the best fresh orange juice. I go to an art exhibition at the Padiglione d'Arte Contemporanea (see page 111). For lunch, because I'm a vegetarian I have Japanese; I love Osaka on corso Garibaldi, which makes vegetarian sushi and serves great green tea. In the afternoon I go shopping. I head to piazzale Cinque Giornate on corso Vercilli for shoes. I am a big reader so I go to Libracco for old editions you can't get anywhere else and Hoepli for new books, on philosophy, other religions, cookbooks. I never try other recipes – for me to cook is to express myself – but I take inspiration from Japanese food as I lived in Japan for a year, also China and India. I admire the Japanese because they maintain contact with the essence of life: nature. In the early evening I go to Trussardi alla Scala (see page 124) for fresh fruit and a vegetable juice, and later I'll see a performance, perhaps theatre or opera. I love all the arts, I love to feel the emotions of the performers. After theatre I eat gelato. My favourite is Gelateria Umberto at piazzale Cinque Giornate as it's very old: I love the hazelnut! Then I stroll around Brera. It's beautiful at night, very lively with all the bars.

Pietro Leeman,
Michelin-starred Chef at Joia, describes his perfect day in Milan.

South

El Brellin €€
Vicolo Dei Lavandai & Alzaia Naviglio Grande 14,
T02-5810 1351.
Map: Milan, C7, p82.
One of the heavyweight restaurants along the Navigli, this ristorante and popular aperitivo bar, situated in an old mill, is perfect for pre-dinner drinks followed by classic Milanese dishes. The outdoor garden is great for lunch.

Cantina Della Vetra €€
Papa Pio IV, T02-8940 3843.
Closed Sat lunch.
Map: Milan, D6, p82.
This rustic food and wine bar has a strong local following for the delights of the frequently changing blackboard menu. Excellent mixed plates of salami and accompanying *gnocco fritto* (puffy fried dough), as well as great wines, make this a good stop on the Navigli.

Officina 12 €€
Alzaia Naviglio Grande 12,
T02-8942 2261.
Closed Mon & Sat-Tue lunch.
Map: Milan, C7, p82.
There is nothing modest about this massively popular Navigli

eatery: from the size of the local groups that come here, to the size of the tasty pizzas, to the size of the restaurant itself. While it's more romantic sitting alfresco, inside the atmosphere is contagious.

Fabbrica €
Via Alzaia Naviglio Grande 70,
T02-835 8297.
Map: Milan, C7, p82.
The attraction is pretty straightforward at this popular pizza place – wonderful, simple wood-fired pizzas constantly heading out to two floors of hungry locals. It's open late, too, making it a solid choice after a few aperitivo rounds along the Navigli.

Gnocco Fritto €
Via Pasquale Paoli 2,
T02-5810 0216.
Map: Milan, B7, p82.
Just off the Navigli, this is the place where groups of locals go to line their stomachs before a night out, or head after they've realised that aperitivo snacks only go so far. The big attraction is huge plates of fresh *gnocco fritto* (puffy fried dough) which shares equal billing with delicious plates of cheese and cold cuts.

Luca & Andrea €
Alzaia Naviglio Grande 34,
T02-5810 1142.
Map: Milan, C7, p82.
A long-time favourite on the Navigli, the languid nature of this *enoteca* belies the quality of the

wines and the outstanding plates of cheese and *salumi misti* (mixed salami and ham).

Pizzeria Naturale €
Via Edmondo de Amicis 24,
T02-839 5710.
Map: Milan, D6, p82.
The fantastic wood-fired oven front and centre gives diners a big hint as to what the specialty is here, but it's the wholemeal and gluten-free options that set this pizza place apart. Only a few tables, so get in early for some of the best pizza in town.

Pizzeria Tradizionale €
Ripa di Porta Ticinese 7,
T02-839 5133.
Map: Milan, D6, p82.
One of the key eateries on the Navigli, Pizzeria Tradizionale does a roaring trade, with its outside tables packed with locals and visitors half an hour after opening every night. The big, puffy pizzas make their way to just about every table, but the locals also swear by the *fritto misto* (fried seafood).

Le Vigne €
Ripa di Porta Ticinese 61,
T02-837 5617.
Closed Sun.
Map: Milan, B7, p82.
This honest little osteria is an endearing one, with a *piccolo* menu and a wine list that's a real page-turner for the grape buffs. Fantastic fresh pastas and great seasonal specials.

Planning a picnic?

Pick up some gourmet delights from Peck (see page 137) or simply some cold meats and cheeses from local markets and head to:

Parco Sempione Milan's best park is a beautiful expanse of green boasting big shady trees, meandering paths and pretty ponds. See page 100.

Sant'Eustorgio Neighbourhood green, popular with locals walking their dogs and drinking beers, extends from behind Sant'Eustorgio north to via Molino delle Armi. See page 116.

Giardini Pubblici Picnic on the park benches at this central park. Not the best, but handy for sightseeing. See page 111.

Giardini Pubblici.

Entertainment

Cafés
Rinomata Gelateria
Corner of Ripa di Porta Ticinese & viale Glorizia, T02-5811 3877.
Map: Milan, D7, p82.
One of the defining moments of summer in Milan is taking the edge off the sweltering heat at this venerable gelateria. Delightfully old-fashioned with fantastic flavours.

East

Da Giacomo €€
Via Sottocorno 6, T02-7602 3313.
Closed Mon & Tue lunch.
Map: Milan, H4, p83.
While this inconspicuous trattoria is ever-popular with Milan's business elite and fashion's heavy hitters, it's all about excellent seafood in convivial surroundings. The *gnocchetti* with prawns alone makes the trip to this unassuming neighbourhood worth the effort.

Da Giannino L'Angolo d'Abruzzo €€
Via Rosolino Pilo 20, T02-2940 6526.
Closed Mon.
Map: Milan, H3, p82.
Unapologetically old-fashioned, this family-run trattoria serves up dishes from the Abruzzo region of central Italy. While some of the customers look older than time itself, the cooking is timeless.

West

Boccondivino €€
Via Giosué Carducci 17, T02-866 040.
Closed Sun.
Map: Milan, D5, p82.
If you're wondering why Italy is so revered for its cheeses, wines, hams and salamis, Boccondivino answers the question. Popular with locals who pick their way through plates of wonderful produce and select hard-to-source wines from the wine list.

Cafés
Caffè Litta
Corso Magenta 25, T02-805 7596.
Map: Milan, D4, p82.
This lovely old café is an institution in Milan, as much for its art nouveau interior as its excellent coffee and snacks. The outdoor seating is just as popular for the corso Magenta people-watching.

Marchesi
Via S M alla Porta 11a, T02-876730.
Map: Milan, E4, p82.
Don't let the endearingly old-fashioned window display and original interior here distract you from the excellent coffee and snacks – popular since 1824!

Apart from aperitivo of course – which begins after work or before dinner – the Milanese hit the bars late (after 2200) and hit the clubs even later (rarely before midnight). While bars are free, and there'll often be free snacks for drinkers, clubs often charge an admission fee (from around €10-20) however, this usually includes a drink. Some clubs have free nights, while others offer annual membership (check online) which is sometimes little more than the cost of an entry fee yet guarantees you free entry and other perks. Many venues are closed during August.

Bars
Bhangra Bar
Piazza Sempione 1, T02-3310 0824, bhangrabarmilano.com.
Wed-Sun.
Probably Milan's only Indian-inspired aperitivo spread. Low-key hipsters frequent this bar, which turns more club-like as the night wears on.

Bar Brera
Via Brera 23, T02-877091.
Daily 0700-0300.
A Milan institution, it's hard to beat a sunny afternoon here people-watching on the cobblestone streets.

Bar Magenta
Via Carducci 13, T02-805 3808.
Daily 0800-0300.
The antidote for those who say Milan is reserved, this traditional

remedy is best taken between 1700 and 2100, when aperitivo heats up.

Beige
Largo La Foppa 5, T02-659 9487.
Mon-Sat 1200-0200.
A relaxing bar and *enoteca*, it's reliable for a glass of good wine and excellent finger food for aperitivo.

Le Biciclette
Via Torti 1, T02- 839 4177, lebiciclette.com.
Mon-Sat 1800-0200, Sun 1230-0200.
This former bicycle workshop pedals some of the best of aperitivo atmosphere in Milan – get there early.

Boccascena Café
Teatro Litta, corso Magenta 24, T02-805 5882.
Daily 1000 till curtain close.
Set in an 18th-century palazzo, this groovy bar belies all that's stuffy about theatre. Go for pre- or post-play drinks.

hclub>diana Bar
Sheraton Diana MajesticHotel, viale Piave 42, T02-20581, sheraton.com.
Daily 1000-0200
The grande dame of aperitivo just keeps marching along with a stylish crowd, excellent cocktails and the choice of garden or groovy interior settings.

Five of the best

Fashion spots

Milan's fashionistas flock to the city's chic designer bar-cum-restaurant-cum-clubs. Dress to impress. Seriously.

❶ Dolce & Gabbana's **Martini Bar** *corso Venezia 15, T02-7601 1154.*

❷ Armani's **Nobu Bar and Restaurant** *via Pisoni 1, T02-6231 2645.*

❸ Armani **Privé** *via Pisoni 1, T02-6231 2645.*

❹ **Just Cavalli Café** *Torre Branca, Parco Sempione, T02-313 817.*

❺ Trussardi's **Alla Scala Café & Restaurant** *piazza della Scala 5, T02-8068 8295.*

The Navigli

Aperitivo is first and foremost a Milanese ritual – don't let anyone tell you differently. So your night out sampling aperitivo spots – essentially a bar hop! – should begin with a stroll from the centre of Milan, starting from the **Duomo**, in the lovely late afternoon. This way you can do as the Milanese do and follow the locals who saunter here after work, taking it especially slowly during summer.

To get to the Navigli from the Duomo, follow shopping street **via Torino** until you come to a

fork in the road: take the left prong, **corso di Porta Ticinese**. You'll soon come across the 16 striking columns of **San Lorenzo Maggiore** on your left. If it's a Friday or Saturday night, the piazza in front of the church, a popular meeting place, will be crowded with people sipping beers and sitting at the base of the columns chatting to their friends.

Walk under the arch where – if you're ready to start – you can imbibe at a local favourite, **Luca's Bar**. Continuing further down the street you'll no doubt see the neoclassical columns of **Porta Ticinese**.

Your first aperitivo stop is **El Brellin** (see page 126), one of the local favourites for its much-coveted seating overlooking the water. Next you'll pass **Officina 12** (see page 126) where they do great pizzas (and even better steaks) – the atmosphere is lively, making it popular with groups. Next up is a local institution, **Luca & Andrea** (see page 127), where they serve delicious plates of cheese and meats as well as great wines. By now the place will be buzzing with locals perched on stools by the water or spilling across the pavement, so you can settle in and do some people-watching.

Next, if you're ready to have something serious to eat, you can keep heading down Alzaia Naviglio Grande to **Fabbrica** (see page 127), where the pizzas are some of Milan's best, or you can head over to the other side of the canal, crossing the footbridge at via Casale. On the other side of the canal there are a couple of casual eateries that are worth a look, including **Le Vigne** (see page 127), a friendly rustic osteria and **Gnocco Fritto** (see page 127), a buzzy place where you can soak up the liquor with some simple filling fare. Alternatively, you can head up Ripa di Porta Ticinese. There are a few more bars you can stop at en route and if you still haven't found something that tempts your tastebuds, **Pizzeria Tradizionale** (see page 127) has plenty of atmosphere and outdoor cobblestone seating.

By now you might have seen crowds gathering a few doors up at **Rinomata Gelateria** (see page 128). Make a beeline here when you're ready for dessert. If you're not in the mood for gelato, you can check out the trinkets being sold outside by the stallholders at the head of Naviglio Pavese. Or, if you want to kick on, head down Naviglio Pavese and do a lap of the outdoor bars with their pumping soundtracks, which will provide you with plenty of options well into the night. You can also head back along corso di Porta Ticinese where wandering beside the canal, sipping a beer (bought from one of the late-night shops), is a local tradition – as is a toast to a good night out.

Continue on, then head right along piazza 24 Maggio. You'll now come across three bodies of water, the Darsena on your right, the **Naviglio Grande** directly ahead and the Naviglio Pavese to your left. Walk towards the Naviglio Grande where you'll see that there are streets running down each side of the waterway, the one on the left being Ripa di Porta Ticinese and the one on the right Alzaia Naviglio Grande. You can grab a quick drink at the outdoor bars that spill onto the bridge or head down **Alzaia Naviglio Grande** where some of Milan's best aperitivo bars are.

Huggy Bear
Piazza Sempione 3, T02-345 1614.
Seventies mood, great cocktails, plenty of retro music, and a cuddly vibe, of course.

Living
Piazza Sempione 2, 02-3310 0824, livingmilano.com.
This former post office can have lines as long as its former incarnation did for the excellent aperitivo snacks. Arrive about 1700.

Luca's Bar
Colonne di S Lorenzo, corso di Porta Ticinese, T02-5810 0409.
Far from the world of shiny hip bars full of designer furniture, low-key Luca's bar is all about the liquor. Go late.

Yguana
Via Papa Gregorio XIV 6, T02-8940 4195.
Jungle-boogie vibe with wicker chairs, wicked cocktails and wonderful snacks.

Cinema
Arcobaleno Film Centre
Viale Tunisia 11, T02-2940 6054, cinenauta.it.
Plays the latest releases – but bear in mind Italian cinemas have a tendency to dub rather than use subtitles.

Anteospazio Cinema
Via Milazzo 9, T02-659 7732, spaziocinema.info.
This art house film centre has three screens, a bookshop and café.

Cineteca Italiana
Viale Vittorio Veneto 2, T02-7740 6300, cinetecamilano.it.
This stronghold of Italian cinema has classics in the library – projected in their original language.

Clubs
La Banque
Via B Porrone 6, T02-8699 6565, labanque.it.
Tue-Thu 1800-0200, Fri-Sat 1800-0400, Sun 1900-0000, closed Aug.
This former bank is a quite formal, club-style restaurant, bar and dance venue.

Café L'Atlantique
Viale Umbria 42, T02-5519 3925, cafeatlantique.it.
Tue, Wed, Fri & Sat 2100-0400, Thu & Sun 1930-0400, closed Jul & Aug.
An upmarket club for the well heeled and well dressed, with quality DJs and drinks.

Casablanca Café
Corso Como 14, T02-6269 0186, casablancacafe.it.
Wed-Sun 1800-0200, closed Aug.
A strict door policy and commercial house music awaits at this club – it's often a pre-clubbing favourite.

Gasoline Club
Via Bonnet 11a, T02-2901 3245, discogasoline.it.
Thu-Sun 2230-0400, closed Aug.
This small club has fabulous gay nights.

Il Gattopardo Café
Via Piero della Francesca 47, T02-3453 7699, ilgattopardocafe.com.
Tue-Sun 1800-0400.
Located in a deconsecrated church, this club has plenty of baroque charm.

Hollywood
Corso Como 15, T02-659 8996, discotecahollywood.com.
Tue-Sun 2230-0400, closed Jul & Aug.
Somewhat dated, this legendary club still manages to attract the rich and fatuous, from footballers to fashionistas. Dress accordingly.

Magazzini Generali
Via Pietrasanta 14, T02-5521 1313, magazzinigenerali.it.
Wed-Sun 2200-0400, closed Jul & Aug.
This converted warehouse is a happy home to everything from concerts to club nights. *JetLag* on Fridays is a mixed-crowd marvel.

Old Fashion Café
Viale Emillio Alemagna 6, T02-805 6231, oldfashion.it.
Daily 2300-0400.
Labelling itself 'restaurant & rhythmic bar' is truth in

advertising – great DJs, great drinks, and good vibe, even on weeknights.

Plastic
Viale Umbria 120, T02-733996, clubplastic.it.
Thu-Sun 2200-0400, closed Aug.
Once past the fire breathing door dragons (arrive early or fabulously late), you'll find durable Plastic one of the best mixed-crowd clubs in Italy.

Gay & lesbian
Gay and lesbian Milan has a notoriously fickle bar and club scene. Many bars and clubs are straight six nights of the week and have one great gay-friendly night a week, but the nights and the clubs change. The best thing to do is to contact Arcigay di Milano (arcigaymilano.org) which has membership cards to most gay venues. Despite the changeable nature, Afterline is a good choice for men, while Sottomarino Giallo is a dependable choice for women.

Afterline
Via Sammartini 25, T02-669 2130, afterline.it.
Mon-Sat 2100-0200, Sun 1800-0200.
The granddaddy of gay venues, this club has the best theme nights on what is essentially Milan's 'gay street'.

Ricci
Piazza della Republica 27, T02-6698 2536.
Tue-Sun 2000-0200, closed Aug.
A café and cake shop by day, the setting of the sun sees this place turn into one of Milan's most popular gay venues in the city.

Sottomarino Giallo
Via Donatello 2, T02-6311 8654, sottomarinogiallo.it.
Wed & Sun 2300-0300, Fri & Sat 2300-0400, closed Aug.
'Yellow Submarine' remains the premier hangout for lesbian women of all ages who mingle over two floors with a bar and disco. Weekends are strictly gay.

Music
Alcatraz
Via Valtellina 25, T02-6901 6352, alcatrazmilano.com.
Fri-Sat 2200-0400. Club closed Jul & Aug.
A venue that hosts big international acts such as Kanye West during the week, it's generally a dance club on weekends.

Blue Note
Via Borsieri 37, T02-6901 6888, bluenotemilano.com.
Performances Mon-Sat 2100 & 2330, Sun 1800 & 2100.
This Italian branch of the Blue Note franchise is an excellent one, with real atmosphere and great local and international acts.

Blues House
Via S Uguzzone 26, Villa San Giovanni, T02-2799 3621, blueshouse.it.
Wed-Mon 2245-late.
Way off the radar of inner-city Milan, this blues club is worth the trek if you know the players on the bill – not so much for the 'tribute' bands.

Forum
Via di Vittorio, Agasso, T02-488571, forumnet.it.
A big, soulless, and acoustically challenged venue for major acts such as Bob Dylan.

Pala Sharp
Viale Sant'Elia 33, San Siro stadium, T02-3340 0551, mazdapalace.it.
The venue formerly known as Mazda Palace is a popular spot for international artists such as Fall Out Boy.

Rolling Stone
Corso XXII Marzo 32, T02-733172, rollingstone.it.
Thu & Fri 2200-0300, Sat 2100-0400, Sun 2200-0400.
Milan's most unpretentious rock venue is set over three floors with DJs on the weekends.

Scimmie
Via Cardinale Ascanio Sforza 49, T02-8940 2874, scimmie.it.
Daily 2000-0300.
An atmospheric bar on the Navigli, Scimmie specializes in live music – especially jazz.

Theatre, opera & ballet

Auditorium di Milano

Largo Gustav Mahler, corso San Gottardo 42a, T02-8338 9401, auditoriumdimilano.org.
Box office open Thu-Sun 1000-1900.
This delightful former cinema is home to the Giuseppe Verde Symphonic Orchestra and hosts others.

Piccolo Teatro di Milano: Teatro Strehler & Teatro Grassi

Via Rovello 2, T02-7233 3222, piccoloteatro.org.
Box office open Mon-Sat 1000-1845.
These two highly regarded theatres host quality productions as well as ballet.

Serate Al Museo

T02-8846 4526, comune.milano. it/dseserver/labellaestate/.
These summer 'Night at the Museum' events are held across the city and feature concerts and workshops. See the tourist office for programmes.

Teatro alla Scala

Via Filodrammatici 2, T02-7200 3744, teatroallascala.org.
This sumptuous 18th-century opera house has been restored to its former glory after a restoration and controversial additions (see page 90). Off-stage dramas have matched the onstage melodrama, but when the curtain goes up each year on 7 December for the start of the season that now runs most of the year – thanks to the renovations – all is forgiven. With the expanded backstage areas of the theatre, the sets can be works of art themselves – just like the performances of operas by Verdi, who had a wonderful creative career based in this very opera house. Sub-title screens built into the backs of the seats have also improved the experience of those coming to the opera for the first time. When you're in Milan, the best place to get tickets is the ticket office at Galleria del Sagrato, Piazza del Duomo, in the metro underpass (1200-1800). You can also purchase online from their website.

Teatro dal Verme

Via San Giovanni sul Muro 2, T02-8790 5201, dalverme.org.
Box office open Tue-Sun 1100-2100.
This delightful venue, built in the 1870s, has had several lives, but today it's home to theatrical events, concerts and operas.

Teatro Manzoni

Via Alessandro Manzoni 42, T02-763 6901, teatromanzoni.it.
Box office open Mon-Sat 1000-1900, Sun 1100-1700.
A favourite for its light comedies, musicals and Sunday morning performances.

A much-coveted private box at La Scala.

Teatro Smeraldo

Piazza XX Aprile 10, T02-2900 6767, teatrosmeraldo.it.
Box office open Mon-Sat 1000-1815, Sun 1200-1630.
Musicals, theatre, and pop and jazz concerts are generally what are on offer at this busy theatre.

Le Voci della Città

Located at various historic churches around Milan, T02-3910 4149, levocidellacitta.org.
'The Voices of the City' concert programme includes orchestras, vocal ensembles, organ, choral and chamber music concerts, which take place in Milan's splendid churches, such as the Basilica di Sant'Ambrogio throughout the year. There's information online or available at the tourist office.

Shopping

Opening hours vary remarkably from the enormous emporiums on corso Vittorio Emanuele II, which never seem to close, to the smaller stores which generally do business Monday to Saturday 0930 or 1000, close for lunch at 1200 or 1300, then reopen 1600-1900. Those staying open on Sunday close one weekday (usually Monday) and open late another afternoon (often Tuesday).

Art & antiques
The cobblestone streets of Brera, northeast of the Duomo, on via Brera and Solferino in particular, are crammed with fine art galleries and antique shops, while those lining the Naviglio Grande tend to specialise in bric-a-brac and emerging artists. For more antique shops try the area around Sant'Ambrogio, on San Maurilio and via San Giovani. Milan also hosts a number of regular antique markets. If you're serious about buying local art, look out for the booklets 'Start Milano: Guida All'Arte Contemporanea' (start-mi.net).

Books
Messaggerie Musicali
Galleria del Corso 2, corso Vittorio Emanuele II, T02-7605 5404, messaggeriemusicali.it.
An unparalleled range of travel guides, maps and magazines, CDs and DVDs, and English-language novels and translations of Italian literature.

Sleek & unique

Design junkies should make a beeline for the cutting-edge contemporary design stores on corsos Venezia, Monforte and Europa.

Alessi
Corso Matteotti 9, T02-795726, alessi.com.
Pick up a quirky souvenir from the flagship store of the makers of the Magic Bunny toothpick holder and iconic products such as their Starck-designed three-legged juicer.

Da Driade
Via Manzoni 30, T02-7602 0398, driade.com.
This frescoed neoclassical mansion is home to Antonia and Enrico Astori's contemporary design solutions, as well as chic furniture and lighting products from international designers who share their style philosophy.

Ricordi Media Stores
Galleria Vittorio Emanuele II, T02-8646 0272, lafeltrinelli.it.
If Messaggerie Musicali doesn't have what you're looking for, find it here.

The English Bookshop
Via Mascheroni 12, Angolo via Ariosto, T02-469 4468, englishbookshop.it
Author Peter Panton opened this cluttered English bookstore (Milan's first) in 1979. Specializes in rare and second-hand books.

Kartell
Via Turati & Carlo Porta 1, T02-659 7916, kartell.it.
Milan's plastic pioneer, Kartell is synonymous with clever designs, from Ron Arad's Bookworm shelf (1994) to the Louis Ghost chair (2002) and Optic cubes (2006).

Momo Design
Galleria San Babila 4/A, T02-7601 6168, momodesign.com.
Sleek motorcycle helmets, sunglasses, leatherwear, watches and other cool accessories to go with that Vespa you're planning on taking home.

SAG '80
Via Giovanni Boccaccio 4, T02-481 5380, sag.com.
Covet contemporary design products by the biggest names – Artemide, B&B Italia, Boffi, Cappellini, Dada, Driade, Flos, Knoll, Matteograssi, Minotti, Vitra and Zanotta – at this one-stop design shop.

Clothing & accessories
You'll find fabulous fashion, shoes, accessories and jewellery on corso Vittorio Emanuele II. For exclusive designer wear, your first stop should naturally be the chic fashion quarter, the **Quadrilatero d'Oro** (see page 104). For more interesting fashion and jewellery, hit the hip boutiques on via Torino, corso di Porta Ticinese, and in and around Naviglio Grande.

10 Corso Como

Corso Como 10, T02-2900 0760, 10corsocomo.com.

When Italian Vogue editor Carla Sozzani opened this groundbreaking store in 1991 she started an inspired retail trend. This multi-brand fashion boutique, art gallery, gift store, book and music shop, restaurant, café and bar remains as stylish as ever.

Borsalino

Galleria Vittorio Emanuele 92, T02-804337, borsalino.com.

One of the country's oldest hat-makers, Giuseppe Borsalino started making beautifully-crafted men's and women's hats in 1857. They're renowned for their fedoras.

Cavalli e Nastri

Via Brera 2, T02-7200 0449.

Fashion discoveries are a real delight here, one of Milan's first and still one of its best vintage clothing stores.

Colomba Leddi

Via Revere 3, T02-4801 4146.

Colomba Leddi has been creating stunning bespoke clothes for over a decade from her gorgeous atelier. Select your own fabrics and design or seek advice from a professional stylist.

Purple

Corso di Porta Ticinese 22, T02-8942 4476.

The racks bulge with labels by sassy local designers, much of them stitched together from recycled fabrics, some created exclusively for Purple.

Sermoneta

Via della Spiga 46, T02-7631 8303, sermonetagloves.com.

An Italian institution, Sermoneta has been producing the finest quality Italian leather and suede gloves since 1965. The driving gloves are a must on a Lakes road trip. There's a mind-boggling array of colours and styles and staff ensure your gloves are properly fitted.

Cosmetics & perfume

Acqua di Parma
Via Gesù 3, T02-7602 3307, acquadiparma.it.
Created in the 1930s, and originally made for men, this one-of-a-kind fragrance now has a female counterpart, Profumo, and a line of sensual body products.

Calé Fragranze d'Autore
Via S Maria Alla Porta 5, T02-8050 9449, cale.it.
Let the aromas of rare European perfumes waft over you at this elegant store – then take some home!

La Speziale
Corso Buenos Aires 59, T02-2940 0644, laspeziale.it.
Can't find that special scent? Then have a personalized fragrance made just for you – or your own essential oils prepared.

Department stores
With so many fabulous and fascinating shops in Milan, it's hard to imagine why you'd want a department store other than during the end-of-season sales when they're known for their bargains. Try swish **La Rinascente** (piazza del Duomo, T02-875653, Mon-Sat 0900-2200 & Sun 1000-2000) or the more affordable **COIN** (piazza Cinque Giornate, T02-5519 2083, Mon-Sat 0900-2000).

Food & drink

Enoteca Cotti
Via Solferino 42, T02-6572 995, enotecacotti.it.
The Cotti brothers have run these atmospheric cellars since 1952, supplying wine buffs with fine Italian offerings – a great source for collection-quality vintages, especially those of Lombard growers.

Giovanni Galli
Victor Hugo 2, T02-8646 4833, giovannigalli.com.
Specializing in *'maronni, canditi, fondenti'* (chestnuts, candies, fondants). There are also delectable chocolates, pralines, marzipan, amaretti, and tinned pastels.

Peck
Via Spadari 9, T02-802 3161, peck.it.
Established in 1883, elegant Peck boasts three floors of gastronomic goodies, making it a perfect for picnics or gourmet gift-shopping. Ground floor counters and shelves are crammed with aged proscuitto, Parma ham, truffles, olive oil, pastries, gelato and freshly-prepared meals for the picnic basket. Upstairs there's a café, chocolates, sweets, teas and fresh coffee beans, while downstairs is a wine cellar and champagne bar.

Five of the best

Markets in Milan

❶ **Viale Gabriele d'Annunzio** (Sat all day) Lively flea market crammed with unusual stuff.

❷ **Viale Papiniano** (Tue & Sat mornings) Fresh local produce (perfect for picnic supplies) and cheap clothes.

❸ **Ripa di Porta Ticinese, Naviglio Grande** (last Sun of month) Huge art, antiques and bric-a-brac market lines the canal.

❹ **Via Fiori Chiari**, Brera (third Sat of month) High quality antique market specialising in fine antiques and art.

❺ **Mercato Comunale**, Darsena, piazza XXIV Maggio (Mon-Sat) Covered market for fresh fruit and veg on the Darsena.

Above: Market stall on viale Papiniano.
Opposite page: Sermoneta.

Activities & tours

Novelty

Luisa Cevese Riedizioni
Via San Maurilio 3,
T02-801088, riedizioni.com
This Milanese designer creates innovative recycled plastic and textile products, from handbags and raincoats to notebooks and cushions, all delightfully embedded with vibrant scraps of fabric, yarn and threads – it's all industrial waste!

Moroni Gomma
Corso Matteotti 14,
T02-7600 1932
Fun stuff for home and leisure-time that makes fabulous gifts and souvenirs, from retro-looking Tivoli radios to Mini Gioco Football games.

Jewellery

Mon Bijou
Via Pontaccio 2, T02-8058 3197.
Milanese jewellery designer Alessandra Moro creates feminine jewellery from semi-precious gems that is charmingly retro in style.

Pellini
Corso Magenta, T02-7201 0569.
With its antique furniture, this delightful shop is the perfect setting for owner Donatella Pellini's unique pieces.

Kidswear & toys

Città del Sole
Via Orefici 13, T02-866131,
cittadelsole.it.
Need to keep the kids busy in the back seat on those long drives? This fantastic toy shop stocks a huge range of good old-fashioned toys including frisbees, board games, jigsaw puzzles, model kits, activity books, and hand puppets.

I Pinco Pallino
Via della Spiga 42, T02-781931,
ipincopallino.it.
This children's clothes store, complete with crystal chandelier and kiddie fashion TV, specialises in the most fashionable Italian kids' wear around.

Stationery

Fabriano
Via Pietro Verri 3, T02-7631 8754,
fabrianoboutique.com.
Handmade paper manufacturers since 1872, Fabriano also stocks fine quality, handmade, Italian leather-bound photo albums, diaries, notepads, business-card holders and wallets.

Papier
Via Maurilio, off Via Torino,
T02-865221, papier-milano.it.
Beautiful handmade textured writing and wrapping paper embedded with flower petals, leaves and the like, along with exquisite pens, desk-sets, and photo frames with gems and beads.

Football

San Siro Stadium
Via Piccolomini 5, T02-4870 0457,
stadiosansiro.it.
Milan's two major league football clubs, AC Milan (acmilan.com) and FC Internazionale Milano (generally known as 'Inter' or 'Inter Milan', inter.it) play at this famous stadium, which is hardly ever called its real name – Stadio Giuseppe Meazza. Football fans will enjoy the museum and tour (T02-404 2432, sansirotour.com, open daily 1000-1700, €18 adults, €10 under 18) dedicated to the stadium and the two teams that built their reputation here. Tickets to matches are available from branches of Banca Popolare di Milano or from the websites of the two teams.

Language

Dante Alighieri
Piazza le Cadorna 9, T02-7201
1294, dantealighieri.org.
This long-established school offers an extensive range of Italian courses suitable for beginners or for those wishing to study at an Italian-speaking university.

Motoring

Autodromo Nazionale Monza
Via Vedano 5, Parco di Monza,
T039-24821, monzanet.it.
This legendary car racing track, generally known just as 'Monza', is only a short drive away from Milan and is the host of a round of the Formula One Grand Prix

Stadio Giuseppe Meazza – better known as San Siro.

circus. The race is seen as the 'home' grand prix of Ferrari. If you're not there for this red flag waving Ferrari love-fest in September, you can actually take a lap of the famous circuit in your street vehicle for just €40. Specific dates are available from the website.

Italian Motors
Foro Bonaparte 76, T02-867131, zaniviaggi.it.
For those who love anything with an engine, tour company Zani Viaggi operates visits to the Galleria Ferrari in Maranello and the Ducati museum in Bologna.

Sightseeing
A Friend in Milan
T02-2952 0570, friendinmilan.co.uk.
This company specializes in bespoke tours of the major Milan sights as well as the less visited attractions and driving tours of the region.

Autostradale
Departure point at via Marconi, nr Duomo, T02-3391 0794, autostradale.it.
The Autostradale bus company runs a three-hour bus tour of the city (except Mondays). Perfect if you want to knock over the key sights of the city quickly before going shopping guilt-free. One of the best aspects of the tour is the guaranteed visit to da Vinci's *The Last Supper* – it can be hard to get tickets at short notice otherwise. **MaTM** (T02-4803 6999, matmbus.com) offer a tour with a similar itinerary.

Centro Guide
T02-8645 0433, centroguidemilano.net.
Centro Guide provides official guides who are proficient in English (and a number of other languages) and are experts in their chosen field. The cost of €100 for three hours covers up to 25 people.

Ciao Milano Tourist Tram
Departure point at piazza Castello T02-7252 4301.
Several restored 1920s-era trams

run from April to October, going past the main points of interest, with headphones and multilingual commentary.

Navigli Cruises
Via Copernico 42, T02-667 9131, naviglilombardi.it.
Running in the warmer months on weekends, these tours glide down the Navigli waterways, which were originally designed by da Vinci in the 1400s to transport goods and were still active until the Second World War.

Sightseeing Milano
Foro Bonaparte 76, T02-867131, milano.city-sightseeing.it.
This 'Hop-On Hop-Off' bus has two lines around the city with tickets valid for 24 hours (€20 adults, €10 ages 5-15) and commentary in several languages. Some sections of the trips do overlap, so it's best to check the routes to decide which satisfies your interests.

Zani Viaggi
Foro Bonaparte 76, T02-867131, zaniviaggi.it.
This well-established travel agency is a one-stop-shop for a wide range of trips, including Milan shopping expeditions and aperitivo tours. This excellent travel agency also organises tours to other parts of Lombardy including all the lakes, Como, Bergamo and Verona, as well as visits further afield.

Contents

143 Introduction
144 Lake Maggiore
146 Great days out:
    Island hopping – Lake Maggiore
152 Lake Orta
154 Listings:
154 Sleeping
156 Eating
159 Entertainment
160 Shopping
161 Activities & tours

There are many tiny and intriguing villages,
such as Belgirate, on Lake Maggiore.

Introduction

What to see in…

…one day
If you only have one day, **island-hop** on Lake Maggiore. Start at **Stresa**, from where you can catch the ferry to **Isola Bella**, **Isola Superiore**, and **Isola Madre** respectively, taking time to wander about each island. Return to **Montarrone** and walk back along the waterfront to Stresa.

…a weekend or more
Drive to **Verbania** and explore **Villa Taranto**'s sprawling gardens, have coffee in the old town centre and stroll along the lakeside promenade. Stay overnight in **Cannobio**, exploring the *centro storico* and its delightful waterfront. Enjoy an amble before dinner and stroll with gelato for dessert.

Spend a day exploring medieval village **Orta San Giulio** and idyllic little **Isola di San Giulio**. Do a circuit of **Lake Orta**, stopping at **Omegna** on the northern tip, from where you'll have splendid views to Isola San Giulio; pretty **Pella** also warrants a stop. Back on Maggiore, you could travel from **Stresa** down to **Arona** and the **Rocca di Angera**.

The grandest of all the lakes, Lago Maggiore is also one of the more peaceful lakes, lacking the development that sometimes conspires to spoil the Lake Garda experience. The highlight is no doubt the triplet of atmospheric islands owned by the influential Borromeo dynasty, with Isola Bella and its palatial grounds a breathtakingly beautiful sight and one full of history.

Back on shore, the pleasant town of Verbania has a lively waterfront lined with lovely emerald parks, while Stresa has a maze of pedestrianized streets and charming buildings. Both towns come to life on their weekly market days. Cannobio has a charismatic waterfront lined with equally characterful buildings and alfresco cafés, while the steep lanes leading off the waterfront are also enigmatic. Its small lakeside beach sees the locals sunbathing on the lawn beside the town promenade during summer, while the foreign visitors look on in bemusement.

Petite and picturesque Lake Orta is arguably the most alluring of all the lakes in northern Italy. Popular with wealthy Italians and northern Europeans, the lakeside village of Orta San Giulo is pretty as a postcard and if a little touristy during the middle of the day, it's enchanting by the late afternoon when everyone is out for a stroll. Opposite, the island of Isola di San Giulio, with the splendid Basilica of St Giulio, is a highlight of these lakes.

Canoeing on Orta San Giulio, Lake Orta.

Lake Maggiore

Most foreign travellers visiting Lake Maggiore make their base on the western shore, either at Stresa – an elegant, albeit faded fin-de-siècle resort – at pretty Verbania across the water, or at charming Cannobio further upstream with its colourful old buildings skirting the waterfront.

The mountains rise above lakeside Cannobio.

The grande dame of lake resorts, Stresa has been a popular holiday spot since Napoleon carved a route through the mountains in the early 19th century, and the Simplon tunnel and railway line opened the way for the Grand Tour travellers heading south (see page 37). Two centuries later and tourists are still flocking here, but while the Stresa that Stendhal, Dickens and Byron waxed lyrical about has long gone, the place still has a certain retro-charm and undeniable allure – largely due to its grand old hotels, temperate Mediterranean climate, and an archipelago of lovely islands off-shore.

Boasting pastel buildings and pretty piazzas where people linger at alfresco cafés to eat enormous dishes of gelato, Stresa is still an undeniably attractive town – in spite of the traffic, tacky souvenir shops and hordes of tourists in summer. Pass through in winter when the hotels are closed up and the craggy limestone mountains appear even more dramatic blanketed in snow, and you can better picture the tranquil, isolated place that has inspired poets and writers (after visiting in 1948 Ernest Hemingway set part of *A Farewell to Arms* at the Grand Hotel des Iles Borromees) and drew aristocrats to build elegant villas here. Villa Pallavicino can be visited, and indeed, apart from strolling Stresa's picturesque lakeside promenade, lined with vibrant-coloured flowerbeds, visiting the luxuriant Borromeo islands, and taking a

The Borromeo family

An important and influential family throughout Milan's history has been the Borromeo family, but their rise to prominence only came after the death of the head of the family, Filippo, who was decapitated by the Florentines after a revolt in 1370, his children having fled to Milan. Once the family became established in Milan, Vitaliano I (c 1391–1449) put in place the foundations of what was to become a great legacy. Vitaliano, due to his savvy business dealings, purchased the family's first land near Lake Maggiore. The next major player in the family was Giberto II (c 1511-1558) who, as a cardinal, strengthened the family image. But it wasn't until the next generation that the family's name was cemented in history.

Carlo Borromeo (1538-1584) became a very popular Reformist archbishop in 1564 and after his death his cousin Federico (1564-1631) worked tirelessly to have his cousin canonised, which he eventually succeeded in doing in 1610. In 1593 Federico had been made a cardinal and went on to become archbishop of Milan in 1595 and continued the reforms initiated by his cousin. He notably set up the Biblioteca Ambrosiana and its gallery in Milan (see page 145). The family continued its good work and good fortune under Carlo III (1586-1652), the nephew and heir of Cardinal Federico. Today the dynasty still survives and the interests of the family are concentrated on preserving their heritage.

hike up **Monte Mottarone** (see page 162), there's little else to do but explore the gracious villa and its fragrant gardens.

Villa Pallavicino

Via Sempione Sud 8, Stresa, T0323-31533, parcozoopallavicino.it.
Mar-Oct, daily 0900-1800, €9/€6 4-13.

These splendid villa grounds near the lake were opened to the public after the Second World War. The villa sits atop a hill with distant views of the eastern shore of Lake Maggiore. There's an abundance of flora, animals and birdlife in the lush 20-ha botanical gardens and zoo, including peacocks and ostriches that roam at will, and a wonderful park with picnic areas, a café-bar and a playground for the kids.

Essentials

☻ **Train station** Via Giosuè Carducci, T892021, trenitalia.it.

⊝ **ATM** Piazza Cavour.

⊕ **Hospital** Verbania is the closest.

✛ **Pharmacy** Farmacia Dr Polisseni, via Cavour 16, T0323-933833, Mon-Wed & Fri-Sat 0830-1300 & 1530-2000, Thu 0830-1300.

⌁ **Post office** Via Anna Maria Bolongaro 40, T0323-30065, Mon-Fri 0830-1900, Sat 0830-1300.

❶ **Tourist information** Piazza Marconi 16, T0323-30150, distrettolaghi.it, Mar-Oct daily 1000-1230 & 1500-1830, Nov-Feb Mon-Fri only.

Island hopping – Lake Maggiore

The bewitching Borromean Islands, situated just off Stresa on Lake Maggiore's western shore, are arguably the most enchanting of any on the lakes. The islands are owned by the Borromeo family (see page 145), who started buying them up in the 16th century. A day spent hopping between them by boat, exploring their beautifully landscaped gardens and gracious *palazzi* and enjoying the gorgeous vistas is an absolute delight. Especially when punctuated by a sublime seafood lunch!

There are three islands: **Isola Bella** (the beautiful island), **Isola dei Pescatori** (the island of fishermen, also called Isola Superiore), and **Isola Madre** (the mother island), the largest. It makes most sense to visit them in this order, but if you want a full day exploring and don't want to rush around, then you'll need to catch the earliest boat you can from Stresa. Note that you need to buy your tickets for entry to the island's museums and villas when you buy your boat tickets at the Stresa dock.

Isola Bella, named after Countess Isabella Borromeo, boasts a sumptuous baroque summer palace and stunning terraced gardens. The richly decorated palace, which Count Vitaliano Borromeo began building in 1632, is now a Pinacoteca (art gallery) with priceless paintings, sculptures, antique furniture and tapestries on display; however, it's the gardens that most people come to see.

Essentials

borromeoturismo.it
Isola Bella & Isola Madre: end Mar-Oct, daily 0900-1730; Isola Bella €12, Isola Madre €10, combined ticket €16.50. Isola Bella Pinacoteca: daily 0900-1300 & 1330-1700, €4. Guided island visits (booking essential) €35, T0331-931300 or online.

Tip...

Boat services to the islands are operated by Navigazione Lago Maggiore (T0322-233200, navigazionelaghi.it) but don't panic if you miss a boat or you decide to spend longer on one island as there are also private boatmen on all of the islands.

Above: Diminutive Isola dei Pescatori. Opposite page: Aptly named Isola Bella.

Considered to be a fine example of the 17th-century Italian garden style, they have ornate arrangements of flowers and plants set out on overlapping terraces (10 in all!), all carefully selected to ensure something is always in bloom from spring to autumn. Don't miss the chapel with the family tombs and the quirky mosaic grotto. Allow one or two hours to see the palace and gardens; picnics aren't allowed so you probably won't feel the need to stay any longer.

Isola dei Pescatori, said to be a favourite spot of Hemingway's, is tiny – just 90 m wide and 500 m long – yet it's a busy little fishing village of an island, where fishermen still live and work. Wander the lanes first (it won't take long) where you'll find Madonnas in shrines (to protect the fishermen) and nets strewn about the place. There are a handful of excellent seafood restaurants, which makes it a great place to stop for lunch.

The largest island, **Isola Madre**, boasts the most luxuriant gardens of all. Nicknamed the 'Botanical

Island', it's home to an array of exotic plants and flowers, including the biggest kashmir cypress tree in Europe. The island also boasts an elegant villa which can be explored, with plush furnishings and paintings, and – the highlight for many – an enormous room-size puppet theatre with elaborately painted sets, beautifully-made marionettes, and various bits and pieces of puppet paraphernalia on display.

But once again, it's the glorious gardens that most come for – these ones boasting dense forest with shaded paths and fine lake views, exotic palm trees and towering cacti, and whatever time of year you visit, flowers cascading all about the place. For garden enthusiasts the times to visit are April for the camellias and May for the azaleas and rhododendrons, although you're guaranteed to find something blooming throughout the year.

Verbania, like its neighbour Stresa across the Gulf of Pallanza, is all about the waterfront, with a picturesque promenade around the promontory that's a fine place for a stroll, particularly on balmy summer evenings. Like Stresa, Verbania has a long history of tourism, with its piazzas lined with alfresco cafes and gelaterias, crammed with postcard stands, and uncomfortably crowded with people in high summer. It also sports what the 19th-century travel writers who visited might have called 'gaily-painted' buildings. Decorated with flowerboxes and bold awnings, the gelato-coloured edifices have a quaint charm very different to the grandeur and splendour of Stresa. But like its neighbour, Verbania – actually three towns in one, Suna, Intra and Pallanza (Mussolini named them all 'Verbania' in 1939) – has its fair share of gracious villas with luxuriant gardens, the most famous of which is Villa Taranto.

Giardini Botanici Villa Taranto

Pallanza, T0323-556667, villataranto.it.
Daily Mar-Sep 0830-1830, Oct 0830-1700, €9.

Boasting verdant terraces dotted with waterfalls, fountains, and pools floating with lilies, these botanical gardens on the Pallanza promontory are simply bewitching. If there's one local attraction you shouldn't miss, it's this lifetime labour of love of intriguing Scotsman Captain Neil Boyd McEacharn. Born in 1884 to an affluent shipping and mining family with business interests in Australia, McEacharn visited Italy as a child, an experience that forever changed the life of this member of the Royal Company of Archers, who decided to pursue his passion for botany. Travelling to Italy in 1928 to source land to establish a research garden, McEacharn purchased La Crocetta from the Marquise of Sant'Elia, and began planting the 16 acres of land with seeds and plants from around the world. Forced to leave during the Second

Villa Taranto.

Stops on the Lake Maggiore circuit

If you're driving a circuit of Lake Maggiore, as many people do, head south from Stresa along the western shore to Arona, then loop around to the eastern shore and head north to Locarno, Switzerland, returning south on the western shore via Cannobio and Verbania. The drive alone will take half a day; however, it can stretch to a full day with the following detours along the way:

❶ Start by driving to **Arona**, 17 km south of Stresa. A Borromeo dynasty stronghold before Napoleon arrived, Arona is famous for its gigantic 17th-century bronze statue of Carlo Borromeo (you can climb inside and look out his pupils!).

❷ Drive on to the Borromeos' medieval castle, **Rocca di Angera** (T0331-931300, daily 0900-1730, €7), 16 km northeast from Arona, on the opposite shore from Stresa. It has frescoes in the Sala della Giustizia dating to 1342 (some of Lombardy's oldest) a splendid tower with fabulous lake vistas, and a doll museum.

❸ **Santa Caterina del Sasso** (Mar-Oct daily 0830-1200 & 1430-1800, Nov-Feb weekends only, free) lies 15 km north from Rocca di Angera and is your next stop. There are frescoes inside dating to the 12th century, but it's the dramatic setting of this monastic complex, built into a cliff face, that people come to marvel.

❹ Sitting 60 km further north, in Switzerland, are **Locarno & Ascona**. Locarno's modern glass buildings obscure a medieval centre that's worth seeking out, especially the 14th-century Castello Visconteo, while neighbouring Ascona, once an artists' haunt, has streets lined with chic boutiques.

❺ Finally, crossing back to Italy is **Cannero Riviera** (23 km south). With its hilly lanes, vivid houses, bougainvillea and fruit trees, Cannero has Mediterranean ambiance that makes it a pleasure to explore. Don't miss the little castle islands off shore. From Cannero Riviera, the drive south to Stresa is 30 km and takes around 40 minutes.

Above: Passing the day on Cannobio's waterfront.
Opposite page: Colourful old houses of Cannobio.

more than 8,500 plant varieties, including rare specimens collected from around the globe, and acclimatized over long periods, it's a superb example of a botanic garden where plants are settled into microclimates. Highlights include the dahlia gardens (with over 300 varieties), avenues of azaleas, maple, rhododendron and camellia, carpets of heathers, greenhouse treasures, including the enormous *Victoria amazonica*, and rare lilies. All plants are labelled; you can also buy a guidebook at the entrance and follow the numbered arrows. Allow an hour or so to stroll the gardens.

Cannobio

Boasting a labyrinthine *centro storico* of medieval stone houses, elegant arcades, and skinny pebble streets that crawl down the hillside, Cannobio is the most charming town on Lake Maggiore. But it's the glimpses of cobalt water between the colourful old houses that line the lakefront and the alfresco cafés along the tranquil pedestrian-only waterside promenade that really make Cannobio captivating.

There's very little to actually do here but that's part of the charm of the place and what makes it a wonderful spot for a relaxing summer break. Locals spend their days sunbathing on the patch of grass that serves as a 'beach', while the teenagers dive from the concrete ruin that juts into the lake, and the older folk chat on the shady benches overlooking the sparkling water.

In the evening everyone comes out for the *passeggiatta* and aperitivi at the waterside bars, afterwards cramming the restaurant terraces for their fish meals, and then once again doing laps of the promenade with a gelato in hand. If you get bored with this, Verbania is a 30-minute drive south, and Switzerland 10 minutes north, or you can head up to the hills for some fresh mountain air (see page 162).

World War, he gifted the Italian State his garden on the condition it remained private, and set sail for Australia. Returning after the war, McEacharn was begged by the Italians to open the gates to the public, which he did in 1952. In return, he was honoured with the keys to the city in 1963. The Captain died a year later at his villa on a veranda overlooking the stunning views of his garden.

McEacharn's garden is much admired for its combination of wild beauty and elegant symmetry – the result of his blending of natural English Romantic garden and the classic Italian style based on formal terraces and geometric patterns – but also his decades-long efforts to establish the garden on chestnut fields. With

Take a drive from Cannobio

If you're keen to get your head in the clouds and inhale some fresh mountain air, there's a wonderful drive to do from Cannobio that encircles the *Parco Nazionale della Val Grande* (Great Valley National Park) in Piedmont. The park itself is not easy to explore unless you slip on some skis (during winter) or take a hike (during the warmer months), best organized with a guide through one of the tourist offices. But you can enjoy the craggy mountains of the park from the comfort of your car, and punctuate the journey with invigorating walks along the way. In spring, the velvety meadows are blanketed with wildflowers and in autumn, the trees are all shades of brown and gold. Take extra caution on this route during summer when every cyclist in Italy seems to be out on the roads.

From the southern side of Cannobio, take the turn-off west, signposted with a brown tourist marker saying 'Val Cannobio'. You won't miss it but if you do, there's another road on the northern side of town also heading west that meets up with it. The moment you get off the main road, you'll notice the landscape change immediately as you quickly ascend along narrow winding roads, crawling across old stone arched bridges, through lush dense forest to high mountainous wilderness. The slender road trims right down to a thin stick of a lane in parts where it can be near impossible to pass other cars, so do take care, but for some this is part of the fun. If you see a spot to pull over, take it, as they're few and far between and getting out and stretching your legs as you breathe in the crisp air is glorious. After an hour or so hugging the hills and snaking through tunnels of trees, you'll join up to the main road at Malesco, and, if you're not careful, the freeway at Domodóssola. It's much more enjoyable to stick with the smaller roads though, even though they run right near the freeway, as these allow you to stop and explore the ruins of castle towers and churches. Otherwise, blink and you'll be back in Cannobio. You will come to Verbania first, or you can head south instead to Omegna and visit Lake Orta.

Lake Orta

The most bewitching of all of Italy's northern lakes, Lake Orta
is an absolute delight to explore. There is really only one place
that makes an engaging base here and that's the delightful
Orta San Giulio. If you drive around the lake, Omegna and
Pella are worth a look, although the best part of the drive will
be the views from Pella across to Isola di San Giulio. At the
northern end of the lake, Omegna has an attractive canal and
cafés opposite the waterfront that make a perfect lunch stop,
while laidback Pella, which sees few tourists stopping at all,
has a pleasant café-bar on its lakefront.

Below: Fishing boats at Orta San Giulio. Opposite page: Stunning Lake Orta.

Visit once and you'll find yourself returning to this charismatic little medieval village with its captivating views of Isola di San Giulio (San Giulio Island) just offshore.

Splendidly situated on a tiny promontory jutting into the lake and surrounded by fragrant wooded forests and undulating emerald hills, Orta San Giulio boasts the most stunning setting of any village in the lakes region. It's also one of the quietest. Take a stroll around the tranquil lanes in the early morning or late afternoon and all you'll hear is silence! Add to the dramatic location a lake that is the deepest blue, traffic-free cobblestone streets lined with charming shops, gourmet grocery shops and alfresco cafés, and a mountain dotted with 21 chapels illustrating the life of Saint Francis of Assisi – the **Sacro Monte di San Francisco**, a UNESCO World Heritage Site – which serves as a backdrop.

There's no denying that Orta San Giulio is touristy – at the height of summer tour buses stream in, dropping their passengers at the tourist office to catch the road-train in, and nearly every shop sells useless trinkets and has a postcard stand. However, at the same time its diminutive size and gracious aristocratic villas give the village an air of exclusivity. As does enchanting **Villa Crespi**, a whimsical Moorish-inspired boutique hotel with a Michelin-starred restaurant. Visit in spring or autumn to enjoy the village at its most peaceful, when it will just be you and the locals sunning yourselves at a café, or reclined on one of the park benches watching the boats putter across to the island.

Named after fourth-century patron saint Julius of Novara, and once home to serpents and dragons according to local legend, Isola di San Giulio (San Giulio Island), offshore from Orta San Giulio, is easily one of the lakes' most alluring islets. Only 140 m wide and 275 m long, the island boasts

Essentials

☺ Train station Orta Miasino, T892021, trenitalia.it.

☻ ATM Via Alpino Gustavo Fontana.

✚ Pharmacy **Farmacia Dr Bergamasco**, via Caire Albertolletti 10, T0322-90117, Mon-Wed & Fri-Sat 0900-1230 & 1530-1930.

➔ Post office P Ragazzione 9, T0322-90157, Mon-Fri 0830-1400, Sat 0830-1300.

ⓘ Tourist information Via Panoramica, Orta San Giulio T0322-905614, distrettolaghi.eu.

one sight worth seeing – the **Basilica di Saint Giulio** (0930-1200 & 1400-1845, free) with a splendid Romanesque tower, and adjoining it a whitewashed **Benedictine convent**. Dating to the 14th century, the church interior boasts vaulted ceilings and naïve frescoes that are worth a quick look, but it's just as enjoyable to wander the island's only street and do some reflection – as the multilingual signs the Benedictine nuns have erected suggest. Boats do the five-minute run from Orta's piazza Motta to the island every 15 minutes or when they're full; daily April to September, weekends October to November & March, stopping altogether December-February, €3 return. For further transport details see page 163.

Sleeping

Stresa

Grand Hotel des Iles Borromées €€€€

Corso Umberto I 67, T0323-938938, borromees.it.

This belle époque masterpiece on a vast waterfront property is reason enough to stay in Stresa alone. Originally built in 1861 and exquisitely restored only a few years ago, it's lake opulence at its best, despite the fact that it's popular with groups and conferences. While a lake view room is the most romantic choice, the garden view rooms don't suffer from a lack of attention as they do in some other lakeside hotels. The main restaurant is a fine dining affair with formal dress expected in the evening. Yes, it's that kind of place.

Il Sole di Ranco €€€

Piazza Venezia 5, Ranco, T0331-976507, ilsolediranco.it.

This small hotel spread over two villas is renowned for the excellent cuisine of the Brovelli family who have been here on the lake for more than 150 years. While previously the food was the highlight, the rooms have been upgraded and are now worthy in supporting the creative cuisine of Davide Brovelli. It's a lovely spot to relax at and the hotel has views from the suites and a decent swimming pool to work off those calories.

Hotel Residence La Luna Nel Porto €€

Corso Italia 60, T0323-934466, lalunanelporto.it.

This cross between a hotel and studio apartments is best experienced for a week or more so you can settle in and enjoy the lakefront position. The spacious apartments have modern furnishings, excellent views and all facilities suitable for a long stay, including broadband internet. Shared kitchen facilities available.

Verbania

Villa Dal Pozzo d'Annone €€€€

S Strada del Sempione 5, T0322-7255, villadalpozzo.com.

This property is actually two separate structures, the villa and the *Borgo* (longer-stay accommodation), dating from the 18th century; both overlook the lake. There are six suites available in the exclusive villa with period furniture and all mod cons (except air conditioning), while the comfy *Borgo* has 12 rooms with air conditioning and hot tubs. There is also a well-regarded bistro, if you find the premises too hard to leave.

Hotel Pallanzo €€

Viale Magnolie 8, T0323-503202, pallanzahotels.com.

A great location across from the ferry dock, this handsome art nouveau style four-star hotel has been recently refurbished. There

Tip...

The lakes are generally seen as a summer destination, so many of these hotels (and their restaurants) close completely in winter, opening again around end of March.

are 48 rooms, most with views and a variety of configurations and colour schemes, and all have air conditioning. They also have a good value three-star hotel, the Belvedere San Gottardo.

Cannobio

Hotel Cannobio €€

Piazza Vittorio Emanuele III 6, T0323-739639, hotelcannobio.com.

This elegant hotel has one of the best locations in town, right on the waterfront (ask for a lake view room with balcony) overlooking the promenade. Private parking, a great breakfast, and fine alfresco restaurant. There is a very appealing junior suite with a double balcony and jacuzzi.

Pironi Hotel €€

Via Marconi 35, T0323-70624, pironihotel.it.

This former 15th-century palace has had a thoughtful restoration and boasts original frescoes, vaulted ceilings, well-placed antiques and a beautiful breakfast room. There are 12 individually decorated rooms (some with lake views) and while it's not directly on the waterfront, the atmospheric medieval village setting is fitting.

Antica Stallera €
Via P Zacchero 7, T0323-71595, anticastallera.com.
This small hotel and restaurant has modern rooms with en-suite and an attractive and well-regarded garden restaurant.

Isola dei Pescatori

Hotel Ristorante Verbano €€
Via Ugo Ara 2, T0323-30408, hotelverbano.it.
The best value option here, this hotel has a wonderful, romantic atmosphere and a lovely garden restaurant. The rooms are cosy and have excellent views and it's a great place to hole up for a few days – but perhaps not during the height of the tourist season.

Orta San Giulio

Villa Crespi €€€€
Via G Fava 18, Orta San Giulio, T0322-911902, hotelvillacrespi.it.
If nothing else, the sight of Villa Crespi, a Moorish-style villa built in 1879, is a startling one. And if the idea of the Middle East adjacent to Lake Orta is fantastic, the exotic interior details keep the suspension of belief alive a little longer. Fourteen ornate rooms of varying size and detail are on offer, but topping the magical atmosphere is the cuisine of star chef Antonio

Villa Crespi is a unique and romantic property.

Cannavacciuolo whose creativity outshines the whimsicality of the accommodation.

Hotel San Rocco €€€
Via Gippini 11, T0322-911977, hotelsanrocco.it.
A four-star hotel with an enviable lake location, this is a popular retreat for honeymooners, with a spa, private swimming pool and lake views the main incentives. Over half the rooms have watery vistas but book early and reconfirm. While the decoration of the rooms in the old convent is fine, the 11 rooms in the villa are superb.

Hotel Orta €€
Piazza Motta 1, T0322-90253, hotelorta.it.
With a prime position right on the main square and overlooking the lake, this hotel can't be beaten for location. The languid nature of the lake, however, is reflected in the running of the hotel and while the room rates are reasonable for the location, the rooms themselves are uninspiring – only the rooms with balconies overlooking the lake make this a good-value option.

Eating

Stresa

Piemontese €€€€
Via Mazzini 25, T0323-30235.
This family-run restaurant is a local favourite, offering a choice between the elegant dining room or the vine-shaded courtyard. The cuisine consists of local classics presented with modern flair, and the service and wine list are the best in town.

Ristorante del Pescatore €€€€
Vialo del Poncivo 3, T0323-31986.
Renowned for its excellent seafood and while the grilled lake and ocean fish are excellent, they also do a Spanish paella, as well as fish stew – a tribute to the owners' Spanish origin. The seafood pastas are also a highlight of this petite restaurant.

Osteria degli Amici €€
Via Bolongaro 33, T0323-30453.
This genial osteria is spread out over several rooms and has a tiny outdoor area where you can indulge in anything from a delicious pizza to a multiple course blow out. Menu highlights include risotto with porcini mushrooms or local fish.

Cafés
Most of Stresa's cafés and gelaterias are on and around the lake, such as **Pasticceria Jolly Bar** (via Principe Tomaso 17, Stresa), a big bustling place which also sells scrumptious pastries and sweets, and **L'Idrovolante** (piazzale Lido, 6, Stresa, T323-31384), a busy café-cum-bar-cum-restaurant on the water near the ferry dock that's popular for its superb coffee and pastries.

Verbania

Verbania is really divided into three areas: Pallanza, Suna and Intra, but most things of interest to visitors – diners especially – are in Pallanza, which is the area running along the waterfront and creeping up the hill behind. Due to the number of foreign visitors that invade Verbania each summer, you'll find a wide range of ethnic eateries, including Chinese, Indian, Japanese and Greek, most of which are mediocre and inauthentic. Unless you really need to satisfy a craving, it's best to stick to Italian fare.

Il Sole di Ranco €€€€
Piazza Venezia 5, Ranco, T0331-976507, ilsolediranco.it.
Chef Davide Brovelli continues a family legacy at this restaurant with a summer and winter garden and an elegant interior. Expect premium ingredients to appear on the surprisingly lengthy menu, alongside creatively presented lake fish. With such an excellent wine cellar, it's probably a good idea to stay the night in one of the rooms upstairs.

Tip...
Regional dishes, delicious seafood and great wines await, but make sure that the restaurant of your desires is open – opening times vary, although most open for lunch (1200-1500) and dinner (1900-2300) at least six days and nights a week. Keep in mind that most lakes restaurants close from December through to January, some staying shut as late as March, and some also close one night a week, generally a Monday or Tuesday.

Il Monastero €€€
Via Castelfidardo 5/7, Suna, T0323-502544.
This highly regarded restaurant has plenty of rustic elegance – not easy to achieve – and classic versions of local fish and meat dishes.

Milano €€€
Corso Zanitello 2, Pallanza, T0323-556816.
A peaceful lakeside terrace is the setting for this local favourite. Not surprisingly the lake fish dishes are the hit of the menu, which also includes a fair share of classic regional specialities.

Da Cesare €€
Via Mazzini 14, Verbania, T0323-31386.
From the hotel of the same name, this restaurant has a good reputation for dishes such as risotto with local fish, best taken on the outside terrace.

Cafés

There are myriad cafés and gelaterias on and around the waterfront in Pallanza but locals and tourists alike love **Gelateria Pasticceria Ciao Bella** (via San Vittore 61, T0323-519585).

Cannobio

Lo Scalo €€€
Piazza Vittoria Emanuele II 32, T0323-71480.

The best expression of the cooking style of the region is to be found at this elegant restaurant, with excellent seafood (lake fish a speciality), painstaking presentation and a well-chosen wine list.

Porto Vecchio €€
Piazza Vittorio Emanuele II, Cannobio, T0323-739639.

The restaurant of the Hotel Cannobio, Porto Vecchio, is on a wonderful outdoor terrace that sets the scene for a romantic meal. The food (local specialities and Italian classics) is fine, as is the service and wine list.

Cafés

Cannobio has an array of alfresco cafés with tables overlooking the lake, and excellent gelaterie, conveniently located near the waterfront for when you're in the mood for a moonlit stroll with icecream in hand. For the best handmade gelato try **Gelateria Bar La Piazza** (piazza Vittorio Emanuele II 33, T0323-70496),

Gelatiere Di Zaccheo Dario (via Magistris 63, T0323-71090) or **Bar Jolly Gelateria** (via Vittorio Emanuele II 24, T0323-71022), which also does good coffee.

Orta San Giulio

Villa Crespi €€€€
Via G Fava 18, Orta San Giulio, T0322-911902.

If you need to rub your eyes in disbelief when you first sight the Moorish-themed Villa Crespi, the cuisine of chef Antonino Cannavacciuolo will have you repeating the gesture when each course of his perfectly crafted dishes arrive at the table. The skilful use of local ingredients and the balance of flavours sets a chef of this calibre well and truly apart from the rest.

Venus Ristorante €€€
Piazza Motta 50, T0322-90362.

It's hard to beat the summer terrace at this restaurant. Excellent local fare is on offer (and a good tasting menu), with a fine wine cellar and stellar desserts that will have you ordering that extra course.

Taverna Antico Agnello €€
Via Olina 18, T0322-90259.

This family-run, relaxed and intimate taverna serves up fantastic versions of old favourites – some quite unexpected – to a crowd of locals and visitors in-the-know.

Above and below: Villa Crespi.

Sun-drenched cafés in Orta San Giulio.

Osteria al Boeuc €€
Via Bersani 28, Novara,
T0322-915854.
This ancient wine bar is worth visiting for the vino alone. They also do a selection of great cold cuts and snacks that perfectly compliment the local wines.

Cafés
Leon d'Oro
Piazza Motta 43, Orta San Giulio,
T0322-941991.
Simple meals and snacks are served at this rather old-fashioned place on the main piazza. It won't win any gastronomic awards, and is much better for a coffee in the morning or an aperitivo in the evening. Pull up a chair at one of the floral covered tables under a shady umbrella and you can easily while away a couple of hours people-watching on the square.

Arianna
Via Domodossola 10/12,
Orta San Giulio Nordovest,
T0332-911956.
It may not be in the centre of the old village, but it's worth a trip for their delicious biscuits, the most famous of which is their *Amaretti del Sacro Monte* (moist almond biscuits).

Arte del Gelato
Via Olina 30, Orta San Giulio,
T335-832 9298.
Don't make a special trip, but if you are driving in or out of town, this superb gelateria in the modern centre, known as Orta San Giulio Nordovest, is worth a stop for their delicious artisanal gelato.

Omegna

Salera 16 €
Piazza Salera 16, Omegna,
T349-215 1632.
A pleasingly modish café opposite the lake, it does great business with locals who drop in for its excellent coffee, substantial salads, fresh pastas and daily specials.

Entertainment

Maggiore and Orta aren't exactly the most happening lakes when it comes to entertainment, tending to attract more mature travellers or couples seeking romance. If you're after dance clubs, best head to the beaches or stay in Milan. However, no matter where you are on the lakes the thing to do in the late afternoon during the warmer months is to enjoy an aperitivo or two at a waterfront café-bar. Regardless of what you order, drinks often come with tiny complimentary dishes of snacks such as potato crisps, nuts, olives, cheese and salami cubes, and grissini. After dinner, head to the nearest gelateria for a gelato and a stroll along the lake's edge.

Lake Maggiore

Bars

Enoteca da Giannino
Via Garibaldi 32, Stresa.
This busy little place might not be the most atmospheric of bars, but they have a good range of wines by the glass and fairly tasty snacks that do the trick.

Birreria Stregatto
Via Cadorna 20, Verbania.
The courtyard here is the best place in town for a cold beer on a hot summer's day, and attracting mostly locals gives it a rare authenticity hard to find on this part of the lake.

Festivals & concerts
There are classical music concerts held frequently throughout the spring and summer months, from March–September, in towns, villages and islands around Lake Maggiore, under the umbrella of the **Stresa Festival** (via Carducci 38, Stresa, T0323-31095, stresafestival.eu, €10-50). Venues range from atmospheric churches and villa gardens to town halls and waterfront promenades. Expect anything from Renaissance and baroque wind music to Mozart concertos, performed by everything from small ensembles to the Stresa Festival Orchestra to the Michael Nyman Band. See the website for programmes with full details.

On both Lake Maggiore and Lake Orta, café-bars are dotted around the waterfront and main squares. Most of the bars doubling as cafés open all day, from morning until fairly late at night, and might close one day a week, often Monday. Bars that mainly serve as wine bars tend to open around lunch and close after midnight.

Lake Orta

Bars

Caffè Jazz
Via Olina 13, Orta San Giulio, Lake Orta, T0322-911700.
This cosy wine bar is the most atmospheric in Orta San Giulio, serving good wines by the glass to a cool jazz soundtrack.

Imbarcadero
Piazza Motta, Pella, Lake Orta, T0322-918003.
Attracting everyone from local old fishermen for a beer to Milanese couples on holiday enjoying a quiet aperitivo, what makes this down-to-earth café-bar special is its tranquil waterfront location in one of the Lake Orta's most peaceful villages.

Festivals & concerts
On Lake Orta, classical concerts are held as part of the **Cusiano Festival of Antique Music** in June, while jazz, blues, rock, folk and classical performances are held in a dozen towns and villages as part of the **Il Lago della Musica** series, from early June through to early November. Contact the tourist offices for details.

Shopping

You'll find loads of little shops in Stresa, Verbania and Cannobio on Lake Maggiore and in Orta San Giulio on Lake Orta selling local crafts but, more often than not, very tacky souvenirs. Crafts include handmade and handpainted ceramics, pottery and glassware. The best shopping on the lakes is found elsewhere, in Como and Bellagio; otherwise people simply head to Milan. Most shops open from Monday-Saturday 0930 or 1000, close for lunch at 1200 or 1300, then reopen 1600-1900. Those staying open on Sunday during the busy summer tourist season may close one weekday (usually Monday) and open late another afternoon (often Tuesday).

Markets on Lakes Maggiore & Orta

Every day there are open-air markets on the lake selling fresh fruit and vegetables, cheeses and cold cuts, flowers, clothes and other items. They are usually held on the main square and surrounding pedestrian streets and are easy enough to find.

Monday Baveno

Tuesday Arona

Wednesday Luino

Thursday Omegna

Friday Stresa and Pallanza

Saturday Intra and Verbania

Sunday Cannobio

Stresa

Food & drink

Salumeria Musso di Bianchetti Augusto
Via Mazzini 1, T0323-30402
This shop boasts a great selection of cold cuts and fantastic regional salami.

Pasticceria Gigi
Corso Italia 30, T0323-30225
In the business for 40 years, this bakery does tasty mini pizzas and pizza slices, which go down very nicely with a bottle of red.

Orta San Giulio

Art & antiques
The delightful village of Orta San Giulio is blessed with myriad shops selling antiques, collectables, and bric-a-brac on via Olina.

Food & drink
There's no shortage of atmospheric picnic spots at and around Orta San Giulio (from one of the benches under the shady trees on the main square to Isola di San Giulio itself) and there's no shortage of shops where you can stock your picnic basket.

Panetteria Sappa
Piazza Motta 7, T0322-90416
Makes delicious fresh bread and *focacce*, tasty pizza slices, as well as pastries and cakes.

Il Buongustaio
Piazza Ragazzoni, 8/10, Orta San Giulio, T0322-905626
A great one-stop-shop which boasts the best of the region including cheeses and cold cuts. The specialty is their salami, and there's a wide array to choose from, including salami of donkey, deer, wild boar, goat and goose,

Below: Elegant Orta San Giulio. Opposite page: Local delis are fantastic at Orta San Giulio.

Activities & tours

Boating
Navigazione Lago Maggiore
Via F Baracca 1, Arona,
T322-233200,
navigazionelaghi.it.
The government-operated water transport for Lake Maggiore offers regular daily shuttle boats from Carciano (Stresa's lido) to Isola Bella and Isola Pescatori, as well as a range of cruises. These include excursions from Stresa or Laveno to Isola Bella, Isola Pescatori, and Isola Madre; tours to Switzerland, including a boat to Locarno; and the famous Lago Maggiore Express, a combined boat-train trip to Locarno from Thursday through to Sunday that trundles through stunning mountain and lake scenery. March-September only.

Food & drink
Il Gusto è a Monte
Tomassucci Travel Agency,
piazza Marconi 3, Stresa,
T323-933621, gustoamonte.it.
This initiative by Verbano Ossola Province tourism offers 25 organized excursions, named 'Flavours of the Mountains', that provide a chance to taste and learn about local produce. Maggiore and Orta's gastronomic specialties include cured meats such as *violino di capra* (cured goat leg ham), alpine goats cheeses like Bettelmatt, wild game including roe deer and boar, and Ossolano

---

with truffles and with Barolo wine. Their wild boar bresaola and local mortadella are very good.

Souvenirs
Ricordi Orta San Giulio
Piazza Motta 30, Orta San Giulio,
T0322-90337
This delightful shop has baskets out front overflowing with a huge array of fragrant handmade soaps, perfumes, essential oils and incense for the body and home, along with local crafts and souvenirs.

Silvia Rizzi
Piazza Motta 30, Orta San Giulio,
T0322-90337
This young artisan uses traditional techniques to paint delicate fairies and maidens on porcelain. Not to everyone's taste but they make wonderful gifts for grandmothers and children, and her skills are impressive.

Vetroe' Di Berardi Stefania
Via Giovanetti 2/4,
Orta San Giulio, T0322-905555
You'll find beautiful handmade glassware and other stunning glass objects, of both traditional and contemporary designs, for the home interior at this atelier of a local artist.

Alessi
Via Privata Alessi 6,
Crusinallo di Omegna,
T0323-868648, alessi.com.
Mon-Sat 0930-1800.
This huge store adjoining the Alessi factory stocks the entire product range, the majority of which is at reduced outlet prices.

wine from Nebbiolo grapes. There are art, nature and architecture themed trips that incorporate walks to abandoned villages, ruined castles and lakes. If you speak Italian you can do a self-guided tour using a specially produced brochure to make your own arrangements to visit food producers of your choice.

Sports
Lago Maggiore Adventure Park
Strada Cavalli 18, Baveno, Stresa T0323-919799, lagomaggiore adventurepark.com. Mar-Apr & Sep-Oct weekends & holidays 1000-1900, May-Jun daily 1000-1900, Jul-Aug 1000-2300, closed Nov-Feb. A fun adventure park offering a mountain bike range, climbing walls, junior and senior *percorso* (essentially tightrope walking), acrojumping (the opposite of bungy jumping), and an obstacle course with everything from monkey bars to upturned logs.

Monte Mottarone

Cable car
While Monte Mottarone, between Lake Maggiore and Lake Orta, is not the most impressive of mountains, if you're in the neighbourhood and dying to get your head in the clouds or are simply looking for a picnic spot with some altitude (1491 m) and Alpine and lake views, a

cable car up the mountain for a picnic makes a fine excursion. Take the **cable car** (daily 1930-1730, every 20 mins, €10 return) from **Carciano** (on the shore opposite Isola Bella) up to the summit. There is one stop at **Alpino** for **Giardino Botanico Alpinia** (at 804 m), which makes a pleasant diversion. Once at the top, picnic spots are easy to find; you can also rent bikes (around €25 a day).

Walking & trekking
If you're keen to do some walking or trekking in the mountains, pick up the brochure *Trekking alle pendici del Mottarone* (Trekking the slopes of Mottarone; Italian only but easy to follow) from the Stresa tourist office (via Canonica 8, T0323-31308). There are a handful of marked trails (some paved), ranging from easy walks on the

lower slopes (including walks west to Belgirate at 260 m) to more strenuous treks up to the summit of Mottarone. All begin at **Baveno**, a suburb of Stresa just northeast of Carciano, and take from 1.5 to 5.5 hrs.

Nordic walking
If you want to do as the locals do, 'Nordic walking' (involving more active use of the arms, like cross-country skiing) is the latest craze. The tourist office has a brochure *Trekking e Nordic Walking al Mottarone* (in English) with instructions on the walking technique and style, and several summit walks which leave from Bar Alp near the Mottarone summit; one 1 hr walk, Giro Rossa, takes you through the Cusio Valley for panoramic views of the Apennines to Monte Disgrazia.

Below: Cable car soaring above Isola Bella. Opposite page: Orta San Giulio.

Mountain climbing

Climbers can pick up a brochure (in English) from the tourist office called *Arrampicare al Mottarone*, produced by SnowFun Mottarone (mottaroneski.it) wth diagrams detailing nine different climbs, the degrees of difficulty, duration, and equipment needed.

The climbing area is about a 30-minute walk from the Mottarone summit and the brochure has directions for getting there. For more information see: arrampicando.it and cmvo.it, the website of the Comunita Montana Valle D'Ossola. The officially recommended Alpine climbing guide is Enzio Seppi (T322-900016).

Lake Orta

Boating

Isola di San Giulio

Piazza Motta Pier, Orta San Giulio, T333-605 0288.

Motoscafi (small boats; €4 return, buy tickets from boat captain) depart every 15 mins for the 10-min ride across to Isola di San Giulio between 0900 and 1130 (breaking for lunch) and from 1300 to 1900. You can also opt for the *Giro Turistico* (tourist circuit; €8) which includes a return trip to the lake and town visit. While you'll notice tourists trying to bargain the price down, this is not a good way to make friends – the locals take great offence.

Walking & cycling

Ask at the Tourist Office of Orta San Giulio (see page 153) for a copy of the *Città di Orta San Giulio Map and Tourist Guide*, which includes a map and detailed directions for five return self-guided walks in and around Orta San Giulio, beginning from piazza Motta in the centre of Orta San Giulio: the first, and easiest, does a loop via the lakefront of the Orta San Giulio peninsula; the second takes you through woods and fields via the hamlet of **Carcegna** to the waterfront village of **Pettenasco**; another follows a mule track to the villages of **Vacciagheto** and **Miasino**, while the last follows mule tracks to the hamlets of **Vacciago** and **Lortallo**, visiting two tiny frescoed churches and a Franciscan monastery with views of the lake and Monte Rosa.

Giro Lago

Ecomuseo del Lago d'Orta e Mottarone, piazza Unita d'Italia 2, Pettenasco, T0323-89622, lagodorta.net

Pick up the brochure from the Ecomuseo del Lago d'Orta e Mottarone titled *Giro Lago*. The *Giro Lago* consists of over 500 km of itineraries you can do on bike and on foot, including two scenic circuits of the lake, offering vistas of Orta and other pre-Alpine lakes. The brochure has a map indicating which routes are asphalt and which are unpaved, and which parts are suited to walking or cycling.

Contents

167 Introduction
168 Como
170 *Map: Como*
172 Great days out:
    Lakeside promenade
174 Southern & western Como
176 Great days out:
    Outdoor activities – Lake Como
180 Great days out:
    Lake Como gardens
182 Northern & eastern Como
186 Listings:
186 Sleeping
187 Eating & drinking
190 Entertainment
190 Shopping
191 Activities & tours

Lake Como

A black-headed gull flies past Como's elegant villas.

Introduction

What to see in…

…one day
If you only have one day, spend it on the lake, and explore Como's jewel in the crown, **Bellagio**. Amble about the gardens of **Villa Serbelloni**, explore the charming cobblestone streets, and enjoy lunch overlooking the water. On the return ferry from Bellagio, alight at **Tremezzo** for **Villa Carlotta**.

…a weekend or more
The next day, explore **Como**'s elegant old town, visiting its splendid **Duomo** and museums, and shopping its streets. Enjoy an aperitivo by the waterfront, dine in one of Como's many fine eateries, then stroll the lakeside promenade with a gelato.

On a longer stay, spend a couple of nights at one of the other villages on the lake, such as **Tremezzo** or **Menaggio**. Spend a few days driving around the lake, stopping on the way to visit the gardens of **Villa d'Este** and **Villa del Balbianello**, and to explore villages such as **Lenno** and **Varenna** and the gardens at **Villa Monastero**.

Lake Como is the shining star of the lakes. When people dream of the Italian Lakes, you bet it's Lago di Como that they're envisioning. Its undeniable beauty, as well as its strategic location as a link between Italy, central Europe and beyond, has made it a coveted address through the ages with artists, artisans and, more recently, American actor George Clooney, all of whom have made the villas skirting these turquoise waters a base for inspiration and reflection.

Shaped like an upside down 'Y', Como sits at the lower tip of the western 'arm' and is the most pragmatic of locations on the lake. The pedestrianised area of the centro storico is punctuated by the splendid Duomo; however, it's the attractive waterfront that everyone's attention always returns to.

As you explore the lake further, snaking around the foreshore and hugging the mountains that surround the lake, small towns, villas and sublime vistas appear regularly. Delightful Bellagio has an enviable position and good shopping on its steep cobbled streets, while Tremezzo has the lovely extensive gardens and handsome structures of Villa Carlotta nearby.

There is plenty to explore on Lake Como and while summer is the best weather for enjoying the lakes, the shoulder seasons either side of summer are far less frenetic – after all, you're coming here to relax, aren't you?

Stroll Como's old streets.

Como

Cradled at the base of a mountain and sprawled around a pretty curve of the lake, the town of Como not only has a stunning setting, but it's also one of the lakes' most characterful towns, with atmospheric cobblestone lanes and lively little piazzas where locals like to socialize over coffee or aperitivi. Como also has the added appeal of being one of the lake's few year-round destinations; it is as enjoyable in winter, when there's mist over the lake and the streets are lit with Christmas lights, as it is in the summer, when the place to be is by the water with the locals on a balmy evening.

A ferry ride around Lake Como is essential.

Many visitors make the town of Como their base for exploring the lake, which they do by water, hopping on and off boats over the course of a few days. Other travellers stay a couple of nights in Como's old town, then drive around the perimeter of the lake spending a night or two in each of, say, Cernobbio, Tremezzo or Menaggio on the western shore, Bellagio at the lake's centre, and then perhaps Varenna, on the eastern shore, before returning to Como. Arrive by car, however, and you'll probably push on, the city appearing rather unattractive with industry all around; arrive by train at the edge of the old town with the water opposite, and you won't want to leave.

Once ensconced in Como's *centro storico* you'll soon realise this is one elegant little city. While Como's foreshore is dotted with imposing architectural monuments, lovely waterside parks, and busy bars and gelaterias, the labyrinthine old centre is blessed with lively piazzas, stylish boutiques and atmospheric restaurants – making it very hard to drag oneself away to explore the rest of the lake. While the cobblestone pedestrian-only lanes of Como's compact old town are enjoyable enough to wander, unlike other lakeside towns, Como actually has a handful of sights worth seeing, including some splendid churches and fine museums. Add to that, during the warmer months, Como's piazzas and gardens host jazz, classical music and world music concerts. Opposite the lake and marina, and at the centre of the old town's waterfront, **piazza Cavour** is an elegant square lined with alfresco cafés on one side and the tourist office on the other. From here, the atmospheric streets of Como's old town or *Cortesella* radiate; the city's history is on show everywhere, from its Roman beginnings evident in the grid-like structure and ruins of **Porta Pretoria**, the Roman gate, to the remains of the medieval walls around the old town perimeter, to the Romanesque city gate of **Porta Torre** at piazza Vittoria.

Essentials

© **Train station** Como San Giovanni (main station) or Como Lago (lenord.it) on the lake.

◉ **Bus station** SPT Linea, via Asiago 16/18, T031-247111.

◉ **ATMs** Piazza Cavour, via Plinio, via Vittorio Emanuele II.

⊕ **Hospital** Ospedale Generale Di Zona Valduce, via Dante Alighieri 11, T031-324111.

✛ **Pharmacy** Farmacia Centrale, caio Plinio Secondo 1 (off piazza Cavour), T031-304204, Mon 1530-1930, Tue-Sun 0830-1230 & 1530-1930.

⌒ **Post office** Via Vittorio Emanuele II 113, T031-260210, Mon-Fri 0830-1400, Sat 0830-1230.

❶ **Tourist information** Piazza Cavour, T031-269712, lakecomo.org, Mon-Sat 0900-1300 & 1430-1800, Sun (Summer) 0930-1230.

Il Duomo

Piazza del Duomo, T031-265244.
Daily 0900-1830, free.

The main attraction of Como's *centro storico* is its monumental Duomo. Considered to be a great example of 14th-century transitional architecture, blending Gothic and Renaissance styles, architectural buffs will enjoy identifying elements from the different periods, such as the pretty Gothic rose window or the portal's two Renaissance statues of Como locals Pliny the Elder and Pliny the Younger (protected behind wire mesh). Once inside, there's a beautifully decorated rococo dome, an intricately carved 16th-century choir, and wonderful paintings

Como listings

① Sleeping

1 Albergo Del Duca *piazza Mazzini 12*
2 Albergo Terminus *via Lungo Lario Trieste 14*
3 Barchetta Excelsior *piazza Cavour 1*
4 Le Due Corti *piazza Vittoria 12/13*
5 Palace Hotel *via Lungo Lario Trieste 16*
6 Quarcino *salita Quarcino 4*
7 Tre Re *via Boldoni 20*
8 Villa Flori *via Cernobbio 12*

① Eating

1 Alessandro Volta *piazza A Volta*
2 Bar Del Terme *Lungo Lario Trieste 14*
3 Gelateria Ceccato *Lungo Lago Trieste 16*
4 Il Carrettiere *via Coloniola 18*
5 Il Pinzimonio *via Bonanomi 24*
6 Il Solito Posto *via Lambertenghi 9*
7 Il Vecchio Borgo *piazza Matteotti 1*
8 Joy *via Cernobbio 2*
9 L'Antica Riva *Lungo Lario Trieste 50*
10 Le Soste Ristorante *via A Diaz 52 A*
11 Nova Comum *piazza Duomo 2*
12 Pizzeria La Darsena *Lungo Lario Trieste 54*
13 Raimondi *via Cernobbio 12*
14 Riva Café *via Cairoli 10*

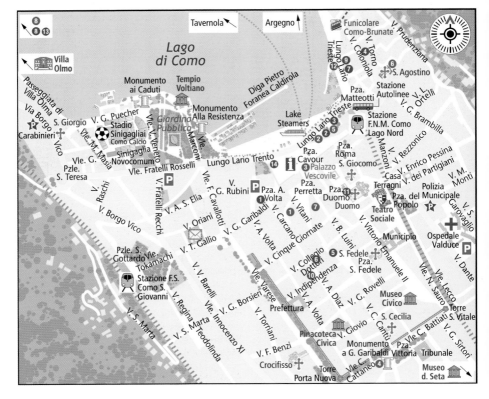

Como's towering Duomo.

and tapestries from the 16th and 17th centuries. Adjoining the Duomo is the striking striped pink, grey and white marble **Broletto**, the old town hall, built in 1215, but reduced in size in 1477 to accommodate the Duomo. The piazza del Duomo cafés provide a perfect spot from which to appreciate both – with a gelato of course!

Musei Civici Como

Museo Archeologico & Museo Storico: Palazzo Giovio, piazza Medaglie d'Oro 1, T031-271343. Civiche Raccolte d'Arte & Palazzo Volpi: via Diaz 86, T031-269869.
Tue-Sat 0930-1230 & 1400-1700,
Sun 1000-1300, €3.

The Musei Civici Como is actually four museums that fall under the umbrella of the Civic Museums of Como: the Museo Archeologico (Archaeological Museum), Museo Storico (Historical Museum), the Civiche Raccolte D'Arte (the Civic Art Gallery, also known simply as the Pinacoteca or Picture Gallery), and **Tempio Voltiano** (the Temple to Alessandro Volta; see page 172). Spread over two palaces, the **Museo Archeologico** is crammed with fascinating artefacts, from Neolithic, Egyptian, Greek, and Roman times. Items of local relevance include decorative vessels from Como dating to the sixth century BC and artefacts from the Italians' battle for liberation from the Austrians that took place in the hills above Como. The **Museo Storico** has an interesting collection of textiles, ceramics and manuscripts, but most impressive are the exhibition of costumes, textiles and lace from the 17th and 19th centuries. The **Pinacoteca** plays host to some absorbing temporary shows but also houses engaging permanent exhibitions of painting, sculpture, graphic design and architectural models from the early medieval period through to the 20th century, including work by local artists. Most notable is the Romanesque collection formed from Como's various churches, abstract art from the Gruppo Como, and the architectural drawings by futurist architect Giuseppe Terragni including those for the Asilo Sant'Elia, a Como school.

Como's finest churches

Chiesa di San Fedele Named after the saint who brought Christianity to Como, this fine Romanesque church, built in 1120 and just a short stroll from the Duomo, has a beautiful, intricately carved medieval door.

Basilica di Sant'Abbondio Another 11th-century Romanesque church with well preserved 13th-century Gothic frescoes; most of the intricate stonework by the famous *Maestri Comacini* is at the Museo Civico.

Chiesa di Sant'Agostino This 14th-century church boasts a beautiful baroque interior, decorated with frescoes, with an elegant cloister.

Lakeside promenade

The waterfront at Como.

Splendidly set around the curve of Lake Como and nestled at the foot of densely wooded mountains, the city of Como has an enviable lakeside location that's best appreciated with an amble along the waterfront.

Start your saunter on the lake's southern side at gracious **Villa Olmo**. This regal 18th-century neoclassical mansion boasts elegant, geometrical-patterned gardens, with manicured lawns at the front overlooking the lake, and a shady forest of parkland out back. Designed in 1780 by celebrated Swiss architect Simone Cantoni as a summer villa for the aristocratic Odescalchi family, it is now owned by Como municipality and used for exhibitions and conferences. It's not always possible to see the sumptuous interior (if nothing's on, it should be open Mon-Fri 0930-1200 & 1500-1800, free), but it's just as enjoyable to wander round the wonderful gardens (summer 0800-2300 & winter 0700-1900, free).

From here, stroll the lovely lakeside path, **Passeggiata di Villa Olmo**, through the elegant

residential Borgovico suburb, passing **Chiesa di San Giorgio** and **Piazzale Somaini**, to via Puecher. Here you'll find three striking landmarks, the **Monumento ai Caduti** (Monument to the Fallen), **Tempio Voltiano** (Temple to Alessandro Volta), and **Monumento alla Resistenza** (Monument to the Resistance). Erected in 1930 as a memorial to Como's 650 fallen First World War heroes, the imposing 33-m high **Monumento ai Caduti** was designed by architect brothers Attilio and Giuseppe Terragni, based on 1914 sketches by futurist architect Antonio Sant'Elia. The white neoclassical **Tempio Voltiano** (viale Marconi, T031-574705, Apr & Sep Tue-Sun 1000-1200 & 1500-1800, Oct & Mar Tue-Sun 1000-1200 & 1400-1600, €3) is a commemorative monument and small museum dedicated to Alessandro Volta, Como's famous scientist. Follow the lakefront Lungolago Mafalda di Savoia to the adjoining leafy public gardens for the **Monumento alla Resistenza**. Inaugurated in 1983, this unusual memorial to victims of the Second World War consists of bronze sheets engraved with the names of the dead, with touching quotations from the victims.

Stroll out to the end of the *diga foranea* (breakwater), a narrow boardwalk opposite the park, for the best views of Como and the action on the water. From here you have a close-up view of the boats coming and going from the *imbarcadero* (jetty).

Continue along the tree-lined lakeside promenade beside Lungo Lario Trento to Lungo Lario Trieste at the end, perhaps the prettiest stretch of all. Seat yourself on a bench beneath the trees, with a view of the bustling lake action framed between the trunks, and you'll think to yourself this is quintessential Como! The promenade is especially lively on summer evenings when locals are out jogging, walking their dogs, canoodling, or, having lined up for ice cream at **Gelateria Ceccato** (see page 189) opposite, out strolling with gelato in hand.

If you're thirsty, grab a waterside table at the simple kiosk-bar **Al Molo** (see page 190), which boasts one of Como's best sunset viewing spots; otherwise, continue along Lungo Lario Trieste,

making a note to return later. At piazza de Gasperi you'll see the **Funicolare per Brunate** (see below).

From hereon, along viale Geno, you'll be strolling one of Como's most tranquil lakefront stretches, with lawn on your left that's ideal for sprawling out on with a picnic (it's a favourite dinner spot for local students sharing beers and take-away), while on your right you'll get a close peek at some of Como's most beautiful and affluent homes. It's hard to know which way to look!

At the end of the street, you'll come to **Villa Geno**, an elegant mansion used for weddings and functions, and from the point, gorgeous views across the lake to the seaplanes landing and taking off. By now it must be time for that aperitivo!

Tip...

For a bird's-eye view of Como and the lake, take a ride up the steep mountainside on the **Funicolare per Brunate** (T031-303608, daily 0600-2230, Sat & summer 0600-2400, every 30 mins; one way €2.50, return €4.35) from piazza de Gasperi, opposite the waterfront.

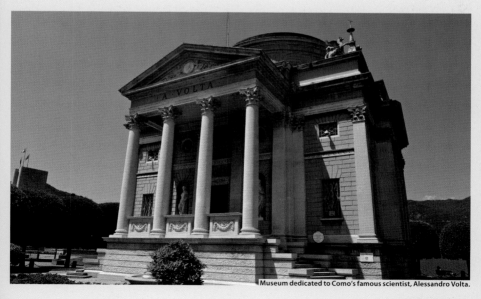

Museum dedicated to Como's famous scientist, Alessandro Volta.

Southern & western Como

Como's western shore is quintessential Lake Como: from refined Cernobbio, at the southern end on the outskirts of Como, with Villa d'Este, the grande dame of hotels, to tiny villages with their stone houses and cobblestone alleys, to colossal villa-gardens that dot the shores all the way up to Tremezzo and Menaggio. Explore by car and you'll be eagerly looking for places to pull up at every turn in the road, so you can peer over fences and snap photos. Explore by boat and you'll be keen to get off at every ferry stop to do the same. Spend a few days (or more) here and you can do both!

Villa d´Este in Cernobbio.

Only 5 km from Como, leafy Cernobbio is like a gracious suburb. Its two main attractions are the sumptuous **Villa d'Este** (see page 187), boasting sprawling gardens dotted with splendid fountains and marble statues that are open to the public and worth exploring, and **Villa Erba**.

Villa Erba

Largo Luchino Visconti 4, Cernobbio, T02-4997 7134 (Milan), villaerba.it.

Film director Luchino Visconti (see box opposite) had fond memories of childhood summers spent at this beautiful villa. His love for the lakeside ancestral home permeated some of his films, most evident in the ball scene in *The Leopard*. Visconti returned to the villa to rehabilitate after becoming ill at the height of his career, but died four years later. Built by the family to entertain illustrious guests, the 19th-century mannerist villa was indeed lavish and in 2003 was restored to its former splendour. Now part of an exhibition and conference complex, the first floor Luchino Visconti rooms have been established as a museum dedicated to the director and the special bond he had with the villa. While the rooms are theoretically open to the public, they close when booked for conferences or special events. Visits are by appointment only, so Visconti fans (and anyone who loves snooping in beautiful houses) should book well in advance.

Cernobbio to Tremezzo

After Cernobbio the narrow road snakes around the coast, which is dotted with palatial villas boasting palm-filled gardens, and delightful diminutive villages. **Colonno** has a labyrinthine old centre of stone arches over cobbled paths. **Sala Comacina** is home to the historic San Rocco chapel, a pretty little marina, and just offshore the overgrown **Isola Comacina**. Smattered with the ruins of old churches, it's Como's only island, and a bit of an artists' retreat. **Mezzegra** is where

Luchino Visconti & Villa Erba

One of Como's favourite sons is renowned film director, Luchino Visconti (1906–1976). Considered the father of Italian Neo-realism, Visconti's films won acclaim for their realistic depiction of social problems in Italy during and after the Second World War. His film *Ossessione* (Obsession, 1942), based on the novel *The Postman Always Rings Twice*, was highly influential for its use of non-professional actors, natural camera movement and an 'authenticity' created by hidden cameras. Born into an aristocratic dynasty, Visconti was able to use his connections and status to further his foray into directing – friendships with Coco Chanel and Maria Callas propelled his career. In later years, Visconti's films became more personal – films such as *Rocco and his Brothers* (1960), *The Leopard* (1963) and *Death in Venice* (1971) are seen as some of his greatest, all reflecting his memories of Lake Como in some way.

Mussolini and his mistress Claretta Petacci were killed in 1944. From the elegant village of **Lenno** you can walk about 20 minutes along the leafy peninsula to the splendid gardens at **Villa del Balbianello** (see page 180), which had a small part in the movie *Casino Royale* – where James Bond recuperated. And speaking of movies, a certain Hollywood star (see page 185) also has a rather grand villa in a certain village somewhere around here, but we'll let the man have his privacy.

The stretch of coast around Tremezzo, known as the Tremezzina Riviera, is quintessential Lake Como, with its verdant hills, luxuriant gardens, belle époque villas and boats bobbing in the tranquil water offshore. Locals and regulars (those who return annually) claim that the air is more fragrant here and the lake is at its most serene. Tremezzo's main sight is elegant **Villa Carlotta** (see page 181) and its lovely botanic gardens.

Outdoor activities – Lake Como

A ferry is an excellent way to see the villages and towns on Lake Como's shores.

Lago di Como offers visitors a wonderful array of ways to enjoy the crisp air, superb scenic vistas, and the languorous lake itself.

One of the first things you should do to get an overview of the area is to take the steep and slightly daunting **funicular** to the town of Brunate, some 720 m above the town of Como. If you're here on a clear day the views are phenomenal and strolling around the village of Brunate is also worth your time. If you're feeling in need of some exercise, you can walk back down to Como or head off into the hills on one of the many hikes that originate from here.

Given that Lake Como is often seen as a glamorous destination, taking a scenic seaplane flight from Como across the lakes is a popular option. **Aero Club Como** (viale Masia, 44, Como, T0315-74495, aeroclubcomo.com) offers scenic flights that do a loop of the Como leg of the lake. On a clear day, the views are spectacular, especially if there is snow around on the mountains.

Staying on the water, there are plenty of ways to enjoy the lake. Catching the **ferry** (navigazionelaghi.it) from Como to Bellagio (one of the must-see destinations on the lake) is an excellent way to see the villages and towns along the way from the water, which is where they look the prettiest. For only €6 it's a bargain, though check the timetables well ahead of time in the winter months to avoid disappointment.

Less of a bargain, but far more Clooney-esque is hiring a **speedboat** (comolakeboats.it, mostesfaggeto.com) and charting your own watery path around the lake. Neither girls in bikinis nor macho James Bond-like men are included in the boat hire fee, which is around €60 per hour for a boat that carries five people.

There are several slower ways of seeing the lake. **Sailing** and **windsurfing** are best at the northern end of the lake due to the better and more consistent winds called the *breva*. Dervio, north of Bellano, is the best base for sailing, where there is a great sailing school, **Orza Minore** (orzaminore.com). Windsurfers tend to congregate at Domaso (further

Going the green way

One of the most enjoyable things to do on Lake Como is simply to walk, whether it's taking a leisurely amble through lush semi-tropical botanical gardens or simply strolling a waterside promenade. Almost all of the lake's villages have cobblestone paths meandering through them, mule trails in the hills above the towns and footpaths that run by the water's edge.
The *Greenway del Lago di Como* is a specially created route connecting these paths all the way from Colonno to Cadenabbia di Griante, allowing you to enjoy a wonderful, uninterrupted 10.5 km walk along the lake, passing palatial villas, sprawling gardens, Roman ruins, and spectacular views en route. The itinerary is set out in a handy little booklet with a map and information in English and Italian, available from Como tourist office.

north and on the west side of the lake), where the windsurfing centre (breva.ch) is highly regarded, offering lessons for all ages and skill levels and they also have catamarans for hire. **Kayaking** (kayaks are also best hired from the windsurf centre) is also a popular way of enjoying the lake while allowing you to be a bit of a water-based snoop, seeing how the rich and nouveau riche decorate their little lakeside villas and gardens.

Back on land, it's important to note that **driving** around the lake can be more frightening than the **funicular** if you're not used to the narrow donkey tracks that sometimes double as roads around the lake.

Riding a **bike** (try **Como Bike** at via Grandi 15) along the lake's waterfront is also a lovely way to spend an afternoon and all the tourist offices have brochures and maps detailing possible itineraries with distances and durations. **Mountain biking** (bellagio-mountains.it), is increasingly popular, particularly around Bellagio. The same company that rents mountain bikes, **The Caval Calario Club** (bellagio-mountains.it) also offers horse-riding – another popular activity around the lakes.

Once you've tackled some of these fun lake-focused activities, you need to try one of the most popular lakeside activities of all – a sunset drink! Wherever you are at the end of the day, toast yourself – you've more than likely earned it.

Around the region

Menaggio is probably one of Lake Como's more bustling villages, with a living, breathing authenticity that the other holiday spots don't have. There's decent shopping and a lively town square lined with restaurants and cafés, and a busy ferry dock, with good connections to all parts of the lake (many residents commute to work in Switzerland or Como). Parking is more plentiful than at most of the villages, making it easier to explore. There's a pretty lakeside promenade that runs the length of the town, boasting benches filled with romantic young Italians reading books and tourists texting home.

Bellagio

Bellagio is bewitching, but while it's decidedly touristy, it's undoubtedly Como's most romantic destination, boasting tranquil parks and meandering paths made for hand-holding, intimate waterfront restaurants and alfresco cafés more suited to couples than families or friends, and lakeside benches apparently installed for canoodling. Besides, apart from strolling the lungolargo (waterside promenade), touring the villa gardens, exploring the steep stairways of the centro storico, and dining in fine restaurants (see box, page 201), there's actually very little to do in Bellagio.

Still, with its pretty pastel buildings spilling down the steep hillside, its quaint centro storico cradled by dense forest and parkland spiked with cypress trees, and its pretty lakeside promenade dotted with palms and flowerbeds, Bellagio offers what for many travellers is the quintessential Como experience.

While the drive from Como, along a hillside-hugging road (little more than one lane in places), is certainly dramatic, it can't beat arriving by water from the western shore. From the ferry, Bellagio is breathtaking, and it appears even more enchanting each moment it comes closer into view. Bellagio's stunning location in the most spectacular part of Lake Como is what makes it so special. On a headland at the tip of the Triangolo Lariano, the mountainous slither of land between Como and Lecco that splits the lake into two branches, it gives fantastic lake and Alpine views.

La Punta Spartivento After alighting from the ferry, day-trippers make a beeline for *La Punta Spartivento* ('the point that divides the wind'), the northernmost tip of the peninsula and most tranquil part of Bellagio. Here you'll find an attractive marina and stupendous views of the lake and Alps. It's an ideal place for a picnic. From lungolargo Mazzoni, walk through piazza Mazzoni, to the entrance of Villa Serbelloni, turn right into via Roma then left onto via E Vitali and follow it to the end. If you're staying overnight, save your stroll for sunset or sunrise.

Centro storico Bellagio is tiny, just ten little streets lengthways, from the Parco Comunale in the south to Villa Serbelloni in the north, and only three small blocks wide at its most concentrated northern half – so it won't take you more than an hour to explore. Start at piazza Mazzoni on the waterfront with its elegant arcades with flowing drapes, then zig-zag your way up and down the stepped cobblestone streets, working your way from one end to the other. There are a surprising number of little stores to detain you, and even if you're not a shopper, you'll be charmed by the delightful buildings lining the narrow lanes with geranium-filled window boxes and bougainvillea tumbling down their walls. Specialties are Como's **famous silk** (Pierangelo Masciadri, salita Mella 19), **handmade glassware** (I Vetri di Bellagio, via Garibaldi 41 & 60), and **handcrafted wood** (Luigi Tacchi, via Garibaldi 22). There are some spots you shouldn't miss for their atmospheric antique interiors alone, including Bar Café Rossi (piazza Mazzini 22) and Enoteca Cava Turaccilio (salita Genazzini).

Villa Serbelloni

Via Roma 1, Bellagio, T031-950216, villaserbelloni.com.

If you're not checking into this grand lakeside hotel (or dining at its Michelin-starred restaurant) then at

Hotel Villa Serbelloni is an icon of Bellagio.

least soak up some old-world atmosphere. Stick your head in and ask nicely if you can see the sweeping staircases, sumptuous salons (where a pianist plays in the evenings) and breakfast room dripping with chandeliers. While there, book a guided walking tour (90 mins; Tue-Sun 1100 & 1530) through the villa's gorgeous 18th-century gardens sprawled on the wooded slopes above the village. The tour takes you on an amble through the park and a hike up to the ruins on the hilltop for arresting lake vistas. Apart from being a stunning setting, the place oozes history – it once belonged to Pliny the Elder!

Villa Melzi

Lungolario Marconi, T0339-457 3838,
giardinidivillamelzi.it.
Apr-Oct 0930-1830, guided tours €6.

A 10-minute stroll along the *lungolargo* to via P Carcano, in the direction of Como, will bring you to the marvellous gardens of the Villa Melzi, once the residence of Duke of Lodi, Francesco Melzi d'Eril, vice-president of Napoleon's Italian republic. The neoclassical mansion was built between 1808 and 1810 and its clean, sober lines allow the eyes to take in the gorgeous countryside and lovely gardens which sprawl along the shoreline. Designed by architect Luigi Canonica and botanist Luigi Villoresi, who were responsible for Villa Reale north of Milan, the beautiful English gardens are dotted with sculptures, while the villa itself is also decorated with paintings and sculptures by some of the most famous artists of the time, including Antonio Canova. The Orangerie, once a greenhouse, is a tiny museum displaying objects from the Napoleonic period, including a bust of Napoleon and the keys to the city of Milan. Highlights include the Japanese gardens with ponds of water lilies, and a white and blue-tiled Moorish pavilion by the water.

Lake Como gardens

Lake Como is most famous for its splendid lakeside villas and their celebrated gardens. Spend any length of time here, especially in spring and summer, and the memories you'll come away with are of the ever-visible splashes of colour from azaleas, camellias, rhododendrons and bougainvillea, and of the fresh woody fragrances of cedar, cypress, juniper and pine. Boat around the lake and you'll be wishing you could hop off, climb over the garden walls, and sneak in for a look. Fortunately, there are a few gardens that are open to the public (so no wall-climbing necessary!), including Villa del Balbianello at Lenno, Villa Carlotta at Tremezzo, and Villa Monastero at Varenna (see page 183).

Villa del Balbianello

Via Comoedia, Lenno, T0344-56110, fondoambiente.it.
Mar-Nov Tue & Thu-Sun 1000-1800; villa €7, garden €5, combined ticket €8/11 (with/without reservation).
Imbarcadero: Lenno.

Stunningly located on the edge of Lenno, on a small, steep headland overlooking the lake, Villa del Balbianello was built in 1787 by Cardinal Angelo Maria Durini, but is more famous as the home of

Above: Villa Carlotta has unparalleled lake views.
Opposite page: Villa Carlotta's wonderful terraces.

20th-century explorer Count Guido Monzino who bequeathed his beloved house to his country. Architecturally, aside from its graceful loggia, there's not a lot that's notable about the enormous lemon villa exterior. Rather, it's the alluring location and enchanting gardens that are special.

Inside the villa there's a fascinating collection of precious objects, art and antiques, including pre-Columbian, Chinese, and African art, and beautiful 18th-century French and English furniture. The Expedition Room contains personal mementoes, photos, flags, and memorabilia from Monzino's trips, including the eight-dog sledge he used to reach the North Pole in 1971. The Map Room in the loggia contains geographical charts Monzino used, along with antique prints of the lake. In the adjoining library are volumes of books Monzino amassed, comprising the research materials he used to plan trips. Today these represent one of the most complete collections of books on alpine and polar expeditions.

The luxuriant gardens are the highlight, however, with their multiple levels, sweeping staircases and panoramic terraces with unparalleled lake and Alpine vistas. Spilling down the steep hillside, with slopes of manicured lawn separated by neat hedges and foliage, the gardens are unique in that they don't fit into either the ornate geometrical Italian form or the wild romantic English garden style that were fashionable at the time. They're an entrancing combination of the two, with shaded paths adorned with marble statues and potted shrubs on the one hand, and the wild wooded parkland on the other.

Villa Carlotta

Via Regina 2, Tremezzo, T0344-40405, villacarlotta.it.
Apr-Sep 0900-1800, Mar & Oct 0900-1130 & 1400-1630, €7.
Imbarcadero: Villa Carlotta or Cadenabbia.

Originally built in 1690 for a Milanese noble, the palatial pale pink Villa Carlotta was sold in 1801 to politician and patron of the arts, Battista Sommariva. It was Sommariva who started to develop the

gardens and establish an exquisite art collection that drew travellers doing the Grand Tour (see page 37). However, it wasn't until the second half of the 19th century, when Princess Marianne of Nassau bought the mansion and gave it to her daughter Carlotta as a wedding gift, that the property was transformed into the thing of splendour it is today.

Carlotta's husband, George II of Saxen-Meiningen, was a passionate botanist and it was he and Carlotta who created the 14 acres of gardens that can be visited today. The front terraced Italian garden is the most dramatic (symmetrical staircases, geometrically arranged flowerbeds, hedges, fishponds, statues, fountains, and its famous 'tunnels' of citrus trees), but the sprawling botanical gardens that encircle the villa are even more impressive. Paths meander through the magnificent woods and gardens, and while there is a café and snack bar in the greenhouse, there are several lovely picnic spots, so bring your hamper.

Also worth an hour or two of your time is the restored neoclassical villa. The ground floor's museum has highlights including a high relief depicting the *Entrance of Alexander the Great in Babylon* commissioned by Napoleon for the Pantheon in Paris in the Marble Room (room 1), fine marble statues of saints from Milan's Duomo in the Cameos room (room 3), a splendid statue of Eros and Psyche, carved from one piece of Carrara marble, by Antonio Tadolini (room 7), the beautiful *Last Adieu of Romeo and Juliet* (1823) by Francesco Hayez (room 8), and an exquisite decorative ceiling (room 9). The first floor has rooms furnished in the original period style, giving a fantastic insight into how Italian aristocrats lived at the time.

Northern & eastern Como

Few foreign travellers explore the northern tip of Lake Como. Gravedona has an old medieval centre and 12th-century Santa Maria del Tiglio church, and nearby at Domaso, there's good windsurfing. Colico is an industrial town with little to interest travellers apart from its 11th-century abbey, the Abbazia di Piona. Bellano is also industrial, the centre for silk and cotton manufacturing, but it has a charming *centro storico*.

Varenna is a handy base for exploring Lake Como by boat.

Varenna is not as lively as the towns on Como's western shore, even at the height of summer – there are few shops, restaurants or cafés to kick back at – and while it's picturesque, it doesn't come close to Bellagio in terms of beauty. Its main square, piazza San Giorgio, is dominated by an imposing 10th-century Romanesque church, but it's now become a car park, and while there are a couple of cafés, they're not the kind of places you want to linger – unless your idea of amusement is watching people squeeze their small cars into miniscule spaces. There's another piazza near the ferry dock from where a waterside promenade takes you on a stroll by boats and ducks and fish swimming about.

Varenna's setting is splendid, however, with a steep mountain providing a dramatic backdrop and the lemon, ochre, salmon and russet buildings colour-coordinating beautifully. Its location opposite Menaggio, midway along the eastern shore between Lecco and the little-visited northern lake area, makes it a handy base for exploring the lake by boat. And for many, the dearth of attractions – it's eerily quiet at night – are its very appeal.

The village's main sight is Villa Monastero, but there's little else to do other than wander the skinny alleys tucked behind the bold villas lining the shore. A stroll will take all of half an hour but explore soon after dawn or just before dusk, and you'll enjoy some brilliant photo opportunities.

You'll also get great views on a hike up the hill behind Varenna on some occasionally precipitous stairs to the ruined medieval **Castello di Vezio** (Perledo, T0335-46518, castellodivezio.it; Apr-Oct 1000-sunset, closed when raining, €4), set amid olive groves, where the Lombard Queen Theodolinda died in the seventh century. If you're lucky you might get to see a bird of prey demonstration by the castle's falconer who cares for an impressive collection of birds of prey.

Villa Monastero

Via IV Novembre, T0341-295450, villamonastero.eu. Mar-May & Sep-Oct Mon-Fri 0900-1300 & 1400-1800 (gardens only), villa museum & gardens Sat, Sun & holidays 0900-1300 & 1400-1800; Jun & Aug Mon-Thu 0900-1900 & Fri 0900-1300 (gardens only), villa museum & gardens Fri 1400-1900 & Sat, Sun & holidays 0900-1900. Mon-Fri €4, Sat, Sun & holidays €6.

A lot less tourist-focused than the other villas on the lake, and more interested in its income from conferences and film shoots, Villa Monastero is nevertheless worth a look if you're lucky enough to find it open. A former Cistercian convent, founded in 1208 by followers of Saint Mary Magdalena from Comacina Island, but was closed in the 16th century by San Carlo Borromeo due to the

What the locals say

Move from one village to the other using the local ferry service – the best way to see the lake is from the lake itself!

Sample one of the best cuisines in Italy, with mouth-watering dishes like *risotto con Pesce Persico*, made with the lake's fish.

Wait for a sunset on the lake's shore – you will immediately understand why Lake Como is one of the most romantic places in the world!

Don't forget your binoculars, especially if you love bird watching. Wild swans, eagles, hawks and many other kind of birds will cross your way during your stay on Lake Como.

Don't forget that Lake Como is perfect also for kids, thanks to its incredible variety of watersports such as wind-surfing, kayaking, canoeing, water-skiing and sailing, so bring all the family with you!

Serena Bertolucci,
Director, Villa Carlotta Museum and Gardens, shares her top tips for tourists.

Around the region

Villa Monastero has delightful gardens and views.

nun's rather licentious behaviour. While the villa's rooms are furnished with antiques and artistic treasures, the highlights are the perfumed gardens with their panoramic lake views, pretty waterfront pathways, and elegant loggias that frame the lake.

Lecco

Mark Twain wrote in *Innocents Abroad* of the 'wild mountain scenery' he enjoyed on his steamer voyage down the Lago di Lecco (the name given to this branch of Lake Como from Bellagio and Varenna south to Lecco) and of 'the towering cliffs on our left, and the pretty Lago di Lecco on our right'. Lecco's setting *is* one of the most dramatic on the lake, best appreciated by boat or on a stroll along the attractive waterfront.

Apart from these two assets, there's little to hold your interest here for longer than an hour or two, unless you're a fan of Lecco's favourite son and Italy's beloved novelist, Alessandro Manzoni (see page 24). In that case, you may want to see the author's statue on the main square and visit the house where the writer lived, **Villa Manzoni** (via Guanella 7, T0341-481247, Tue-Sun 0930-1730, €5), which now comes under the umbrella of the **Musei Civici di Lecco** (museilecco.org) and also houses the **Galleria Comunale d'Arte** and **Fototeca**, while several more museums are located at **Palazzo Belgiojoso** (corso Matteotti 32, T0341-481248, 0930-1400, €3) including the **Museo Archeologico**, **Museo Storico** and **Museo di Storia Naturale**. Unless you're a real lover of museums, you'll be more than satisfied with a visit to Villa Manzoni, where the Fototeca features some stunning old black and white archival images of Lecco and surrounds.

Clooney-spotting

Ever since the silver-haired Hollywood heartthrob George Clooney bought a villa on Lake Como in 2001, things have been a little different on the lake. Clooney has charmed most of the locals – he's a good tipper and is always friendly to everyone – and the attention (of fans and the media) that has come with him hasn't fazed the locals at all. Apart from the downside of paparazzi prowling the lake for shots of a shirtless Clooney steering a speedboat, the boost in publicity for Lake Como hasn't been unwelcome. It appears that Clooney is the kind of celebrity that Lake Como doesn't mind being associated with at all – in fact in 2007 they made him an honorary citizen.

Sleeping

The lakes are generally seen as a summer destination, so many of these hotels (and their restaurants) close completely in winter, opening again around end of March.

Albergo Terminus €€€
Lungo Lario Trieste 14, T031-329111, albergoterminus.com.
The pick of the bunch of Como's endearingly old-fashioned hotels, this 19th-century property overlooking the lake has contemporary rooms that sympathise with the older, classical decor of the rest of the hotel. For a unique experience, there's a delightful (albeit snug) room in the tower with French windows and lake views.

Albergo Terminus has rooms with brilliant views.

Barchetta Excelsior €€€
Piazza Cavour 1, T031-3221, hotelbarchetta.it.
With a brilliant location as the trump card, the chintzy feel of the rooms is easily forgiven if you're in one of the superior rooms with good views, or the suites – but in high season you'll certainly know you're paying for it.

Palace Hotel €€€
Lungo Lario Trieste 16, T031-23391, palacehotel.it.
Run by the same folks as the Barchetta Excelsior, this imposing hotel has 100 rooms, with many of the standard rooms facing the Duomo. Most superior rooms have lake views, but the deluxe rooms are a cert. A good breakfast, decent internet and secure parking.

Le Due Corti €€
Piazza Vittoria 12/13, T031-328111.
While not in the *centro storico*, nor overlooking the lake, this comfortable hotel in a renovated old pink building just outside the pedestrianised old town is still handily placed for sightseeing. Rooms are over-priced during summer, but the rest of the year they're a bargain.

Hotel Tre Re €€
Via Boldoni 20, T031-241349, hoteltrere.com.
This family-run hotel is a good, honest and spacious three-star in a great location near the Duomo. Despite the classic

exterior, the 40 hotel rooms are quite modern (some have balconies) and the hotel has parking. Decent restaurant attached to the hotel as well.

Hotel Villa Flori €€
Via Cernobbio 12, T031-33820, hotelvillaflori.com.
A gracious 45-room hotel (many with a terrace overlooking the lake), this was once an exquisite villa that became a hotel in 1958. The romantic Garibaldi suite is where the famous Italian hero spent the first night of his honeymoon; however, the marriage didn't last long – it appears that his young bride, Giuseppina Raimondi, was experienced beyond her years...

Albergo Del Duca €
Piazza Mazzini 12, T031-264859, albergodelduca.it.
A renovated 17th-century villa, this hotel's rooms have wooden floorboards and exposed beams and are clean and simple. A great location makes it an excellent budget choice in Como. There's parking, but let them know in advance.

Hotel Quarcino €
Salita Quarcino 4, T031-303934, hotelquarcino.it.
Another simple, clean and inexpensive choice in a town not known for great value, Hotel Quarcino has good facilities for the price, including Wi-Fi. Private parking is available.

Eating

Bellagio

Grand Hotel
Villa Serbelloni €€€
Via Roma 1, T031-950216,
villaserbelloni.com.
One of the oldest lake hotels,
Villa Serbelloni offers up the
quintessential Como experience.
The handsome old place exudes
atmosphere, from the gilt-edged
mirrors and chandeliered high
ceilings to the gigantic lakeside
pool. There are verdant grounds
to explore and elegant
restaurants to dress up for
(one with a Michelin Star,
Mistral, see page 189). Book
a room with a view.

Hotel Du Lac €€
Piazza Mazzini 32, T031-950320,
bellagiohoteldulac.com.
Smack bang in the town centre,
this family-run hotel might be
a little old-fashioned, but the
views from the upper floors
(ask for a lake view room on the
fourth) make up for it. Check out
the wonderful rooftop terrace.

Hotel Suisse €€
Piazza Mazzini 23, T031-950335,
bellagio.co.nz/Suisse.
This small, simple, 10-room hotel
above the Ristorante Albergo
Suisse is a pretty good deal for
Bellagio, as is their restaurant.

Cernobbio

Villa d'Este €€€€
Via Regina 40, T031-3481,
villadeste.it.
Villa d'Este is a lavish hotel with
sprawling lawns and a prime
lakeside location that's the envy
of other properties in the region.
The 17th-century hotel has had
many a famous face wander its
whimsical gardens, and while the
character-filled rooms have their
own idiosyncrasies, this is the
kind of hotel where you let
romance dictate your stay.
If you're staying at the height of
summer, book hotel restaurants
in advance and raise your credit
card limit.

Tremezzo

Grand Hotel Tremezzo €€€
Via Regina 8, T034-442491,
grandhoteltremezzo.com.
Close to the delightful Villa
Carlotta, this grand hotel,
dating to 1910, is sumptuously
appointed, with excellent dining
and service. The rooms, superior
level and above, have brilliant
lake views, while the classic
rooms face the garden. All are
beautifully decorated with
period furniture and fittings.
Both indoor and outdoor pools
are a treat.

Regional dishes, delicious
seafood and great wines await,
but make sure that the restaurant
of your desires is open – opening
times vary, although most open
for lunch (1200-1500) and dinner
(1900-2300) at least six days and
nights a week. Keep in mind that
most Lakes restaurants close
from December to January, some
staying shut as late as March, and
some also close one night a
week, generally Monday or
Tuesday.

Como

L'Antica Riva €€
Lungo Lario Trieste 50,
T031-305221, anticariva.it.
Lake Como is a great place
to try seafood and this popular
restaurant delivers with excellent
seafood platters, sublime
carpaccio of tuna, and delicious
seafood pastas. Excellent
lakeside location.

Bar Del Terme €€
Restaurant at Albergo Terminus,
Lungo Lario Trieste 14,
T031- 329111,
albergoterminus.com.
An elegant little restaurant set
in the equally elegant Albergo
Terminus, it's a romantic spot
for dinner. The cuisine is classic
Italian, but with all the usual
dishes handled with exquisite
care and presented beautifully –
try their handmade pastas.

Joy €€

Via Cernobbio 2, T031-572132, joyrestaurant.it.
With its funky purple interior, big wooden deck with brilliant panoramic vistas of the lake, and great pizzas and pastas, this chic casual eatery is currently the local favourite – and it's well off the tourist trail.

Il Pinzimonio €€

Via Bonanomi 24, T031-268667, il-pinzimonio.it.
Set in an historic building in the heart of the centre, the playful contemporary decor melds old wooden beams, exposed stone, brick walls and rustic flowerboxes with contemporary minimalist Italian design. The food equally and effortlessly combines classics with modern interpretations. Locals love the pizzas.

Michelin-starred Mistral.

Raimondi €€

Hotel Villa Flori,
via Cernobbio 12, T031-338233, albergoterminus.com.
With an unbeatable location and a terrace hovering gracefully over the lake, it's the perfect place to try some lake fish – one of the dishes that makes the locals return time and again. Other Italian classics are treated with equal care.

Il Solito Posto €€

Via Lambertenghi 9, T031-271352, ilsolitoposto.net.
The warm glow of lights within beckon customers from beneath the vine-covered entrance at this restaurant on a quiet cobbled lane. Once inside the cosy interior, complete with fireplace, it's hard to leave. The focus is on classic hearty cuisine such as *tagliolini al ragu di coniglio* (pasta with rabbit sauce) and *risotto gamberi e zucchini* (risotto with prawns and zucchini). The €15 two-course lunch menu is popular.

Le Soste Ristorante €€

Via A Diaz 52A, T031-266024.
Closed Sun.
Save this elegant restaurant and equally refined cuisine for an evening meal, when you can take your time enjoying the deliciously simple food, from smoked goose breast served with brioche, foie gras and apple puree, to *gnocchi di patate con burro montate e semi di papavero* (potato dumplings with melted butter and poppy seeds).

Il Vecchio Borgo €€

Piazza Matteotti 1, T031-304522, ilvecchioborgocomo.it.
A good choice when some in your group just want a simple pizza and others some grilled fish or seafood pasta. They do excellent Italian classics, but the local lake seafood – especially the perch – is worth sampling.

Il Carrettiere €

Via Coloniola 18, T031-303478.
Locals love this restaurant for its honest, home-style Sicilian fare and warm ambiance. Tucked away on a back street behind the lake, the wood-fired pizzas are superb and the mixed seafood (*fritto misto*) just one of the excellent seafood dishes on the menu.

Pizzeria La Darsena €

Lungo Lario Trieste 54, T031-301081, la-darsena.it.
Next door to L'Antica Riva, Pizzeria La Darsena is the place to come when you're not in the mood for fuss, and don't want to spend much, yet you still want a lake view – admittedly, overlooking the road too. The pizzas are very good.

Riva Café €

Via Cairoli 10, T031-264325.
This buzzy pizzeria in a sleek contemporary style (cream leather, slate floor, chocolate wood) might not appeal to those looking for the quintessential lakeside restaurant, but it's popular with

locals who come for the 70 types of pizza, from classics to unusual topping combinations, such as salmon, rocket, gorgonzola and walnuts – delicious!

Cafés

Caffè Alessandro Volta
Piazza A Volta.
Named after the Como-born physicist and inventor of the battery, Alessandro Volta (born 1745), this simple café with an alfresco terrace and stand-up bar inside is enormously popular with locals.

Caffè Nova Comum
Piazza Duomo 2, T031-260483.
Popular with locals and tourists alike, the views of Como's striped cathedral don't get much better than from the alfresco terrace of this old-fashioned café. Locals head here for cappuccino for breakfast or a prosecco in the afternoon, while tourists fill up on the fresh panini.

Gelateria Ceccato
Lungo Lario Trieste 16, next to the Palace Hotel Lake Como.
Situated in an elegant building opposite the waterfront, this gelateria is easily Como's most popular – just look for the people spilling out onto the street on a summer's evening. There's an alfresco area upstairs with pretty iron lacework overlooking the lake; however, locals prefer to stroll by the water while they do their licking.

Bellagio

Mistral €€€
Restaurant at Grand Hotel Villa Serbelloni, via Roma 1, T031-950216, villaserbelloni.com.
Hotel Villa Serbelloni is doubly blessed, with Michelin-starred chef Ettore Bocchia watching over both restaurants in the hotel. However, it's his Mistral restaurant where Bocchia spreads his gastronomic wings. Mistral is his laboratory of molecular gastronomy and even though Bocchia isn't afraid of culinary fireworks and flashy presentation, the flavour is firmly on the plate – right up to his innovative gelato!

Ristorante Barchetta €€
Salita Mella 13, T031-951389.
Book ahead for this wildly popular restaurant – locals are either dining here themselves or sending guests here. Fish fresh from the lake is a favourite (try the local perch) and the meat dishes excellent for those who have had their fill of seafood.

La Grotta €
Salita Cernaia 14, T031-951152.
Another local favourite, this comfy and welcoming restaurant does a roaring trade with its excellent thin pizzas (try the one with capers and anchovies) and fish main courses.

Menaggio

Le Tout Paris €€€
Lungolago Castelli 9, Grand Hotel Victoria, T03-443 2003.
With its crisp white linen tablecloths and flower arrangements, this is a very elegant restaurant serving up reasonably-priced regional and Italian classics. The location opposite the waterfront makes it a romantic spot – especially if the musicians are playing.

Varenna

Vecchia Varenna €€€
Contrada Scoscesa 10, T03-4183 0793.
Vecchia Varenna is widely considered to be one of the most romantic restaurants on the lake – if you're a couple book for dinner, otherwise a relaxing (long) lunch here is recommended for the excellent fresh seafood and calming lake views.

Lecco

Nicolin €€€
Via Ponchielli 54, T03-4142 2122.
This homely, inviting, family-run restaurant has lovely garden seating in summer and a fine wine list. The food is classic northern Italian with the occasional imaginative twist.

Entertainment

The thing to do on Lake Como, and it doesn't matter which part of the lake you're on, is to have a late afternoon aperitivo and nibbles (generally a few small dishes of chips, nuts and olives) at a waterfront café-bar. After dinner, head to the nearest gelateria to buy a gelato and take a saunter along the water's edge.

Bars

Café-bars are located on the waterfront at Como and the towns and villages all around the lake, as well as lining the perimeters of most piazzas. Most of the bars doubling as cafés open all day, from morning until fairly late at night, and might close one day a week (often Monday). Bars that mainly serve as wine bars tend to open around lunch and close after midnight. Como has the most interesting bars and a fairly lively bar scene compared to the other towns, while Bellagio's waterfront bar-cafés are probably the most romantic for a pre- or post-dinner drink. During summer, some of the villa gardens, such as Villa del Balbianello (see page 180), host happy hours (generally from 1830-2030) which will feature an alfresco cocktail bar and live jazz or other music.

Al Molo
Lungo Lario Trieste, Como (opposite the Stazione Nord train terminus).
Little more than a stand-up bar with a handful of tables and chairs outside covered in red-checked tablecloths, Al Molo boasts one of Como's best locations for sunset-watching with a glass of something in hand. Little dishes of snacks are also served during aperitivo hour. It may not be flash but this is the kind of place you can settle in for a while.

Mesa Redonda
Via A Diaz 28, Como.
The red country'n'western-style typeface on the black portico may seem out of place in Como's elegant old town, and this dark bar may seem an odd fit too, but it's hugely popular with young arty types, especially late on a weekend night; by day anybody and everybody drops in for a drink.

Osteria del Gallo
Via Vitani 16, Como, T031-272591.
Look for the delightfully old-fashioned osteria sign above the arched doors to find this atmospheric wine bar, a favourite with locals, which serves a good selection of local wines alongside plates of cold cuts and cheeses.

Shopping

Most shops on Lake Como open from Monday-Saturday 0930 or 1000, close for lunch at 1200 or 1300, then reopen from 1600-1900, although in Como town and Bellagio many shops stay open all day, especially throughout the busy summer tourist season. You'll find the most sophisticated shopping at Como and Bellagio, where the cobblestone streets are crammed with chic boutiques selling fashion, jewellery, shoes and handbags, and shops

Markets on Lake Como

There is a market on each day at at least one town on Lake Como. These open-air street markets sell fresh produce, plants, clothes and accessories, and household items. They're usually held from early in the morning until around noon, although on Saturdays they're often held all day. You'll often find them on the main piazza and in surrounding pedestrian streets.

Monday Argegno (am only)

Tuesday Como and Lenno (am only)

Wednesday Varenna, Lecco (am only), Gravedona (1st & 3rd Wed am)

Thursday Como and Bellano (am only)

Friday Menaggio (2nd & 4th Fri am), Colico (every Fri am)

Saturday Lecco and Como (all day)

Activities & tours

specializing in Italian crafts and souvenirs, including hand-painted ceramics, pottery and glassware, as well as gourmet food and wine.

Lake Como is famous for its silk, and Como and Bellagio are the best places to shop for silk scarves, shawls, foulards, cravats and ties. In Como, **A Picci** (via Vittorio Emanuele 54, T031-261369) is a well-regarded, old-fashioned store stocking fine quality classic pieces, while in Bellagio, **Pierangelo Masciadri** (salita Mella 19, T031-950067, masciadri.tv), a Brera Academy graduate (see page 107), creates beautiful silk creations using his own prints with designs inspired by history, art and architecture; his shop displays photos of the rich and famous who have come here to buy his products.

Language

Inlingua
Via Luini 3, Como,
T031-431 0092, inlingua.it.
This highly regarded Italian language school, in operation for 30 years, offers packages of 10 lessons over one, two or three-day periods, aimed at foreigners on holidays. You can arrange one-on-one lessons, or in pairs, or small groups of five people.

Sport & outdoor
For watersports such as sailing, windsurfing and kayaking, and outdoor activities including mountain biking and rides on the Brunate funicular, see Outdoor Activities: Lake Como (see page 176)

Lakes Excursions & Cruises
Via per Cernobbio 18, Como,
T031-579211, navigazionelaghi.it
The government-operated water transport service for Lake Como offers frequent services from Como to various towns, villages and sights around the lake, including Cernobbio, Colico, Argegno, Lenno, Tremezzo, Villa Carlotta, Bellagio, Menaggio, Varenna, Bellano, Gravedona, and Lecco, on several different types of boat: *servizio rapido* (fast catamaran), *servizio autotraghetto* (a slower ferry), and *corso battello* (an even slower 'ship'). During summer, there are also daily excursions and themed cruises (€15-22), some of which offer lunch and dinner (€15-19).

Rent A Boat
Various marinas and docks
around Lake Como,
T038-0843 5253, rentland.it.
You can rent easy-to-drive speed boats, water skis, wake boards and wet suits, from one hour to one week, from a number of marinas and docks around the lake. Call to find the nearest location to where you're staying. Prices range from €75 per hour to €2,250 for six days.

Seaplane Tours
Aero Club Como, viale Masia 44,
Como, T031-574495,
aeroclubcomo.com.
Probably the most popular activity to do on the lake is to take a scenic flight on a sea plane. This company has been offering flights since 1930 and has an excellent reputation.

Shopping and sipping on the streets of Bellagio.

Contents

195 Introduction
196 Southern Lake Garda
198 *Map: Lake Garda*
200 Western Lake Garda
204 Northern & eastern Lake Garda
206 Great days out:
     Outdoor activities – Lake Garda
208 Listings:
208 Sleeping
210 Eating & drinking
212 Entertainment
212 Shopping
213 Activities & tours

Lake Garda

Statues at Il Vittoriale, house of Gabriele d'Annunzio.

Introduction

Lake Garda is Italy's largest lake and while it's popular with retired couples and those in the mood for romance, it's also a favourite with sporting enthusiasts and families. Theme parks, grand hotels, spas, excellent restaurants, as well as superb sailing and windsurfing are all on offer – and all are set amidst some spectacular scenery, particularly at the north of the lake. Sirmione, on the southern shore, is perhaps the most photographed town here because of its magnificent castle with a real moat and drawbridge. Spas, restaurants, shopping and Roman ruins are the attractions at Sirmione – although kids will probably want to head to nearby Gardaland, considered to be the best theme park in Italy. Heading clockwise, we pass the pretty town of Salò where Mussolini retreated to on the lake's west coast, and Gardone Riviera where Il Vittoriale, an ostentatious villa once owned by Italy's famously eccentric poet Gabriele d'Annunzio, is to be found. The northern end of the lake is where the sailing action is concentrated, and where everything from dinghies to yachts can be found tacking with a backdrop of spectacular mountains that work as a wind tunnel, providing reliable gusts almost every day. Riva del Garda and Torbole are the favourite haunts of sailing types, as is Malcesine on the eastern side of the lake.

Family activities centre on the water at Lake Garda.

What to see in...

...one day

If you only have one day, you're going to have to spend it at **Sirmione**. While it's touristy, its moat and castle, the **Rocca Scaligera**, are stunning. Buy a giant gelato, then stroll through the *centro storico* to the far end of the peninsula to see the ruins of **Grotte di Catullo** and take in the aquamarine shallow waters.

...a weekend or more

Stay the night at **Gardone Riviera**, which has one of the prettiest aspects of the lake. Tour **Il Vittoriale**, the bizarre villa of eccentric poet Gabriele d'Annunzio, explore the charming village, as well as picturesque **Salò** nearby, then dine in one of the area's many superb restaurants.

A longer visit will allow you more time to explore and you can stop off at villages along the way, such as **Desenzano**, **Riva del Garda** and **Torri del Benaco**. Sporty types: get on the water for some **windsurfing** or **sailing**. Families will need to take the kids to **Gardaland**. Everyone should set aside time to do nothing, arguably one of the most pleasurable things to do on the lake.

Southern Lake Garda

The southern shore – Basso Garda to the locals – is the most tourist-focused, attracting hordes of tourists to Sirmione for its castle and Roman sights, and to Peschiera del Garda for its nearby theme parks.

Rocca Scaligera, Sirmione.

Little more than a slender finger poking into Lake Garda, Sirmione is undeniably stunning. From the moment you see the spectacular castle at its entrance and enter the village across a wooden drawbridge, you imagine you're in for a treat. Once inside, however, unless you're here early or late in the season (March or October), it's sheer chaos, the pedestrian streets of the village teeming with tourists, the crush especially overwhelming at the height of summer. Prepare yourself for the crowds of sunburnt tourists slurping Sirmione's famous over-sized gelato cones and your risk of disappointment is lowered. Stay here overnight and spend the day sunning yourself on the lake

Tip…

If you're not staying at one of Sirmione's lovely hotels with a sundeck right on the lake, then **Lido delle Bionde** (May-Oct 0800-2400), just beyond **Parco Maria Callas**, is a lovely spot for a swim with its crystal clear water and pontoons. We can't explain why the sunburnt tourists prefer sunbaking under the olive groves on the hillside to joining the Italians on the beach. Parco Maria Callas is a fine spot for a picnic too.

Essentials

🚆 **Train station** Desenzano is the closest, reached from the bus station.

🚌 **Bus station** Via Marconi 26.

💲 **ATMs** Opposite entrance to Rocca Scaligera.

➕ **Hospital** Azienda Ospedaliera Di Desenzano Del Garda, via Monte Croce, Desenzano Del Garda, T030-91451.

✚ **Pharmacy** Farmacia Internazionale Di Cornacchione Arnaldo, via S. Maria Maggiore 18, T030-916004, Mon-Wed & Fri-Sun 0945-1215 & 1630-1900, Thu 0945-1215.

✂ **Post office** Largo Faselo Bitinico 1, T030-916195, Mon-Fri 0830-1400, Sat 0830-1230.

ℹ **Tourist information** Viale G Marconi 2, T030-916114, Mon, Wed, Thu 0900-1200 & 1500-1900, Tue & Fri 0900-1200, sirmionebs.it.

and only slip out at night (when the daytrippers have gone) to explore the village's labyrinthine streets, lined with cafés and elegant boutiques (and, naturally, store after store selling tourist trinkets), and you'll find Sirmione considerably more charming.

Rocca Scaligera

Piazza Castello, T030-916468.
Mar-Oct Tue-Sun 0830-1900,
Nov-Feb Tue-Sun 0830-1700, €5.

Kids (or the big kids in all of us) love Sirmione's 13th-century stone citadel, with its crenellated walls, squat towers, drawbridges and moats that are the stuff of fairytales. Strategically located and splendidly preserved, the castle served as a fortress as late as the 19th century. Built by the Verona-based della Scala dynasty (see page 243), who constructed many of the splendid fortresses in this region, it was seized in 1402 by the Visconti family. Once over the drawbridge to the town, you'll find a second moat and drawbridge leading to the castle itself. While the interior is not as impressive as the striking exterior, there are gorgeous views.

Grotte di Catullo

Via Catullo, T030-916157.
Mar-Oct Tue-Sun 0830-1900,
Nov-Feb Tue-Sun 0830-1700, €5.

According to local legend, these cave-like ruins are those of the Roman villa of the pleasure-seeking poet Catullus (87-54 BC). More recent archaeological evidence suggests the ruins belonged to two villas, both dating to around the first century AD. You'll find them by walking to the very end of via Caio Valerio Catullo, then taking a left at piazzale Orti Manara, or by walking through Parco Maria Callas to Lido della Bionde and climbing up through the olive groves to the grotto. Avoid a visit in the midday sun, when the walk is a challenge in the sweltering heat as there's little shade apart from in the park. If you must, there's a small tourist train that will take you there but it's preferable to do the visit in the early morning or late afternoon.

Lake Garda

Torbole.

Il Vittoriale, Gardone Riviera.

Riva del Garda.

Sirmione.

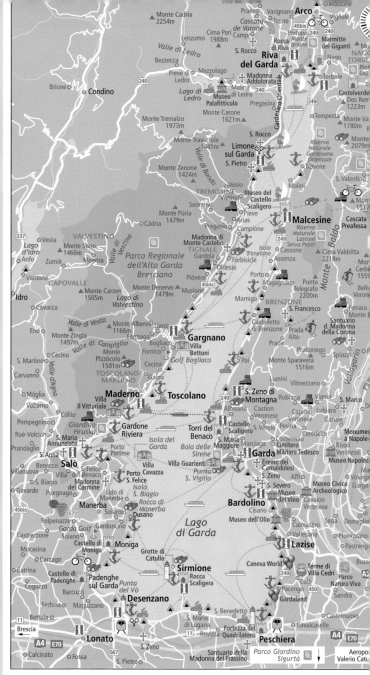

A pier makes for a decent sunbake at Sirmione.

Desenzano

More formally known as Desenzano del Garda, this rather delightful town on the southwestern shore of Lake Garda is the lake's largest – and busiest. While it's certainly an attractive town with its picturesque old harbour, waterfront cafés and restaurants, and 17th-century **Duomo** on piazza Malvezzi, what's most appealing about it is that it's a working town that is alive outside of the tourist season. However, this is also one of the most frustrating things about Desenzano if you're after a peaceful holiday, because the roads are heavy with traffic (especially on market days) and parking is impossible to find. It's definitely one of those towns you need to stay the night at, so you can wander the tranquil streets early morning or evening to fully appreciate it.

What's most appealing about Desenzano is that it's a working town that is alive outside of the tourist season.

Villa Romana

Via Crocefisso 22, T030-914 3547.
Mar-Oct Tue-Sun 0830-1900, €3.

These ruins of a late imperial Roman villa, considered some of Italy's most important, give a great insight into the majestic rural estates where those with the means to do so retreated as anarchy began to spread in Rome in the fourth century AD. Built in the first century AD, the most impressive aspect of the site to the untrained eye is the beautiful decorative mosaics, although some remain only partially excavated.

Peschiera del Garda

Situated on the southeastern corner of Lake Garda, Peschiera's *centro storico*, situated within the well-preserved old walls, is worth a look if you're here to take the kids to the theme parks (see page 213), but there's little else to hold your interest. The town gets uncomfortably busy in summer, and even if you are here for the theme parks, you're better off basing yourself somewhere else on the lake.

Western Lake Garda

The area on the western shore, north of Desenzano (known as the Valtenesi) is an idyllic area of gently undulating hills dotted with olive groves. The main road lies inland; however, there are a couple of diversions on the way worth a quick peek including Moniga, which has a pretty harbour, and the area around Manerba, where there are picturesque beaches. The northern two-thirds of the lake, beginning around Salò, is known as the Alto Garda, or upper shore, and has a decidedly different look and feel to the south, attracting a more affluent traveller to the romantic and refined villages of Gardone Riviera and Gargnano along the mid-west shore.

Below: Summer means swimming at Lake Garda. Opposite page: Antonino Cannavacciuolo.

Salò

Salò is certainly a sight for sore eyes. The first glimpse you get of this genteel village skirting a gorgeous bay lined with elegant buildings and palatial art nouveau villas will have you eagerly figuring out a way to get closer for a look – which is not an easy task. When you see a parking space, grab it, as wherever you park you won't have far to walk, and a stroll here along what is arguably Italy's longest lakeside promenade, Lungolago G Zanardelli, is one of the delights of visiting Salò anyway.

Perhaps because it has few sights to speak of – the **Torre dell'Orologio** (ancient city gate) and the Gothic-Renaissance **Duomo** (0830-1900) are about all that could be considered 'attractions' – and maybe because it appeals largely to well-to-do Italians and affluent Americans, Salò is generally overlooked by English-language guidebooks, which is all the more reason to stay.

Even if you're out and about most of the day exploring the lake, you'll know your evenings will be very pleasantly spent with a promenade along the leafy lakeside, browsing the chic shops hidden within the elegant waterfront arcades, checking out the sleek yachts anchored at the marina, and kicking back in the pretty piazzas with a gelato. Try the lively piazza Dal Vittoria, where the ferry docks and where you'll find most of the cafés and restaurants. Kids also seem to enjoy thumping across the wooden boardwalks and feeding the ducks.

Gardone Riviera

Leafy Gardone Riviera, a couple of kilometres north of Salò, was once the most glamorous resort on Lake Garda. While it's no longer fashionable, its grand old hotels with their luxuriant gardens, lakeside swimming pools and superlative restaurants (see box, opposite) still have a certain faded grandeur that make them a must-do for romantics and travellers nostalgic for the glorious early days of Grand Tour travel. After climbing up the hill to explore the charming village, eat at Agli Angeli (see page 211); amble about the verdant

Michelin stars over the Lakes

The lakes of northern Italy have wonderful surprises in store for food-lovers with some highly creative chefs in restaurants that are destinations in themselves. On Lake Garda, La Rucola at Sirmione serves up refined seafood dishes and whimsical desserts that are beautifully created and presented by the **Bignotti family**, who also have a great wine cellar as well as a Michelin star to their name. On the western shore of the lake, elegant neoclassical Villa Fiordaliso is a wonderful setting for a romantic dinner overlooking the water, but your attention will be drawn to the beautiful plates of chef **Riccardo Camanini** whose seafood dishes are impeccable and have earned the restaurant a very worthy Michelin star. At the Grand Hotel Villa Serbelloni in Bellagio on Lake Como, serious chef **Ettore Bocchia** has earned a Michelin star for his experimental Mistral restaurant, but as he also oversees the hotel's other restaurant, La Terrazza, it's hard to go wrong eating anywhere at the hotel. At the exotic Moorish Villa Crespi at Lake Orta, foodies come to worship at the gastronomic temple run by chef **Antonino Cannavacciuolo**, whose light touch with seafood and extraordinary creativity is a highlight of eating on the lakes – and Michelin agrees, delivering the chef two sparkling stars. Apart from La Rucola, all the restaurants have accommodation – perfect if you want to stagger upstairs to a romantic room after a full degustation menu with accompanying wines.

Giardino Botanico Hruska (T0365-20347, Mar-Oct 0900-1900, €6) and do a tour of Il Vittoriale (see below), there is little else to do except stroll along the palm-lined promenade, but that's the way most travellers like it.

Il Vittoriale

Via Vittoriale, Gardone di Sopra,
T0365-296511, vittoriale.it.
Apr-Sep 0830-2000, guided tours of house (Tue-Sun) & War Museum (Thu-Tue) 0930-1900; Oct-Mar 0900-1700, guided tours of house (Tue-Sun) & War Museum (Thu-Tue) 0900-1300 & 1400-1700. Gardens only €5, garden & tour of house/War Museum €12, garden & tour of house & War Museum €16.

Gardone Riviera's main attraction is the magnificent Il Vittoriale, with its lavish gardens, curious war museum and whimsical villa where eccentric poet Gabriele d'Annunzio lived in the

Gabriele d'Annuzio's quirky home, Il Vittoriale.

Gabriele D'Annunzio

A leading poet and writer in the late 19th and early 20th century as well as a war hero and political heavyweight, Gabriele D'Annunzio (1863-1938) was one of the most intriguing figures in Italian history. D'Annunzio's talent was obvious very early on when he became a published poet while still at school. Plays and poems consumed him as a young adult, as did women and a decadent lifestyle that saw him relocate to Paris to avoid creditors.

When the First World War broke out, D'Annunzio urged Italy to join the war, and he too joined up, earning kudos for his bold deeds and pranks, but losing an eye in a flying accident. Perhaps his most bold deed occurred after the war in 1919, when he and a small band of fighters took and held a Croatian port that Italy was considering giving up as part of the Treaty of Versailles. D'Annunzio 'ruled' Fiume until December 1920.

Becoming a committed Fascist, he was an influential political figure until he was pushed out of a window in 1922, in an apparent murder attempt. Before he fully recovered, another political figure and colleague, Benito Mussolini, became Prime Minister. Essentially bought off by Mussolini, D'Annunzio's public political career ended and he retired to Gardone Riviera. Today he is a greatly admired figure in Italy, as much for his poetic works as for his fierce nationalism and free-spiritedness – and knowing the Italians, probably also a little for his idiosyncratic taste, original style, and extraordinary decorating abilities.

dark for 17 years – he was photophobic. A guided tour moves fairly rapidly through the many inter-connecting rooms, each decorated in a different theme or style, all crammed with a compelling jumble of art, antiques and curiosities that d'Annunzio collected.

The only way to see Il Vittoriale's interior is on a guided tour; however, tour scheduling is poorly organised. Scheduling seems to be dictated according to the guide's convenience so this means sometimes the wait is long. You can join Italian tours and read a translation collected from the locker room; bags and cameras must be stored. Otherwise, take a picnic lunch, buy your tickets, put your names down on a tour, then explore the shady gardens.

The tour begins in The Vestibule with its ancient walnut choir stalls before proceeding to two waiting rooms, one for friends, the other for unwelcome visitors like Mussolini and creditors. Next is The Music Room where pianist Luisa Baccara used to play, its fabric-draped walls resembling an Arabian tent. D'Annunzio's bedroom is probably the most fascinating room, jammed with intriguing objects, cushions, and Persian carpets, while the Blue Bathroom is probably the most cluttered you'll ever see, packed with over 900 objects. At the end of it all, you'll either be ready to scan the nearest antique market for some re-decorating when you get back home or be yearning to check into a minimalist hotel!

Spread over five terraces, the sprawling nine-hectare gardens are dotted with strange sculptures, statues, ponds and fountains, but the most unusual features must be the poet's extraordinary wedding cake monument to himself, and, below it, the navy ship embedded into the hillside; this was a memorial to two of d'Annunzio's comrades who died during their invasion of Fiume (orchestrated by d'Annunzio himself), where he and his followers set up a (short-lived) government of their own!

Gargnano

More so than any other spot on the lake, lovely Gargnano, a former 13th-century Franciscan centre, seems to have its loyal devotees who return to spend their summers relaxing at this easy-going lakeside resort with its small pebble beach and tiny harbour. You can pick them out a mile away – they're the foreign travellers (many German who own villas here) who look right at home, speak enough Italian to get by, and always know all the waiters by name. Unlike Gardone Riviera, the main road runs a bit of a distance inland, leaving the waterfront area relatively tranquil and traffic-free, which is part of the reason for its popularity. Apart from stroll the tree-lined promenade, read a book from one of the many shady park benches or go sailing on the lake,

there is very little to do. But, once again, like in Gardone Riviera that's exactly the way people here like it!

Lake Iseo

Lying west of Lake Garda, northwest of Brescia and a little under halfway to Lake Como, Lago d'Iseo is often overlooked by visitors to Garda and Como, yet it's worth dropping into en route between lakes if you're doing a driving holiday. Lake Iseo may not boast the refined beauty of lakes Como or Orta, nor does it have the dramatic surroundings of lakes Garda or Maggiore, but its mountain setting is stunning and the waterfront at Iseo town is lovely. The lake also has a laid-back attitude many visitors find appealing. Despite the low-key vibe, it's very touristy, its camping spots and holiday resorts inundated with Italian and foreign package tourists throughout the summer months, and away from the shore the modern towns and heavy industry are unattractive.

Four lakes' drive

From Gargnano on Lake Garda's western shore, a turn-off takes you on an engaging edge-of-your-seat drive – be prepared for never-ending switchbacks and hairpin turns – through jaw-dropping scenery to narrow **Lago di Valvestino** deep within a lofty valley. From here the road takes you over a high pass before dropping through dense woods to the tranquil Alpine fjord-like **Lago d'Idro** – at 370 m, Lombardy's highest lake, although a pond compared to the other watery expanses, but nevertheless spectacular with steep mountains either side. Nearby, little **Bagolino** with its stone houses is a gem, while **Storo** is stunningly set beneath sheer cliffs. Once through a dramatic cleft by a rocky river and waterfall, you traverse a lush valley, **Passa Ampola**, before descending to diminutive **Lago di Ledro** surrounded by forest parks, and the lush vineyards of **Pre** to **Riva del Garda** back on the big lake.

Northern & eastern Lake Garda

With its reliable winds, which locals swear breeze in like clockwork, the northern end of Lake Garda is the favoured destination of windsurfers, sailors, and other water-sports enthusiasts. Its villages and towns may not be as attractive or refined as elsewhere in the lakes, but the mountains are still very striking, so if getting on the water is your priority, this is the place to head. Popular with Italian families on camping and caravanning holidays, and northern European package tourists on a budget, the eastern side of Garda may not be pretty but there's still plenty of opportunities for swimming and paddling on its shores.

Below: Limone sul Garda. Opposite page: Windsuring and sailing happens mainly at Torbole.

Northern Lake Garda

While fragrant **Limone sul Garda** is set among citrus groves and was a centre for lemon growing until the 1920s, locals claim its name comes from the Latin *limen* (frontier), as it was once a Roman border outpost. It's now Lombardy's last town – Trentino's border is close by – and while it boasts a stunning location on a slim strip of land beneath colossal rocky mountains, its streets have been given over to tourism of the ugliest kind. You'd do well to stay away except during the first days of the season (March) before the shopkeepers have wheeled out their clothes racks of cheap jeans and shelves of tourist tat. Just as dramatically sited at the foot of jagged mountains, **Riva del Garda** is also touristy, but its reliable winds and beaches bring in athletic holidaymakers who settle in for a summer of watersports, somehow making Riva's brand of tourism slightly more palatable. If you're not here for the windsurfing and sailing (most of which happens at nearby **Torbole**), once you've explored the walled *centro storico* and promenaded around the attractive medieval piazza III Novembre, you'll find the rest of Riva dreary with very little to do. Once part of Austria, Riva is more Teutonic culturally, German is widely spoken, most tourists are German (and British), and many Germans and Austrians have holiday homes here, so it might not suit tourists looking for the quintessential Italian Lakes experience.

Eastern Lake Garda

Located in the Verona province of the Veneto region, Lake Garda's eastern shore has an altogether different atmosphere and little of the western shore's allure, with much of the lakefront lined with ugly resorts and dreary-looking camping and caravan parks. While **Malcesine** has a pleasant *centro storico*, the popular windsurfing spot is overrun with package tourists, having totally given over to tourism. **Torri del Benaco** is the most appealing spot, with a tiny but delightful historic core, a picturesque waterfront lined with citrus trees which buzzes during the summer evening's see-and-be-seen stroll, the *passeggiata*, and some ruined towers

and battlements remaining from its 10th century walls. Nearby, **Punta San Vigilio** boasts pretty pebble beaches at a lido backed by cypress and pine trees, **Parco Baia delle Sirene** (Mermaid's Bay Park, T39045-725 5884, Apr-Sep, times and prices vary throughout the season). Further south, the former fishing village of **Garda** is the only other attractive town this side of the lake, with a little warren of lanes worth exploring in its *centro storico* and a beautiful waterfront promenade with cafés and gelaterias to rival that of Como.

Lake Garda's Winds

Garda's sailors and windsurfers swear you can set your watch by these winds:

Pelèr This gentle breeze (also known as the Vento or Suer) starts around 0200-0300, comes in waves, and lasts until 1100; blowing from the north it brings cool air and clear blue skies to the lake.

Ora Felt mainly in the lake's northern and central parts, this southerly wind picks up where the Pelèr leaves off, around 1200-1300, lasting until sunset; if blowing in the south during summer, it creates cloud on the mountaintops.

Ponale A small chilly wind from the Valle di Ledro.

Ander A small gust blowing from Desenzano across to Garda.

Vent da Mût A blustery wind following storms.

Vinezza A southerly wind blowing from Peschiera to Maderno; in the late afternoon it's a sign bad weather's on its way.

Balì This turbulent 24-hr wind blows south in winter after snowfalls, creating a choppy lake.

Outdoor activities – Lake Garda

Lake Garda is the home of watersports for the northern Italian lakes and the waters teem with vessels of all kinds during the warmer spring and summer months. Mountain biking, climbing and paragliding are also popular here, and all the sports afford spectacular vistas along with the crisp fresh air of the lake.

The lake has some of the best conditions for all forms of sailing in Europe, with a regular breeze arriving nearly every afternoon due to the land around the lake heating up during the day and creating a thermal breeze that funnels through the lake in the afternoon, directed by the mountains either side of the lake. This breeze is called the 'Ora' and in the early morning another breeze often blows, the 'Pelér' or 'Vento', which goes in the opposite direction (north to south). The 'Ora' can measure 4–5 on the Beaufort scale and the 'Pelér' 6–7, but the early surfer or sailor gets the best winds! For full details of the lake's winds, see page 205.

Riva del Garda, or simply Riva to the locals, is sailing central, with almost every type of vessel with a sail found here and dozens of sailing clubs dotted around the pretty shoreline. Further down the lake, where the winds are less heavy, Malcesine is also a popular spot for sailing, as is Sirmione, but none can beat Riva for the breeze. There are plenty of opportunities to rent a *barca a vela* (sailing boat) and take some lessons. One highly recommended centre, **Sailing du Lac** by **Surf Segnana** (T0464-552453, sailingdulac.com), has both catamarans and dinghy-based sailing vessels. For something larger, try **Garda See Charter** (T335-527 4554, gscharter.com), which has yachts as well as smaller vessels, and offers tuition alongside rental and charter. For swapping stories and having a beer after a hard day on the water, head to **Fraglia Vela Riva** (via Giancarlo Maroni 2, T0464-552460, fragliavelariva.it) where most of the area's regattas are headquartered.

The main centre for windsurfing is Torbole, around the north end of the lake from Riva. Torbole

held the RSX world championships in 2006. The best places to head here are **Circolo Surf Torbole** (T0464-505385, circolosurftorbole.com), as well as **Vasco Renna** (T0464-505993, vascorenna.com), where you can rent a full rig for around €45 a day. **Surf Segnana** (T0464-505963, surfsegnana.it), whose main centre is at Lido di Torbole, offers courses, regardless of level, and children are well catered for if they want to start surfing. All the centres mentioned have excellent and up-to-date equipment. The area is very safe too, as powered leisure craft activities such as water-skiing and jet-skiing are not allowed. If the winds are too much up here, then head down to Malcesine and see the guys at **Stickl** (T045-740 1697, stickl.com), who have been operating here since 1976.

Kitesurfers are increasingly finding Lake Garda a great place for kiting even if landing and launching can feel a little daunting with those tall trees and sheer cliffs all around. Campione del Garda is a very popular place to kite surf and has an association there, **Kite Surf Campione** (kitesurfcampione.com),

while for lessons it's best to head to **Kite School Xkite** (T338-828 7886, xkite.it), at Brenzone on the opposite side of the lake.

If you're keen to get even more airtime and want to try paragliding, head to **Arco** (Volo Libero Alto Garda, via Ravazzone 87, T0464-910579) at the head of the lake or **Malcesine** (Paragliding Club Malcesine, via Gardesana 228, T335-611 2902).

If you prefer to stay on the ground, but fancy venturing out with some views of the lake, then perhaps do a spot of mountain biking, climbing or Nordic walking. Mountain bikes can be rented just about anywhere on the lake and the **Visit Garda** website (visitgarda.com) has maps of the many different (and very extensive) paths around the lake. Rock climbers and Nordic walkers head to **Arco**, where it's best to start at **Guide Alpine Arco** (via S Caterina 40, T0464-507075, guidealpinearco. com), where they can give you all the information you need to embark upon mountain activities safely.

Sleeping

Southern Lake Garda

Sirmione

Hotel Sirmione €€€€
*Piazza Castello 19, T030-916192,
termedisirmione.com.*
This four-star is as about as close
to the crowded Castello as you
want to get, but it's quite a
retreat with lake-facing rooms.
A fine breakfast and renowned
spa, the Aquaria Club.

Flaminia Hotel €€€
*Piazza Flaminia 8, T030-916078,
hotelflaminia.com.*
This elegant four-star is a friendly,
family-run affair with 43 rooms in
a waterfront building. Standard
rooms are conservatively
decorated with side views of
the lake, while the superior
rooms and spacious junior suites
boast full lake vistas. There's a
wonderful sunbathing terrace
and their Ristorante Signori is a
good option.

Hotel Eden €€
*Piazza Carducci 3, T030-916481,
cerinihotels.it.*
It's not often that you arrive over
a moat to a hotel recommended
by Ezra Pound in a letter to
James Joyce, but it's true in this
case. Near the old town centre
action, this four-star is a cosy
oasis with rooms boasting views
of the lake or historic pedestrian
square. Friendly staff, wonderful
breakfasts, unbeatable location.

Desenzano

Park Hotel €€€
*Lungolago Cesare Battisti 19,
T030-914 3351, cerinihotels.it.*
This elegant four-star is the best
in town, beautifully furnished
in a fab location. The stylish
executive rooms were renovated
in 2008. Great facilities include
Wi-Fi and a good restaurant.
In 2009 there'll be a rooftop
swimming pool. Breakfast is not
included at standard prices, but
hotel garage parking is free.

Hotel Tripoli €€
*Piazza Matteotti 18,
T030-914 1305, hotel-tripoli.it.*
This delightful old building is
home to a three-star hotel facing
the waterside promenade. While
the rooms don't possess the
charm the façade suggests, it's
still an agreeable hotel and the
location is excellent. First floor
lake-facing rooms boast small
private balconies. Private parking
200 metres away.

Western Lake Garda

Salò

Hotel Bellerive €€
*Via Pietro da Salò 11,
T0365-520410, hotelbellerive.it.*
Tastefully renovated, this hotel
on the marina dates to 1933 –
the feel is fresh and bright but
still soulful. The swimming pool
is just large enough for the
summer crowd and the
waterfront restaurant demands
alfresco dining. They have villa

Tip...

While the grand hotels
offer the quintessential lakes
experience, and some of the
most luxurious ones are on
Lake Garda, both Garda and Iseo
are also popular family camping
destinations. Holiday parks are
well equipped, although some
distance from towns; see **Top
Campings** (topcampings.it).
All accommodation should
be booked well in advance for
June to September, when you
can expect both lakes to be
crowded with Italian families
and European package tourists.
Most accommodation shuts
down for winter.

apartments for three-day stays
or longer – perfect for
unwinding while watching
the boats bob on the harbour.

Gardone Riviera

Grand Hotel Fasano €€€€
*Corso Zantelli 190,
T0365-290220, ghf.it.*
Garda's most famous hotel
offers what many believe to
be the quintessential lakeside
experience. There are several
price categories, with lake-view
rooms being more expensive
but worth every euro. Lovely
gardens, fine restaurant, and the
Aqva Spa make it difficult to
leave. For romantics there are
rooms in an old hunting lodge.

Villa Fiordaliso €€€€
Via Zanardelli 150,
T0365-20158, villafiordaliso.it.
This pink neoclassical villa has been transformed into an exquisite hotel, the lake's most romantic. An exclusive Relais and Châteaux property with only five suites, its bragging rights go to the sumptuous 'Claretta' suite, named after Mussolini's mistress who lived here. A stay isn't complete without visiting their Michelin-starred waterfront restaurant and a drink at the piano bar atop the medieval San Marco Tower.

Gran Hotel Gardone €€€
Via Zanardelli 84, T0365-20261,
grangardone.it.
One of the classic hotels of the region, a visit is such a time warp you half expect Churchill to be here painting, as he actually did many years ago. The fact that not much appears to have changed since will either have you excited or looking elsewhere. Splendid pool, lovely breakfast area, helpful front desk staff, but waiters are surly. Dinner is best taken elsewhere.

Grand Hotel Gardone.

Locanda Agli Angeli €€
Piazza Garibaldi 2,
T0365-20832, agliangeli.com.
Located in a lovely part of the upper town of Gardone Riviera, this is a friendly family-run hotel. All rooms have exposed beam ceilings and a pared-down elegance. The superb restaurant is a must with an outdoor terrace with tables spilling onto the atmospheric square.

Gargnano
Hotel Villa Feltrinelli €€€€
Via Rimembranza 38/40,
T0365-798000,
villafeltrinelli.com.
This beautiful villa and gardens, built by the prominent Feltrinelli family in 1892, served as their summer escape. And this was some summer shack! In 1977 noted hotelier Bob Burns bought the villa, restoring it to its former splendour – integrating historical fittings with mod cons. But it's the notion of croquet on the lawn, cocktails in the elegant bar, and pretending this is all your very own that has the greatest appeal. It's ideal for that special holiday.

Hotel du Lac €€
Via Colletta 21, T0365-71107,
hotel-dulac.it.
Located on the water, this intimate family-run hotel has only 11 rooms. Recently renovated, six have balconies overlooking the lake while the others face the fascinating village streets. Each is decorated

with local 19th or early 20th century furniture. The lovely shaded terrace, where you take breakfast, and the hotel restaurant boast water views.

Riva del Garda
Hotel Bellariva €
Via Franz Kafka 13, T0464-553620, hotelbellariva.com.
This three-star is a good-value option for those taking advantage of the nearby sailing and windsurfing opportunities. The 30 rooms are good value and their restaurant does decent pizzas.

Lake Iseo
Hotel Milano €
Lungolago G. Marconi 4,
T0309-80449, hotelmilano.info.
A good option in Iseo, this hotel-restaurant has decent rooms, some with balcony and lake views. The restaurant's summer terrace is pleasant and the food honest.

Northern & eastern Lake Garda

Apart from the charming villages of Torri del Benaco and Garda, the towns of the eastern shore from Riva del Garda to Sirmione are fairly characterless, inundated with package tourists, and best avoided.

Eating

Torri del Benaco

Hotel Ristorante Gardesana €€

Piazza Calderini 20, T0457-225411, hotel-gardesana.com.
An elegant three-star across the road from the small harbour, the 34 rooms are furnished in a 19th-century Venetian style, with modern air conditioning and Wi-Fi. Book one with balcony. Breakfast is excellent, as is their well-regarded restaurant.

Garni Onda €

Via per Albisano 28, T0457-225895, garnionda.com.
This little family-run budget B&B-style place is a 100-m walk from the centre and a short stroll to the water. The spacious rooms are sparse but spotless and breakfast is good, as is the service.

Garda

Albergo Ancora €

Via Manzoni 7, T0457-255202, allancora.com.
While there are plenty of package resorts and holiday parks around here with handy access to the theme parks, this family-run two-star has far more character. Many of the rooms have lake views, some with balcony or terrace. There's private parking and a bar-restaurant overlooking the lake.

Southern Lake Garda

Sirmione

La Rucola €€€€

Via Strentelle 3, T030-916326, ristorantelarucola.it.
A refined Michelin-starred restaurant situated in streets crammed with gelaterias is quite a surprise. So is the polished seasonal Mediterranean-focused menu. Expect attentive service, a spot-on wine list, and delightful desserts.

Il Girasole €€€

Via Vittorio Emanuele 72, T030-919182, ilgirasole.info.
Easy to spot by its plant-covered terrace, the 'sunflower' is an elegant restaurant in one of the liveliest areas of town. The speciality is seafood, which appears throughout the menu, or for a series of local seafood tasters try the *Menù Degustazione del Lago*.

Risorgimento €€

Piazza Carducci 5/6, T030-916325, ristorante-risorgimento.com.
A local favourite, this restaurant has a homely interior and tables on the square in good weather. The food is mostly northern Italian and seafood is a speciality, so try their spaghetti with lobster (*spaghetti all'astice*) or their baked sea bass in salt crust.

Desenzano

Esplanade €€€€

Via Lario 10, T030-914 3361.
This Michelin-starred restaurant combines jaw-dropping lake views with equally breathtaking cuisine. The emphasis is fresh seasonal produce and the cooking is sublime, with creative touches that don't overwhelm the fine ingredients. Excellent wine list and service.

Cavallino €€€€

Via Murachette 29, T030-912 0217, ristorantecavallino.it.
An elegant and distinctive restaurant specializing in lake fish and other highly fancied seafood such as scallops and lobster. Impressive tasting menus and fine desserts and wines.

Michelin-starred La Rucola.

Salò

Gallo Rosso €€€
Vicolo Tomacelli 4,
T036-552 0757.
Your best bet, this local favourite has earned its reputation with excellent fish and other delicious seafood dishes turned out by accomplished chefs.

Osteria dell'Orologio €€
Via Butturini 25, T036-529 0158.
A great choice for a casual meal, you can't go wrong with the fresh seafood and seasonal game dishes, or simply a pasta with a glass of wine. Excellent value.

Gardone Riviera

Villa Fiordaliso €€€€
Via Zanardelli 150, T036-520158,
villafiordaliso.it.
If the hotel itself doesn't tempt you (see page 208), gastronomes shouldn't miss this delightful restaurant with meals served on the terrace in summer with magical views of the lake – *very* romantic. There's magic in the kitchen as well, as this Michelin-starred restaurant turns out highly creative seafood dishes. Their desserts are a little over the top, though, so don't be disappointed if you can't quite finish them off!

Locanda Agli Angeli €€€
Piazza Garibaldi 2, T0365-20832,
agliangeli.com.
What appears to be a lovely eatery, with tables spilling out onto the piazza in summer, has gastronomic surprises aplenty – seasonal specials are excellent, with plenty of invention and skill. Service is warm and attentive and there's a surprisingly relaxed atmosphere, considering the quality of the cuisine.

Gargnano

Hotel Villa Feltrinelli €€€€
Via Rimembranza 38/40,
T0365-798000,
villafeltrinelli.com.
The restaurant at this eye-poppingly pretty villa has a superb pedigree, with young chef Stefano Baiocco having worked with some of the greatest chefs of the era, such as Alain Ducasse, Pierre Gagnaire and Ferran Adrià. Everyone with a passing interest in great gastronomy should book a table to see what the fuss is about. Expect refined cuisine with fine flavours, and painstaking presentation with garnishes from the chef's garden.

La Tortuga €€€
Via XXIV Maggio 5, T0365-71251.
This unassuming and cosy restaurant would be fine if it offered good cuisine, but it does so much more, to the point that the restaurant has become a must-do for foodies visiting the area. This is one restaurant on the lake where meat gets as much attention as fish.

Tip...

The highlights of dining on Lake Garda are clearly the fine dining restaurants and family-run trattorias of Sirmione and Gardone Riviera. Like the other lakes, regional dishes and fresh seafood are a highlight. Always check in advance to make sure your restaurant of choice is open, as opening times can vary, although most open for lunch (1200–1500) and dinner (1900–2300) at least six days and nights a week. Most restaurants on these lakes close from December-February with some staying shut through to March. Many close one night a week, generally Monday or Tuesday.

Riva del Garda

Al Volt €€€
Via Fiume 73, T0464-552570,
ristorantealvolt.com.
A tastefully decorated old restaurant in the historic centre, Al Volt specialises in creative cuisine based on the cooking from Trentino. Try the homemade pasta or the local fish dishes. Sweet-toothed patrons should make sure to peruse the dessert menu filled with classics.

Bella Napoli €€
Via de Fabbri 34, T0464-552139.
Wood-fired pizzas are the order of the day here. They appear to come out of the oven every 30 seconds and are just as quickly devoured by hungry locals and visitors who have worked up an appetite sailing and surfing on the lake.

Entertainment

Shopping

Lake Iseo
Il Paiolo €€€
Piazza Mazzini 9, 0309-821074.
A local favourite in the historic centre, it's gained a reputation for local dishes as well as *culatello* (the finest cut of parma ham) and other cold cuts.

Northern & eastern Lake Garda

Apart from Torri del Benaco, most of the towns of the eastern shore of Lake Garda, from Riva del Garda down to Sirmione, are characterless and inundated with package tourists, and are best avoided.

Torri del Benaco
Hotel Ristorante Gardesana €€€
Piazza Calderini 20, T0457-225411, hotel-gardesana.com.
This place really has things covered with a refined ristorante in the hotel, as well as a smart pizzeria and café. The restaurant has wonderful views from the balcony and refined local cuisine on the menu as well as a smattering of international dishes.

As Lake Garda and Lake Iseo attract a combination of couples in the mood for romance, mature aged travellers, and camping families, there's little in the way of nightlife. Entertainment tends to be focused on the refined, such as a summer classical music concert, or the laid-back, quiet aperitivo at a lakeside bar or a gelato and stroll after dinner. No matter where you are on the lake come early evening in the warmer months it's time to enjoy an aperitivo or two, whether it's at a casual kiosk on a waterfront promenade or a swish waterside terrace at a grand hotel. After dinner, everyone heads to the nearest gelateria for an icecream and stroll by the water.

Bars
Lake Garda and Lake Iseo's towns all boast café-bars overlooking the lake or on main squares. Café-bars tend to open most days from early in the morning until late at night, with their patrons drinking coffee by day and aperitivi in the evenings. Bars that mainly operate as wine bars tend to open just before lunch and close after midnight.

Music, Dance, Theatre, Opera
Teatro del Vittoriale
Via Vittoriale 12, Gardone Riviera, T036-529 6506, teatrodelvittoriale.it.
An annual summer festival is hosted by this theatre in July and August with everything from opera to jazz and dance.

The shopping around Lake Garda isn't anything special. The best towns for shopping are Sirmione and Desenzano, where there are fashion boutiques, shops selling linens and silks, handpainted ceramics, pottery, glassware, souvenirs, and gourmet food and wine. Most shops open from Monday-Saturday 0930 or 1000, close for lunch at 1200 or 1300, then reopen from 1600-1900, although in Sirmione, the most touristy of Garda's towns, many shops stay open throughout the day during summer to take advantage of the huge crowds of tourists.

Markets on Lake Garda

There are open-air street markets on in the mornings at towns and villages around the lake selling fresh produce, plants, clothes and accessories, and household items. They are usually held on the main square and surrounding pedestrian streets and are easy enough to find.

Monday Sirmione, Peschiera del Garda, Torri del Benaco

Tuesday Desenzano

Wednesday Riva del Garda, Gargnano, San Felice del Benaco (near Salò)

Thursday Toscolano & Maderno

Friday Garda, Lugana di Sirmione (south of Sirmione)

Saturday Salò, Malcesine

Sunday Rivoltella (east of Desenzano)

Activities & tours

Sport & outdoor
For watersports such as sailing, windsurfing and kite-surfing, and outdoor activities such as mountain biking, rock-climbing and walking, see page 206: Outdoor Activities.

Navigazione Lago di Garda
Piazza Matteotti, Desenzano, T030-914 9511, navigazionelaghi.it. Mar-Sep only.
The lakes' government-operated water transport service for Lake Garda offers fairly frequent services to lake towns, and several daily full-day tourist cruises (from €17-22) departing from Desenzano for Sirmione & Gardone; Salò & Sirmione; Riva del Garda; and Peschiera & Riva del Garda. They also offer a full day Isola del Garda excursion (€35) several days a week.

Navigazione Lago d'Iseo
Via Nazionale 16, Costa Vopino, T035-971483, navigazionelagoiseo.it. Jun-Sep mainly, services outside this period limited to local needs only.
The government-operated water transport service for Lake Iseo offers fairly regular boats between Iseo and a handful of lakeside towns. They also offer several tourist cruises with guides, including the full day Sebino's Cruise (Jul-Aug, one cruise, Wed & Fri only, €15) which does a full circuit of the lake,

Three Islands Tour (Jun-Aug, Sun only, €5.50), a night cruise (Jun-Aug, Fri & Sat only, €35) and special themed excursions, including Franciacorta wine-tastings, and tasting dinners with local products.

Theme parks
Many Italian families base themselves at camping areas around Lake Garda so they have easy access to the various theme parks near the lake, including the Disneyland-like **Gardaland** (gardaland.it), **Movieland** (movieland.it), **Medieval Times** (medievaltimes.it), **Sea Life Aquarium** (seaeurope.com), **AquaParadise** (aquaparadise.it), **Il Parco Acquatico Cavour** (parcoacquaticocavour.it), **Jungle Adventure** (jungleadventure.it), and the animal safari park called **Parco Natura Viva** (parconaturaviva.it). You can drive to these, which gives you greater flexibility (after all, these are not Disneyland), or do a tour (see below).

Themed tours
Sirmione ProLoco tourist office
at entrance to centro storico, T030-919322, comune.sirmione.bs.it.
In conjunction with the Hotels and Restaurants Association, Sirmione ProLoco offers an array of interesting guided tours in Sirmione and around Lake Garda, from history and archaeological-

Sailing and fishing are popular at Riva del Garda.

themed tours to wine-tasting tours such as **A Glass of History** which includes visits to the best wineries in the area.

Well-being
Lake Garda boasts a number of thermal spas, but the best to visit is **Aquaria** (piazza Don A Piatti 1, T030-916044, termedisirmione. com) which boasts swimming pools, whirlpools, and myriad spa treatments, from massage to aromatherapy.

Contents

216 Introduction
218 Bergamo
219 *Map: Bergamo*
224 Brescia
225 *Map: Brescia*
230 Cremona
236 Mantua
240 Verona
242 *Map: Verona*
246 Great days out: An amble around romantic Verona
248 Listings:
258 Sleeping
252 Eating
257 Entertainment
260 Shopping
264 Activities & tours

Art displayed on the streets of Bergamo.

Towns of the Po Valley

Introduction

If you're visiting the lakes of northern Italy, it wouldn't do to leave out some of the wonderful towns close to the lakes. Bergamo, Brescia, Cremona, Mantua and Verona all make great bases from which to visit the lakes or, conversely, excellent day trips or overnight stays while lake-hopping. Compact and pretty as postcards, these are all fine towns, each with a charming *centro storico* and plenty of good shopping and eating. Verona is the most famous of the lot, with its colossal Roman amphitheatre playing host to a lively summer opera and concert season, and the legend of Romeo and Juliet helps make this a romantic stop. Bergamo has one of the most atmospheric medieval town centres in the north of Italy, with splendidly preserved architecture and fine food and wine on offer in its restaurants. Brescia too has oodles of medieval and Renaissance charm and historic architecture aplenty. Cremona is a cultured centre of music and home to violin-making since the 17th century when Antonio Stradivari took instrument-making to another level. The town is not about to lose that legacy any time soon, with plenty of fine instruments in museums and ateliers around this attractive town. Mantua has handsome palaces, pretty piazzas, art galore, and some splendid churches, as well as a culinary circuit of gastronomic restaurants in the surrounding area.

…one day

Visit **Bergamo** and explore the hilly cobblestone pedestrian streets of the medieval *centro storico*. While there are plenty of historic *palazzi*, a splendid **Duomo** and striking tower, and superb museums, one of the real delights of Bergamo is the regional cuisine, so make sure you eat out for both lunch and dinner.

…a weekend or more

Spend the second night at **Verona**, a romantic city with cobblestone streets to stroll, pretty piazzas to loaf about, a Roman **Arena**, the colossal **Castelvecchio**, and several vantage points from which to enjoy stunning views.

With a longer visit you could do a loop of all the towns, which are some of Italy's most refined and cultured. Arrange to see the opera and classical concerts for which some of the cities are famous, or visit lakes **Como** and **Iseo** from Bergamo, and call into **Garda** on your way to Verona.

Bergamo's playful *polenta e osei* – a sweet pun on a regional savoury dish (see box on page 220).

Bergamo

Beguiling Bergamo makes for a brilliant diversion from the lakes or an absorbing break from Milan. The bewitching town boasts a character that's unique, and in evidence from the moment you set foot on its fascinating cobblestone streets. The rich hearty cuisine you'll taste in its cosy *trattorie* and the incomprehensible dialect you'll detect as you explore its hilly lanes are the result of centuries of resistance to outsiders that has given Bergamo its robust cultural identity.

Beautifully located at the foothills of the snow-covered Alps where it hugs the hillside, Bergamo is actually comprised of two very compelling towns. The spellbinding medieval upper town, or *città alta*, is a labyrinthine little place of narrow, hilly alleyways and lovely piazzas encased in 16th-century walls, while down below is the elegant, neatly laid-out lower town, or *città bassa*, with broad boulevards, graceful buildings, elegant arcades and busy alfresco cafés. It's a prosperous town, as suggested by its grand *palazzi* and majestic public buildings. While most travellers stay in the *città alta* and spend all their time there, art lovers should allocate a few hours to the lower town's impressive galleries, while the shopping is also some of the best in the region.

Start your exploration in the *città alta*, which, if you haven't checked in to one of its atmospheric little hotels, is accessible from the *città bassa* by the 120-year old *funicolare* (funicular), or a less interesting bus ride and hike: take bus 2 from the lower town's station to via Pignolo and walk to Porta Sant'Agostino from where via Porta Dipinta will lead you to piazza Mercato delle Scarpe (Shoe Market Square). While there are several car parks in the *città alta* for those driving, you need to make arrangements with your hotel first to get a pass, and parking can be a challenge on weekends when Bergamo is at its busiest. The tiny alleys of the walled

Bergamo listings

① Sleeping
1 Agnello d'Oro *via Gombito 2*
2 Excelsior San Marco *piazza della Repubblica 6*
3 Mercure Bergamo Palazzo Dolci *viale Papa Giovanni XXIII 100*
4 Piazza Vecchia *via Colleoni 3*
5 Ristorante Il Gourmet *via S Vigilio 1*
6 S Giorgio *via S Giorgio 10*
7 San Lorenzo *piazza Lorenzo Mascheroni 9/A*

① Eating
1 Al Donizetti *via Gombito 17a*
2 Colleoni & Dell'Angelo *piazza Vecchia 7*
3 Da Ornella *via Gombito 15*
4 La Colombina *via Borgo Canale 12*
5 L'Osteria di Via Solata *via Solata 8*
6 Vineria Cozzi *via B Colleoni 22*

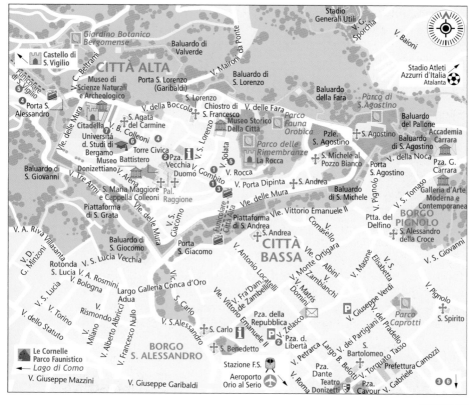

upper town are partly pedestrianized and therefore best navigated on foot anyway. Simply wandering the skinny streets, lined with tall medieval and Renaissance buildings, and browsing in the delightful stores is an absolute delight, but the upper town is also home to some splendid churches and engaging museums crammed with art and sculpture and other fascinating displays, as well as a handful of superb restaurants and *enotecas*.

Via Gombito to piazza Vecchia

Make a beeline for piazza Vecchia, from where you can best get your bearings. Once off the funicular, in the historic cobbler's guildhall, cross **piazza Mercato delle Scarpe**, passing some tempting café tables set up underneath a medieval arcade, to via Gombito. Lined with tall five-storey buildings, their façades decorated with beautiful faded frescoes, Venetian arched windows and flamboyant balconies, and their ground floors occupied by boutiques, bakeries, delicatessens, trattorias and bars, **via Gombito** is the town's pulsating main artery. As tiny as it may be, it bustles during summer, especially on weekends and particularly on Sunday evenings. The rest of the time it's tranquil, a far cry from the traffic-clogged streets of the lower town, and it's a real delight to stroll. In winter, when it can be blanketed in snow, it's positively gorgeous.

Via Gombito leads you to the handsome 15th-century **piazza Vecchia**, after which its name changes to **via Bartolomeo Colleoni** – these streets actually follow the ancient Roman city plans, the *decumanus maximus*, and they still ooze history. Piazza Vecchia is lined with excellent restaurants, cafés and a gelateria. Bergamo's administrative heart for centuries, it remains one of the most splendid squares in the whole of northern Italy, and is considered one of the most perfect Renaissance squares in Italy. Overlooking the piazza on via Gombito is the grand white marble civic library, **Civica Biblioteca Angelo May**. Its stairs are a popular meeting place with locals, and artists often display their paintings under the arches.

At piazza Vecchia's centre is the ornate **Fontana Contarini**, donated by the Venetian *podestà* (governor) in 1780, and decorated with lions, sphinxes and serpents – and tourists snapping photos of each other. On the opposite side of the library, the crenellated 12th-century Gothic grey stone **Palazzo della Ragione**, a civic building and one-time courthouse, presides over the piazza. It boasts a covered stairway and lovely loggia, and 13th-century frescoes inside, only accessible during exhibitions. In the corner of the square the 12th-century **Campanone** or **Torre Civica** (T035-247116, Mon-Fri 0930-1900 & Sat, Sun & holidays 0930-2130, €2), the civic bell tower and clock tower in one, enjoys magnificent vistas of the *centro storico* and surrounding hills. Adjoining it is the attractive palazzo that was once the residence of the Venetian Governor.

A bird in the hand...

Bergamo is a fine eating town with highlights being tasty plates of regional cured meats, salami and cheeses and a rustic local cuisine that features plenty of polenta (cornmeal). However, you must make sure to leave room for some dessert, especially the famous *polenta e osei*. But before you run off screaming that you can't possibly eat any more polenta – *ever* – this Bergamo speciality is very cheekily named. Looking like a golden-yellow polenta cupcake with a little bird (*osei*) on top, the pastry is a playful nod to a favourite local dish of polenta topped with bird meat and is actually one of the sweetest little treats you'll ever try. Made from layers of sponge cake and jam, the dome-shaped cake is rolled in yellow fondant and coated with sugar – just in case it's not sweet enough already! A marzipan 'bird' is added on top and there you have it – a delightfully sweet pun on one of Bergamo's savoury dishes. You won't have to search far to track them down: just look for the crowds around the windows of the pastry shops and bakeries lining via Gombito in the charming upper town (see our recommendations on page 261), and just try not having more than one!

Piazza Duomo

An arched passageway beside Palazzo della Ragione leads to piazza Duomo, once the site of the Roman forum, where you'll find Upper Bergamo's main attractions. Standing under the arch, directly ahead of you is the monumental red-brick **Basilica Santa Maria Maggiore** (T035-223327, Mon-Sat 0900-1230 & 1430-1800 & Sat, Sun & holidays 0900-1300 & 1500-1800); adjoining it is the extravagant marble **Cappella Colleoni** (chapel; T035-223327, Tue-Sun 0900-1200 & 1400-1630, €3); next to it, on your right, is the diminutive apricot marble **Battistero** (baptistery; open for baptisms only); while opposite it, on your left, is the white marble **Duomo** (T035-210223, Mon-Sat 0730-1200).

The stunning brick Basilica Santa Maria Maggiore, dating to 1137, is a splendid example of Lombard Romanesque church architecture. Its pretty marble portal is guarded either side by Venetian lions and above the arch (itself enhanced by intricate decoration) is an equestrian statue of St Alexander. Inside the sumptuous, highly ornamented, late 16th-century interior is an especially lavish example of baroque architecture with all the flamboyancy and theatrical flourishes you expect from the genre, from gilded stucco to carved cherubs.

If that doesn't wow you enough, the adjoining chapel, the Cappella Colleoni, will. The work of Pavian sculptor Giovanni Amadeo, who designed the Certosa di Pavia (see page 118), its extravagantly embellished façade boasts intricate carvings, twisted columns, miniature statues, rows of arcades and balustrades, and a colossal dome, while its splendid interior features masterpieces by Tiepolo and Moroni, including a frescoed ceiling by Tiepolo. Beside the chapel, the pretty baptistery once resided within the basilica but was removed in the 17th century.

The architecture of the elegant white marble Duomo, by contrast, is restrained, and while it might have held your attention had it resided on another square or in another town, here it has difficulty competing with its neighbours. On the site of the 12th-century San Vincenzo, the current structure largely dates to 1886. It was closed for renovation at the time of research.

Top: Ornate ceiling of Basilica Santa Maria Maggiore.
Above: The magnificent marble Cappella Colleoni.

Via Colleoni to piazza della Cittadella

If you make your way back to via Gombito and continue strolling in the direction you were going along via Colleoni, you'll come to the tree-lined piazza Mascheroni and then, beyond it, piazza Cittadella – a square that would be rather grand if it wasn't the car park that it has become.

It's home to the police station and two museums, the fascinating **Museo Archeologico** (piazza della Cittadella 9, T035-242839, Tue-Fri 0900-1230 & 1430-1800 & Sat & Sun 0900-1900, free) and, one for the kids, the **Museo Scienze Naturali** (piazza della Cittadella 10, T035-233154, Tue-Fri 0900-1230 & 1430-1730 & Sat & Sun 0900-1900, free). If you take the opposite exit on piazza Cittadella you will come to busy largo Colle Aperto, which leads to **Porta Sant'Alessandro** and the **San Vigilio Funicular**, which will take you up to the **Castello** (T035-236284, daily 0900-2000, free) where there are a couple of cafés and spectacular views.

Around the *città alta*

From piazza Mascheroni, you can return to piazza Mercato where you started your stroll, through via San Salvatore or its parallel street via Arena. Both are atmospheric lanes lined with elegant *palazzi*, and both will bring you out at the rear of Basilica Santa Maria Maggiore on piazza Rosate, which joins up with piazza Giuliani and piazza Duomo. On via Arena you'll find the **Museo Donizetti** (via Arena 9, T035-428 4769, Tue-Fri 0930-1300 & Sat & Sun 0930-1300 & 1400-1730, free), dedicated to Bergamo-born opera composer Gaetano Donizetti, who, along with Bellini and Rossini, was famous for his rich *bel canto* (literally: fine song) style, typified by his opera *Lucia di Lammermoor*. Continue along via Donizetti to piazza Mercato, which you can cross and turn into via Rocca to visit **La Rocca** (via Rocca, T035-221040, Tue-Sun 0930-1300 & 1400-1730, summer 0900-1900, free). Built on the site of the Roman capitol, the fortress was reinforced in the 14th century, and while the museum inside isn't all that engaging, the views from here are impressive.

Few visitors to Bergamo take the time to discover the elegant *città bassa* or lower town, yet art and architecture buffs will certainly find a few hours here worthwhile. The wide tree-lined avenues are buffered by graceful neoclassical *palazzi* and striking Fascist-era buildings. Enter the **Porta Nuova's** mock Doric-style temple for the **Sentierone**, a leafy piazza with pretty arcades, loggias and porticoes (most secreting chic shops and cafés) that's a lovely place for a stroll, while the **Borgo Pignolo** is another medieval section of town worth a look. Other highlights include the grand 18th-century **Teatro Donizetti** (see page 257), the splendid **Chiesa San Bartolomeo** (largo Belotti 1, T035-383 2411, Mon-Sat 0900-1230 & 1400-1800 & Sat, Sun & holidays 0900-1300 & 1500-1800, free), and the city's superlative museums.

Bergamo Alta.

Accademia Carrara

*Piazza Giacomo Carrara 82, T035-399677,
accademiacarrara.bergamo.it.*
Tue-Sun 1000-1300 & 1430-1730, €2.60.

Bequeathed to the city by Count Giacomo
Carrara at the end of the 18th century, the
collection at this impressive fine arts academy
is considered to be one of northern Italy's finest
collections of medieval, Renaissance and baroque
art. Boasting some 1800 artworks dating from the
15th to the 19th century, the collection includes
paintings by Botticelli, Bellini, Mantegna, Raffaello,
Moroni, Tiepolo, and Canaletto, along with
sculptures, bronzes, drawings, prints, and
decorative arts. Closed for extensive restoration
at the time of writing this book, the impressive
museum, housed in an enormous neoclassical
building, is due to open again in 2010. Until it does,
temporary exhibitions from the Academy will be
on display at the Palazzo della Regione and the
Museo Scienze Naturali in the upper town.

Galleria d'Arte Moderna e
Contemporanea/GAMEC

Via San Tomaso 53, T035-270272, gamec.it.
Tue-Sun 1000-1900 & Thu 1000-2200, €5.

Bergamo's cutting-edge gallery of modern
and contemporary art may not be enormous but
it's world-class. There's an excellent permanent
collection, the highlight of which for many is the
Spajani Collection of around 40 works that give
a great insight into 20th-century Italian painting,
especially the first half of the century, from the
masters of Futurism through to the avant-garde
movement and Italian post-war painting.
The contemporary collection, which features some
300 works collected since the turn of this century,
features many groundbreaking international artists,
while the Finazzi Italian photography collection is
also insightful. There are also frequent temporary
shows, and film and music events.

Controversial Caravaggio

Widely considered to be the most important artist
of the late 16th and early 17th century, Michelangelo
Merisi da Caravaggio (1571-1610) was certainly one
of the most controversial Italian artists to ever live
– both for his art and his personal life. Known as
'Caravaggio', the artist was already apprenticed to
an artist at age 11. He moved from Milan to Rome
at around the age of 18 and lived a tumultuous
existence for several years until the influential
Cardinal Francesco del Monte noticed his work.
It was through del Monte that Caravaggio received
his first large commission in 1597 to decorate the
Contarelli Chapel in the Church of San Luigi dei
Francesi in Rome. The three paintings, *St Matthew
and the Angel*, *The Calling of St Matthew* and *The
Martyrdom of St Matthew* were completed between
1598 and 1601. The paintings caused a sensation and
one, *St Matthew and the Angel*, had to be repainted
as the cardinals were shocked by his depiction of
the saint. What Caravaggio did was to paint in a
manner harsher, more realistic and more striking
than the idealised manner popular at the time.
He used a technique called *chiaroscuro* – the use of
light and dark to show contrast – but took it to a new
level later called *tenebrism*, which had a much more
brutal contrast between light and dark that isolated
the figures from the background, rather than just
highlighting them.

Caravaggio's paintings were a breakthrough
and he became a much sought-after artist, receiving
countless commissions for the churches that were
proliferating. However, Caravaggio's personal
demons were more shocking that any he put onto
canvas, and his combative nature saw him kill a man
in Rome. Caravaggio fled, eventually surfacing in
Naples, then Malta and Sicily, all the while painting
while working through his grief at what he had done.
After being attacked and nearly killed in Naples,
he died on his way back to Rome, where he was to
be pardoned. Controversy still surrounds the artist;
in 2007 the city of Milan determined that they had
found a birth certificate for the painter stating that
he was born in Milan. The town of Caravaggio near
Bergamo (where the painter's name comes from)
claims otherwise, and the Bergameschi themselves
often claim him as their son.

Brescia

Brescia is a buzzing little city. Once the Roman city of Brixia, it's now a living and working town with a vibrant *centro storico* boasting several pedestrian-only shopping thoroughfares and lively interconnecting piazzas that are a delight to wander. It may not be breathtakingly beautiful but it has a handful of architectural gems including an elegant loggia, an old and 'new' Duomo, a splendid Broletto, and a Visconti castle. Despite being brilliantly located between Milan and Verona, if you're travelling by train, or between Lakes Como and Garda on a lakes drive, Brescia gets by-passed by most travellers. A centre for industry and commerce – although that's only visible on the drive in from the *autostrada* – Brescia is home to a multicultural population of immigrant workers from Asia, Africa and the Middle East. It's this grittily authentic, ethno-Italian vibe and lack of tourists that make Brescia so appealing, and a visit here so refreshing.

The impressive dome of the Duomo Nuovo.

Brescia's piazzas

Piazza della Vittoria is as fine a piazza as any from which to begin to explore, and starting here makes sense if you have a car, as there's a public car park. The piazza is surrounded by striking, colossal structures of the movement known as *Novecento* (meaning 1900s, but closely associated with the Fascist era). Designed by Marcello Piacentini, the architect responsible for Rome's impressive EUR district, it's a must-do for architecture and design buffs; note the marble-striped post office and the very cool off-centre clock on the white marble tower.

Brescia listings

❶ Sleeping
1 Ambasciatori *via S Crocifissa Di Rosa 92*
2 Jolly Hotel Igea *viale Stazione 15*
3 Vittoria *via X Giornate 20*

❶ Eating
1 Castello Malvezzi *via Colle S Giuseppe 1*
2 Locanda Dei Guasconi *via C Beccaria 11*
3 Osteria Al Bianchi *via Gasparo da Salò 32*
4 Osteria La Grotta *vicolo del Prezzemelo 10*
5 Vasco Da Gama *via Musei 4*

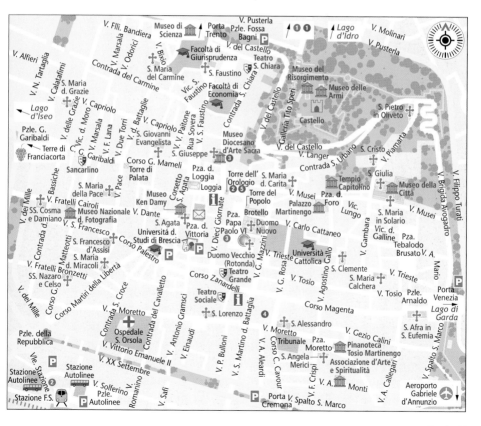

Duomo Nuovo.

From here, head north on via Post to the 15th-century **piazza Loggia**, Brescia's most attractive square. It's home to the enormous elegant Venetian Renaissance **Palazzo della Loggia**, a lovely place to cool off on a sultry summer's day. Spot the Roman stones embedded into the building on the square's southern side, where the tourist office is. The **Torre dell'Orologio** was inspired by Venice's campanile in piazza San Marco and below the clock tower you'll note a memorial to eight people killed and a hundred-odd injured here in the 1974 Fascist bombing of a trade union rally. You should also be able to see some damage to the pillar near where the bomb was left in a rubbish bin.

The tiny lanes immediately north of piazza della Loggia are interesting and worth a look. If you're staying here for a couple of days then explore the area north of here, which is home to Brescia's

immigrant population. While a little rough round the edges (some may even find it intimidating), it's safe: corso Mameli is crammed with shops, delis, cafés and bars and there's a cheap clothes market on piazza Rovetta, while contrada del Carmine is the city's old red light district.

Back on piazza della Loggia, take the bustling passage immediately east, via Dieci Giornate (note the delicatessens under the arcades), to **piazza Papa Paolo VI**, formerly piazza del Duomo. Alternatively, you can take the slightly longer and more interesting way around to the piazza through the medieval tower-gate **Porta Bruciata**, in the northeast corner of the square, to **via del Musei**, an atmospheric street. There are several restaurants full of character here and along **via Beccaria**, which leads down to piazza Papa Paolo VI, and there are good cafés and eateries on and around piazzetta Tito Speri.

Piazza Papa Paolo VI, named after the Brescian-born Pope Paul VI (1897-1978), is a picturesque square that's presided over by the splendid 13th-century **Broletto** (see box, opposite), still a working administrative centre, with a wonderful courtyard that's worth wandering into to admire its carved reliefs and frescoes. Exit on the opposite side of the Broletto and turn left onto via Mazzini to meet back up with via dei Musei to take in **Roman Brixia** (see box, page 228), and on the hill overlooking it, the **Castello**. Or, return to piazza Papa Paolo VI to visit the Duomos.

Duomo Nuovo

Piazza Papa Paolo VI, T030-42714.
Mon-Sat 0730-1200 & 1600-1930,
Sun 0800-1300 & 1600-1930, free.

Rather unusually for Italian towns where a new church is normally built upon an old one, or reconstructed using materials of the former, the enormous Duomo Nuovo (new cathedral) and squat Duomo Vecchio (old cathedral) sit side by side. The old church is dwarfed by the imposing 'new' 17th-century cathedral, which took 200 years to build – which many locals argue was 200 years

The Broletto

One distinctive aspect of northern Italian Gothic public architecture was the *broletto*, a splendid structure featuring spacious halls for meetings and inner courtyards or lower loggias for public gatherings. Often decorated with frescoes and reliefs, you'll notice that this type of Gothic architecture is very different to Gothic architecture in England or France, with rounded arches instead of pointed ones, for example – a practical concern considering the materials used, as well as a carry-over of tradition from the Romanesque era. It was also very different to other traditional Italian Gothic architecture, such as Milan's Duomo, which was more influenced by the Germanic Gothic style. Besides Brescia, there are fine examples of this genre of architecture in Como and Milan, with a particularly wonderful example of a *broletto* in the main square of Orta San Giulio.

Five of the best

A walking tour of Roman Brixia

Remains of the important Roman city of Brixia, designated *Colonia Civica Augusta* in 27 BC, are still in evidence in Brescia today:

❶ *Decumanus maximus* You can begin a walk along the ancient main east-west street, which is now via dei Musei, beginning from the Broletto.

❷ Roman Forum Piazza del Foro was built over the ancient centre of Brixia, thought to have been much larger in its day.

❸ *Tempio Capitolino* The towering marble columns of the *Capitolium*, a partly-reconstructed Roman temple, built in AD 73 by Emperor Vespasian, still

stand and can be visited (via Musei 55, T030-297 7834, Tue-Sun 1000-1300 & 1400-1700, free); the brick parts are from the reconstruction in 1939.

❹ *Teatro Romano* Frescoes from an older temple have been found at this partly-excavated Roman amphitheatre just past *Tempio Capitolino* on the left.

❺ Mosaic floors from Roman villas Well-preserved mosaics are on display in the Museo della Città (Museo di Santa Giulia, via Musei, Tue-Sun 1000-1800, €8) along with other archaeological finds from Brixia.

The Capitolium of Brixia.

Adapted by the Venetians, French and Austrians, the fortress' myriad drawbridges, ramparts, towers and courtyards are a mishmash of military styles.

too long. The exterior has a restrained Renaissance façade with minimal ornamentation other than some elegant statues and carvings, while the interior hosts the tomb of Sant'Apollonio, notable paintings and sculptures, and an enormous 80-m high 19th-century cupola, the third largest in Italy.

Duomo Vecchio

Piazza Papa Paolo VI, T030-42714.
Tue-Sun 0900-1200 & 1600-1900, free.

Many find the old cathedral, also called the Rotonda, far more intriguing than its neighbour. As it's sunk slightly below piazza level, the fine Romanesque structure and features of the circular 11th-century church aren't easily appreciated. Built on top of an early Christian basilica, which in turn was established upon Roman baths (preserved beneath glass inside), it houses fine medieval paintings and the 13th-century red-marble tomb of Berardo Maggi, Bishop of Brescia. The level you enter at was the *matroneum*, a prayer gallery reserved for women. Dress code is strictly adhered to, so dress modestly.

Il Castello

Cidneo Hill, via del Castello 9, T030-293292.
Oct-May Tue-Sun 0930-1700, Jun-Sep Tue-Sun 0930-1700, castle free, museums €3.50 each.

Overlooking the remains of Roman Brixia, and once an early Roman site itself written about by the ancient poet Catullus (and before that a Bronze Age settlement), the 14th-century Visconti castle is accessed from via dei Musei past a lane that winds up to the wooded Cydnean Hill. Adapted by the Venetians, French and Austrians, the fortress'

Strada del Vino Franciacorta

The *Strada del Vino Franciacorta* or Franciacorta Wine Route is a wine drive through the wonderful Franciacorta wine region, between Brescia and Lake d'Iseo; look for the brown tourist signs. For a tiny growing region, Franciacorta wines really pack a punch well above their weight. While wine has been made here for many centuries and was praised by Pliny the Elder (AD 23-79), it wasn't until the 1960s when sparkling wines using the *méthode champenoise* were released that the area became known internationally. Since 1995, only the sparkling wines are Franciacorta DOCG, while the still wines qualify as DOC Terre di Franciacorta. The sparkling wines are made from Chardonnay, Pinot Blanc, Pinot Noir, and Pinot Gris grapes, and there is a sparkling *rosato* (rosé) as well. The still wines are quite French in approach, with a Burgundy-style white based on Chardonnay or Pinot Blanc, or a blend, and a Bordeaux-style red made with Cabernet Sauvignon or Cabernet Franc, with some local Nebbiolo and Barbera grapes in the mix. Given that many of the producers are wealthy part-timers based in Milan or Brescia, the quality of the wines is superlative; they appreciate quality more than chasing the quick money, and avoid the long-term image problems that come from producing cheap wines. Labels to look out for are the traditional ones for the area: Bellavista, Ca del Bosco and Cavalleri. If you prefer to do a tour or be guided through the region, see page 264.

myriad drawbridges, ramparts, towers and courtyards are a mishmash of military styles with its most impressive structure being an imposing keep with a 22-m high cylindrical tower, dating to the 13th century, known as the 'Mirabella'. While the castle's labyrinth of rooms and passages house several small decent museums dedicated to weaponry, astronomy and the Italian Risorgimento, the best thing to do is simply enjoy the views and picnic in the surrounding forested parkland.

Cremona

Compact Cremona is one of the region's most compelling towns. There is no denying that most visitors are drawn here for the little city's fascinating history of violin-making, to appreciate the fine craftsmanship of the masters, the Amati family, and the most famous craftsman of all, Antonio Stradivari, whose violins are the most valuable musical instruments on the planet. But what makes Cremona such a delight to visit is that the violins and violas are not just museum pieces in the city, although there is certainly plenty of polished wood around to admire. Dozens of instrument-makers toil away in workshops dotted around the town to this day, hand-making instruments to a meticulous tradition. The beautiful sound of the instruments being played frequently fills the air, lending Cremona a tone of refinement and sophistication not found in many places.

Cattedrale di Santa Maria Assunta and the Baptistery.

Piazza del Comune

This splendid town might be most famous as the home of violin-making, but it's worth visiting for its stunning architecture alone, most of which is on the main square. The enormous **piazza del Comune** is one of northern Italy's most elegant squares with its breezy arcades, charming loggias and alfresco cafes, and the monumental 12th-century **Cattedrale di Santa Maria Assunta** as its centrepiece. Adjoining the cathedral is the colossal **Torrazzo**, one of the tallest bell towers in Italy (you'll notice it from the *autostrade*), and on the other side of the church, a charming octagonal **Baptistery**, tiny in comparison. There's a crenellated city hall, the **Palazzo Comunale**, and the rather handsome red-brick **Loggia dei Militi**, all of which make a stroll around the square something of an architectural tour in itself.

The piazza del Comune may be where your sightseeing starts but the piazza and its surrounding streets are also the centre of the city's social life and where you'll find yourself hanging out after dark. The streets of Cremona are alive with young music students and aspiring violin-makers who flock here from all around the world to learn the craft and, in summer when school's out, the students cram the squares in the evenings with beers in hand and the city really buzzes. Cremona's families and older folk pull up chairs at the alfresco cafés on the square or simply wander about with gelatos, giving the city a laid-back atmosphere that's addictive. Prepare yourself for staying longer than you planned.

Essentials

- 🚉 **Train station** Via Dante, T892021, trenitalia.it.
- 💲 **ATMs** Via Dante, via Manzoni, corso Mazzini.
- ⊕ **Hospital** Istituti Ospitalieri Di Cremona, viale Concordia 1, T0372-4051.
- ✛ **Pharmacy** Farmacia Leggeri Dr Alberto, corso Matteotti Giacomo 22, T0372-22210.
- ✆ **Main post office** Via Verdi 1, T0372-593551, Mon-Fri 0830-1900, Sat 0830-1230.
- ❶ **Tourist information** Piazza del Comune 5, T0372-23233, aptcremona.it, daily 0900-1230, 1500-1800.

Cattedrale di Santa Maria Assunta

Piazza del Comune, T035-383 2411.
Mon-Sat 1030-1200 & 1530-1800,
Sun 1030-1100 & 1530-1730, free.

While the size of Cremona's enormous red-brick Duomo, the **Cattedrale di Santa Maria Assunta**, dating to 1107, is what initially impresses most – it's truly colossal and it does take time to take it all in – the detail is stunning too. A superb example of

Five of the best

Historical city itineraries

Pick up a detailed city map from Cremona's excellent tourist office (piazza del Comune 5, T0372-23233, aptcremona.it) before setting out to discover these architectural gems from different ages:

❶ **The Roman & Early Middle Ages City** Stroll along via Solferino (the ancient Roman *cardus minor*, or side street), then via Capra Plasio (for the Roman mosaics), before visiting the archaeological section of the Museo Civico Ala Ponzone. Finish with the former Basilica of San Lorenzo and Chiesa di San Michele Vetere.

❷ **The Medieval City** Start on the main piazza with visits to the Cathedral, Torrazzo, Baptistery, Loggia di Militi, Town Hall, Cittanova Palace, then the Chiesa di Sant'Agata and Chiesa di Sant'Agostino.

❸ **The Renaissance City** Enjoy the city's many stunning Renaissance churches, including San Sigismondo, Santa Margherita, San Pietro di Po, and Sant'Abbondio, as well as Raimondi Palace and Affaitati Palace.

❹ **The 18th-Century City** Appreciate some of Cremona's splendid churches, San Vincenzo, Sant'Ilario and Sant'Omobono, before checking out the elegant Stanga-Rossi San Secondo, Silva-Persichelli and Mina-Bolzesi *palazzi*, and the Ponchielli theatre.

❺ **City of Violins** Start with the Stradivari Museum and the Collezione Gli Archi in Sala dei Violini. You could also visit Stradivari's house (corso Garibaldi 57) and grave (in the public gardens), the International School of Violin Making, and the Fodri and Pallavicino *palazzi*.

Around the region

Lombard Romanesque church architecture, its splendid marble façade boasts a beautiful rose window, pretty rows of open galleries, and a portal crowned with statues within niches. Inside there is a brick apse and transepts, but it's the vivid 16th-century frescoes of Mary and Jesus that capture attention. Back outside, an elegant, red-tile-roofed, Renaissance marble loggia, known as 'La Bertazzola', takes you from the cathedral to the lofty **Torrazzo** (Tue-Sun 1000-1300, summer 1530-1730, €5), which at 111 m remains one of the country's tallest medieval bell towers and clock towers, and has magnificent vistas of the town. There is little to see – apart from columns and high balconies – inside the brick interior of the nearby **Baptistery**, dating to 1167, and you are better off heading to the museums.

Collezione Gli Archi in Sala dei Violini

Palazzo Comunale, piazza del Comune 8, T0372-20502.
Tue-Sat 0900-1800, Sun 1000-1800, €6.60, combined ticket including Museo Civica Ala Ponzone €10.

Located at the top of a sweeping staircase in the lavish Palazzo Comunale building in the *Sala dei Violini* (violin room), opposite the cathedral, this small but exquisite collection of musical instruments should send musicians' hearts racing. Perhaps the most prominent pieces of the collection – ones that even those who aren't fans or musicians would want to see – are the instruments crafted by Antonio Stradivari. The surviving instruments of Stradivari are so renowned that they all have 'names' that are often based on famous ex-owners.

The large format *Il Cremonese* is one of only 10 instruments crafted by Stradivari in 1715 during his golden period. The instruments made in this year are amongst his most coveted creations. *Il Cremonese* was once owned by famous violinist and composer of the 19th century, Joseph Joachim, so is sometimes referred to as the *ex-Joachim* Stradivarius.

A second violin, the *Vesuvius*, dates from 1727 when the master was in his most mature period as a violin-maker. Bequeathed to the museum by English violinist and composer Remo Lauricella, it was named *Vesuvius* after its original bright red varnish. The colour of the instrument has turned brown over the years, the apparent result of heat and humidity from a stint in India.

That Stradivarius sound

Cremona has been a centre of violin- and viola-making since the 1500s, with the Amati family being the most well-known name in the art of the luthier (originally, they were lute-makers). However, it was a pupil of the highly respected instrument maker Nicolò Amati who in 1666 pushed the violin to new heights of design, material use and crafting techniques. His name was Antonio Stradivari (1644–1737).

An instrument made by this master during the years that are considered his golden period (1700–1720) can fetch millions of pounds. So just what makes these Stradivari instruments, of which there are still around 600 in circulation, so special? Firstly, Stradivari refined the instrument from the already mature models of the Amati family of luthiers. He changed the proportions of the instrument, which had a larger and shallower body, giving greater projection and better tone. While many luthiers have copied the exact dimensions of the instruments, they never sound quite the same to trained ears. Experts say there are several factors for this. One is the density of the wood used in the Stradivari instruments: a distinguishing feature of a great luthier is choosing the right wood and knowing when that wood is ready, when it has aged enough, to be used. Another factor is the glue that Stradivari used and, most importantly for some researchers, the varnish that Stradivari applied. The thickness of the top piece of wood (the face) is also critical. In the end it could be that Stradivari was a master of all of the above, and after refining the shape and build of his instruments, he was free to concentrate on making his instruments greater than the sum of their parts. The fact that his cellos are also highly sought-after shows that the violins he made were no flukes. He *was* a master craftsman.

Around the region

In contrast to these two instruments of the mature Stradivari, a violin of his from 1669, *Il Clisbee*, shows the clear influence of Nicolò Amati, of whom Stradivari was a pupil. Herbert Axelrod, a famous philanthropist and collector of classical instruments, donated the instrument to the museum in 2003.

Another fascinating instrument is Stradivari's violincello, *Cristiani*, dating to 1700, which was the master's attempt at making a smaller cello. This was one of only two examples of violincellos from this year that are in existence. Note the fine maple wood used by Stradivari and its rich plum-red varnish.

Another instrument of interest is Nicolò Amati's 1658 violin, *L'Hammerle*. This is a classic example of just what fine instruments Stradivari's mentor was capable of, with beautiful workmanship and still some of the original varnish intact.

Museo Civico Ala Ponzone

Palazzo Affaitati, via Ugolani Dati 4, T0372-407269. Tue-Sat 0900-1800, Sun 1000-1800, €7, combined ticket including Collezione Gli Archi in Sala dei Violini €10.

The Museo Civico Ala Ponzone is really three museums in one building: the Sezione Archeologica, the Pinacoteca and the Museo Stradivariano. The compact archaeological section contains exhibits of Egyptian treasures (the amulets are beautiful), ancient Greek finds (the vases and urns are a real highlight), and Roman relics (the glassware is pretty); however, the Pinacoteca (picture gallery), which you can view on your way to the Museo Stradivariano, is of more interest, with works by Caravaggio, Cremonese artists, and notable collections of porcelain, ceramics and ivory.

Above: One of Italy's tallest towers, the Torrazzo gives great views of the city. Opposite page: Museo Stradivariano.

Cremona's craftsmen

Today in Cremona, luthiers still practise the art of hand-making violins and other stringed instruments, and these 'bench-made' instruments – hand-crafted by a master luthier – are made with very little variance from the techniques that Antonio Stradivari used to make his instruments. Many are ordered to the same specifications as the master's finest instrument, perhaps in the hope that some of the magic will appear with the brush of a varnish stroke.

One such master luthier is Stefano Conia, originally from Hungary, who has been crafting violins in Cremona for over 45 years, painstakingly applying coats of varnish – up to thirty coats! – to his beautifully hand-crafted violins. Musicians who covet these instruments order them up to a year in advance and Conia can take that long to deliver. 'Time is not important,' he tells us, 'Musicians understand this. They are interested much more in the quality of the workmanship that comes out.' When we visited his workshop only a handful of violins were in progress, and he makes only around a dozen a year. This is because each instrument is crafted entirely by hand. The only pieces of equipment in his workshop that use electricity are the lights, the radio, and a grinder to sharpen his chisels. Conia works alone too. He feels that's part of his 'signature'. When musicians order an instrument from him, they are getting an instrument that has Conia's DNA.

While his violins go for no less than €10,000, and often a lot more depending on the level of finish and the woods used, Conia puts his money back into what he considers one of his biggest assets, his stockpile of wood – some has been ageing for over 40 years!

While the school for luthiers in Cremona has students that are mostly from overseas, and will go back to their respective countries to craft instruments, the reputation of a handmade instrument from Cremona is harder to duplicate than the dimensions of a Stradivarius. While there is competition from the Chinese who can mass-produce 'playable' instruments for around €20, these can't compare to a Cremonese instrument. And coming to Cremona to order your handcrafted violin, have a couple of fittings and adjustments to ensure the instrument suits your style perfectly, then have the instrument appreciate in value every year you play it – that in itself is priceless.

The **Museo Stradivariano** is what most people come to see. This wonderful collection was started in 1893 after a collection of moulds, patterns and tools of some of the greatest violin-makers, including Antonio Stradivari, were donated to the town of Cremona. The most significant part of the museum is from the collection of Ignazio Alessandro Cozio who had purchased part of the workshop of Stradivari. The museum is in three parts, the first being based around the construction of a contralto viola in the traditional Cremonese manner. The second part is comprised of instruments from violin-makers of the second half of the 19th century and the first half of the 20th century. Finally, the Salabue-Fiorini collection comprises 16 cases containing 710 fascinating artefacts from the workshop of Antonio Stradivari. While the museum is engaging for anyone interested in classical music, woodwork or instrument-making, it might only be a quick visit for others, albeit an insightful one.

Mantua

Diminutive Mantova (Mantua is the anglicized version) must be one of the most magnificently located cities in Italy. The walled city dominates its small peninsula, with water on three sides, the Mincio River having been formed into three man-made lakes – Lago Inferiore, Lago di Mezzo and Lago Superiore – in the 12th century, for defensive purposes. The lakes are both a blessing and a curse; they provide delicious fresh fish to Mantua's tables all year, but send swarms of mosquitoes through the city during the summer. Like Venice and the other cities of the low Po plains, Mantua gets swelteringly hot in summer. However, when there's a breeze blowing across the lake and into the town's arcades and squares on a balmy evening, there are few more pleasant places to be.

Piazza Erbe.

It's hard to imagine how a gorgeous city, dominated by a majestic castle and surrounded by serene lakes, could be a hidden gem, but Mantua certainly is. It's less than 40 km from Lake Garda and 30 km from Verona, yet few visitors include a stay here on their itineraries. Those who drop by on a day trip inevitably wish they'd stayed longer. Mantua's attractions might be obvious – a colossal castle, sumptuous baroque churches, lazy piazzas, and elegant *palazzi* filled with frescoes – yet like Brescia, its real appeal is the distinct lack of tourists (even at the height of the season) and an unassuming elegance. While there's a postcard stand or two outside the old-fashioned *alimentari* (grocery shops) on piazza Sordello, mostly they're inhabited by locals buying bread and a newspaper. The locals ride bikes around the largely pedestrianized streets of the *centro storico* and linger at tables set up on the cobblestones, separated by potted oleander bushes. Like Brescia, Mantua has a sizeable foreign population and it's not unusual to see immigrants lined up at the government offices sorting out their new lives. Yet it's this kind of everyday activity about the city that gives it an authenticity that's hard to find elsewhere in the region. That, combined with the history and beauty, is what makes Mantua so alluring.

Mantua's piazzas

Mantua is a city of handsome squares all interconnecting, making it easy to explore. The spacious cobblestone **piazza Sordello** is Mantua's main square, presided over by the big baroque Duomo at its northern end, the enormous Palazzo Ducale and its lovely arcades and gardens sprawled on the eastern side, and several *palazzi*, including a striking crenellated red-brick façade, on the western side; there are several pleasant alfresco cafés here too. A passageway takes you beneath the brick Broletto and the lofty medieval tower, the Torre della Gabbia, into tiny **piazza Broletto**, which in turn takes you along a laneway lined on both sides by arcades with elegant shops and cafés tucked beneath them to the next square. On **piazza Erbe** you'll find the elegant 13th-century

Tip...

If you're arriving in Mantua from Padua or Ferrara on via Legnago, prepare to grab your camera. Mantua is breathtakingly beautiful from this approach, its muscular castle appearing to float on the water. If you're coming from Lago di Garda, Brescia or Verona, the easiest access to the city is on via Mulini but it's worth going the extra distance and taking the Mantua Nord exit from the A22 simply to enjoy the jaw-dropping views of the city. While there's plenty of parking all over the city, there's nowhere to pull over as you come across the causeway between Lago Inferiore and Lago di Mezzo, so have your camera ready and slow down.

Palazzo della Ragione (with wonderful frescoes inside in the upper chamber) and a beautiful 15th-century **Torre dell'Orologio** (clock tower) with a golden zodiac on its inner 'dial' and faded frescoes on the outer circle. There are several good restaurants under the arcades that neatly spread their tables out on the piazza in warmer weather, while on Thursday mornings there's a busy market here. The piazza is also home to the Rotonda di San Lorenzo (see page 239); opposite is the tourist office. Piazza Erbe joins tiny **piazza Mantegna**, which is dominated by the enormous **Basilica di Sant'Andrea**, which in turn leads down a lovely cobblestone street lined with pavement cafés and smart shops to **piazza Marconi**, and then onto corso Umberto and the busy transport hub (the taxi stand is here) of **piazza Cavallotti**, where you'll find the neoclassical **Teatro Sociale**.

Castello di San Giorgio & Palazzo Ducale

Piazza Sordello, T037-224832, mantovaducale.it. Tue-Sun 0845-1915 (last tickets 1830), €6.50.

Mantua's main attraction is its monumental castle, which is the only thing many visitors to the city see. It's actually a complex of several majestic buildings, including the Castello di San Giorgio, and the Palazzo Ducale, which were seized from the ruling Bonacolsi in 1328 by Luigi Gonzaga, at the start of the dynasty's 300-year period of rule. Once Europe's largest royal residence, at the height of its power over a thousand people lived and worked here in its 500 rooms, and when the Austrians looted the place in 1630 it's said they used 80 carriages to cart off all the riches including 2,000 paintings. While the complex is crammed with room after room of Renaissance treasures, most people make a beeline for the beautifully restored frescoes of the Gonzaga family painted by Andrea Mantegna from 1465-1474 in the Camera degli Sposi ('the bedroom of the wedded couple'). The frescoes are stunning. Considered one of Mantegna's greatest works, they contain all the attributes that made the artist great, from the three-dimensional quality to the exquisite attention to detail. Keep in mind it could easily take you a couple of hours to get there if you stop and spend time in each of the splendid rooms on your way. There are around 40 rooms to see, and if you're a fan of castles you could easily spend the good part of a day here. During winter, when there are few visitors, you're required to do a guided tour (times posted outside), but the rest of the year you have a choice between doing a guided tour, self-guided visit, or an audio guide. Numbers are restricted to 20 people at 10-minute intervals for the Camera degli Sposi, so book ahead if visiting during the peak spring and autumn periods. Also worth viewing are the splendid frescoed summer rooms of Isabella d'Este (see box), which can be seen by anyone but only by appointment on weekends.

Duomo

Piazza Sordello, T0376-320220.
Daily 0700-1200 & 1500-1900, free.

The piazza's other outstanding monument is the striking 14th-century Duomo, also known as the

Renaissance woman: Isabella d'Este

Isabella d'Este (1474-1539) was one of the most famous and fascinating women of the Renaissance. Born in Ferrara, she was the first daughter of Ercole d'Este I and married Francesco Gonzaga, the Marquis of Mantua, at age 16. A precocious young lady, she danced, sang, played musical instruments and was one of the most fashionable women of her time – painted by da Vinci, Titian and Mantegna. Under her patronage, Mantua became a centre of art and culture in the region. However her skill set was found to be even broader when her husband was captured in Venice in 1509 and held hostage. Isabella successfully ran Mantua, including their military forces, until her husband returned in 1512. Somewhat chastened that his wife had upstaged him, Francesco was happy to let her travel as she pleased, as travel was one of her great loves. When Francesco died in 1519, she once again assumed the reins of the city, proving herself an astute politician until her son was old enough to rule. While she was a groundbreaking woman of her time, perhaps a little sibling rivalry contributed to her ambition and capability. Her equally beautiful and talented sister, Beatrice d'Este, became the Duchess of Milan, having married Ludovico Sforza, and also became one of the great patrons of the Italian arts.

Above: Detail from Mantua's Duomo.
Opposite page: Frisky frescoes of the Palazzo Te.

Cattedrale San Pietro. Even travellers who have been in Italy a while and are bored with churches inevitably find themselves drawn inside this intriguing Duomo, eager to see what the interior of such an unusual cathedral might look like. The red-brick Romanesque exterior has minaret-like towers and an austere white late-baroque façade with restrained ornamentation and statues of saints on top, while the interior is richly decorated with fluted columns that hold up elaborately gilded ceilings and a beautiful frescoed cupola.

Rotonda San Lorenzo

Piazza Erbe, T0376-320220.
Daily 1000-1200 & 1430-1630, donations welcome.

The city's oldest church, dating to 1082, was presumed to have been 'lost' until the little round red-brick structure was re-discovered in 1908 when the buildings surrounding it were destroyed. Like the Duomo Vecchio in Brescia, it is sunken beneath piazza level, has bare brick walls, and there is a separate women's prayer gallery. There are also some lovely faded medieval frescoes.

Palazzo Te

Viale Te, T0376-323266.
Mon 1300-1800 & Tue-Sun 0900-1800, €8.

This sumptuous Renaissance-Mannerist palazzo was designed by the celebrated architect-artist Giulio Romano (who spent 10 years from 1525-1535 decorating it). It was built for Federico Gonzaga II as a romantic retreat and pleasure dome to enjoy with his lover Isabella – which explains the exuberant decor and erotic frescoes featuring scenes of bacchanalian excess. It just goes to show what's possible when artistic imaginations are allowed to run wild!

Verona

Verona is a captivating city – and it's the history and romance of the place, real and imagined, that make it so. Both ooze from every polished marble street and cobblestone laneway, from the remnants of the ancient Roman city of *Veronia* that are scattered about the place, to the splendour of the Renaissance palpable on every square presided over by frescoed medieval and Renaissance *palazzi*. Verona is indeed a very handsome city. Gracious buildings overlook beautiful piazzas strewn with finely carved statues and ornate fountains, all watched over by wonderful tombs, while the city's skyline is graced with bridges, spires and towers, providing brilliant vantage points from which to enjoy those breathtaking panoramas. And while there are impressive churches and museums to see, fascinating shops to browse, and excellent restaurants and *enotecas* to enjoy, one of the greatest pleasures of visiting Verona is simply the chance to stroll. Largely pedestrianized, the *centro storico's* atmospheric lanes provide ample opportunities for kicking about the old town. You can also mosey across the many fine bridges spanning the Adige, wander along the waterside promenades, and hike up to the hillside gardens overlooking the city to soak up even more vistas.

Below: The Arena di Verona has hosted gladiators, opera singers and rock bands. Opposite page: Piazza dei signori.

Verona's piazzas

Like all good Italian cities, Verona boasts countless piazzas, with more than its fair share of particularly beautiful ones. **Piazza Brà** is the main semi-circular 'square', dominated by the colossal Roman Arena (see page 243) and the café-lined marble promenade known as the Listone. The chic pedestrian shopping street of via Mazzini connects piazza Brà to **piazza Erbe**, another gorgeous square with vibrantly frescoed buildings around its perimeter, such as elegant Palazzo Maffei. Once a vibrant marketplace proffering fresh fruit, vegetables, flowers and herbs, these days piazza Erbe tends to host stalls selling souvenir t-shirts and tacky trinkets. Crammed with tourists and traders in summer, the piazza is best-appreciated off-season, when empty and tranquil. Accessed via an arched passageway from piazza Erbe, **piazza dei Signori** is Verona's most elegant square. Also known as piazza Dante, at its centre is a 19th-century statue of Dante, who, exiled from Florence, was the guest of Veronese Cangrande I. Dante faces the Romanesque Palazzo della Ragione, while the building behind Dante is the 15th-century Venetian Renaissance Loggia del Consiglio (Portico of the Counsel), and the crenellated edifice is the 13th-century Scaligeri palazzo.

Arche Scaligere

Corner of via delle Arche Scaligeri and via della Costa. No entry to the courtyard.

From quiet piazza dei Signori you'll either be repelled by the crowds of camera-snapping tourists and guides waving umbrellas in the air

and barking at their tour groups, or you'll be mighty curious to see what all the fuss is about. It's the extravagantly decorated and highly ornamented Gothic chapel and marble tombs of the Scaligeri dynasty (see box, page 243) in their palazzo courtyard that command so much attention. Cangrande I's monument, dating to his death in 1329, is a crowd-pleaser: his tomb shows the 'Big Dog' astride his horse with his *cani* (dogs) at his side.

Roman Veronia

Like Rome, it's the remnants of ancient *Veronia* scattered about the city, appearing unexpectedly in places, that makes Verona so atmospheric. The best preserved is the **Roman Arena** (see page 243), while across the River Adige, near Ponte Pietra, the

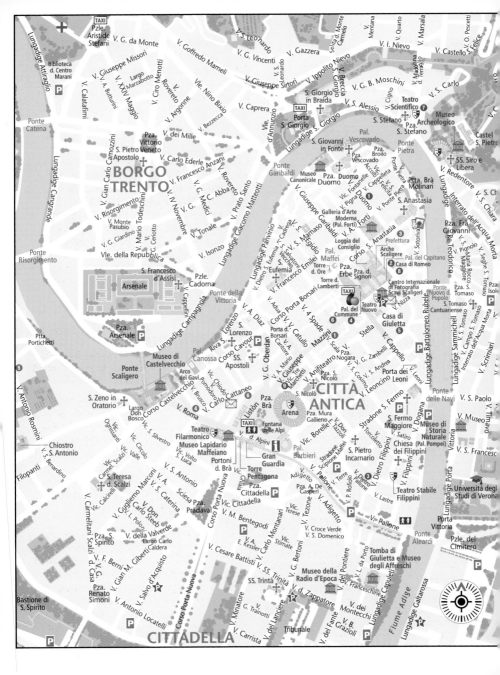

Verona listings

ⓘ Sleeping
1 **Accademia** *via Scala 12*
2 **Appartamenti L'Ospite di Federica De Rossi**
via XX Settembre 3
3 **Due Torri Hotel Baglioni** *piazza S Anastasia 4*
4 **Europa** *via Roma 8*
5 **Residence Antico San Zeno** *via A Rosmini 15*
6 **Torcolo** *vicolo Listone 3*

ⓘ Eating
1 **Antica Osteria Al Duomo** *via Duomo 7a*
2 **Arche** *via Arche Scaligere 6*
3 **Enoteca Al Bersagliere** *via Dietro Pallone 1*
4 **Greppia** *vicolo Samaritana 3*
5 **Il Desco** *via Dietro San Sebastiano 7*
6 **La Bottega del Vino** *vicolo Scudo di Francia 3*
7 **La Fontanina** *via Portichetti Fontanelle 3*
8 **Osteria al Duca** *via Arche Scaligere 2*
9 **Trattoria Tre Marchetti** *vicolo Tre Marchetti 19/b*

Family rule

The della Scala family, also known as Scaligeri or Scaliger, were an important family that ruled Verona in the late 13th and 14th centuries, ushering in a golden age for the city politically and culturally. The first of the family to rule was Mastino I della Scala, who took over from the infamous tyrant Ezzelino da Romano in 1259. In 1277 Mastino was assassinated in Verona and was succeeded by his brother Alberto and then his son Bartolomeo. However, it was his brother Can Francesco, nicknamed Cangrande I ('Big Dog'), who had the biggest impact on Verona. After initially ruling with his brother Alboino, Cangrande became the sole ruler in 1311, launching a series of wars against Padua and Vicenza. While a brave fighter, Cangrande was also a supporter of the arts and a patron of poet Dante Alighieri, who wrote the masterpiece *The Divine Comedy*. After taking Treviso in 1329, Cangrande died under suspicious circumstances and the dynasty dwindled under his successor and nephew, Mastino II.

Apart from the Cansignorio years, 1359 until 1375, when Verona benefited from enhancements, the della Scala rule fizzled out, effectively ending in 1387 when the city was annexed by Milan. Besides the Scaligeri tombs, evidence of the Scaligeri rule is in many of the crenellated fortifications and castles of the region, including those in Verona and the castle at Sirmione on Lake Garda. As you wander around the city, you'll also notice their heraldic emblem, the *scala* or ladder.

Teatro Romano is also in good condition, restored in the 18th century. Behind the Arena, the **Mura di Gallieno** are substantial remains of the Gallieno walls built by Emperor Gallieno. Not far from piazza Brà, and serving as the entrance to corso Porta Borsari, visitors seem to enjoy stumbling upon the white limestone **Porta dei Borsari** (Door of the Bursars), with its striking rows of arches and windows, which seems to take most people by surprise. Dating to the first century AD, it was the entrance to the Roman city; an inscription on the architrave commemorates Emperor Gallieno's restoration of the city walls in AD 265. Amble under the arches along corso Porta Borsari and you're walking the ancient *Decumanus Maximus* (main east-west road). Back beside Castelvecchio is another limestone gate dating to the first century AD, the **Arco dei Gavi**, which once crossed via Postumia. After the French destroyed it in 1805, it was rebuilt in 1932 beside the castle.

Arena di Verona

Piazza Brà, T045-800 3204, arena.it.
Sep-Jun Mon 1400-1930 & Tue-Sun 0830-1900, Jul-Aug (summer concert season) 0900-1530, €4. For concert info see page 259.

This monumental Roman amphitheatre has hosted spectacles of all sorts in its 2,000-odd years; from grisly gladiatorial exhibitions, to spellbinding operas, to concerts by rock bands such as REM. Arguably one of the world's best-preserved Roman amphitheatres, and undisputedly the third largest after Rome's Colosseum and Capua's amphitheatre, the Arena held around 30,000 spectators, the size of Roman *Veronia*'s population at the time. Built in AD 30, the Arena's original limestone façade was almost completely destroyed following two 12th-century earthquakes and sections of it were carted off for other city construction projects. It wasn't until the Renaissance that restoration began. Since 1913 the Arena has hosted its famous summer opera season, although these days there seem to be more music festivals and rock concerts scheduled than opera. If you're an opera buff it's

Around the region

worth paying more for the plush red seats (*poltronissime*) in front of the stage, or the mid-range folding seats (*poltrone*) in the lower rows, where the acoustics are excellent to good. Seated up high you won't hear a thing, because the opera is not amplified. Right at the top you'll actually have a better chance of hearing a conversation at a café on the piazza than you will the opera. If you're going purely for the spectacle – and that's what you'll get with something like *Aïda*, which sees some 400 performers taking to the stage for the *Triumphal March* – then it probably won't matter, just make sure you rent a cushion to soften the discomfort of the marble stones. No matter where you'll be sitting, take a light raincoat and hood (or some coins to buy one), as the chances of it raining are fairly high. If you're going alone, take a book or be prepared to socialize, as the opera won't start until it's dark (or the rain has stopped). And no, it's not a requirement to join in on the 'Mexican wave'. If you're not planning on seeing a performance, then a visit during the day is a must.

Castelvecchio

Corso Castelvecchio 2, T045-806 2611 (guided tours, T045-8040431), comune.verona.it/Castelvecchio. Mon 1330-1900 & Tue-Sun 0900-1900 (last tickets 1800), €7.

Verona's noble rulers have made this stunning crenellated medieval red-brick fortress their home and headquarters since Cangrande II della Scala ordered work to be started on the sturdy defensive structure in 1354. Not the most popular leaders, they wanted to be prepared for popular rebellion, hence the fortified bridge, Ponte Scaligero, in the back yard to enable a swift escape. From the opposite bank there was a secure road to the Adige valley. The Carrara dynasty moved in after the della Scala, followed by the Visconti. It then became a munitions warehouse until the 18th century, when the Venetian military academy took over.

It's now home to the Museo di Castelvecchio, the city's main museum, which boasts a superlative

Top: Castelvecchio's Gothic bridge across the Adige.
Above: View from Castel San Pietro towards Verona's centre.
Opposite page: Lovers' graffiti at the Casa di Giulietta.

collection of paintings, sculptures, textiles, costumes, jewellery, ceramics, metalwork and weapons. Don't miss the equestrian statue of Cangrande I della Scala which came from the Scaliger Tombs in town, and paintings by Jacopo and Gentile Bellini, Mantegna, Pisanello, and Stefano da Verona. Italians come to admire the careful restoration by acclaimed Venetian architect Carlo Scarpa, as much as the castle and its contents. Undertaken by Scarpa from 1959 to 1973, the architect's style is stamped all over the place, from the attention to detail in the furnishings to the fixtures designed especially to display the pieces.

Duomo

Piazza Duomo, T045-592813.
Mar-Oct Mon-Sat 0930-1800 & Sun 1300-1800, Nov-Feb Mon-Sat 1000-1600 & Sun 1330-1600, €2.50.

The most sumptuous of Verona's many splendid churches, construction of the Duomo began in 1139, but while the cathedral was consecrated in 1187, it took more than four centuries before work was properly completed. Mostly Romanesque (note the intricately detailed carvings on the gigantic doors), it's actually a mishmash of styles, with the Gothic and Renaissance features that became fashionable during the building of the Duomo being incorporated into the design. While boasting evidence of exquisite craftsmanship in every respect (note the two-storey portal by celebrated medieval sculptor Nicolo and the beautiful choir screen by Veronese Michele Sanmicheli) and a wealth of art (such as Titian's vivid *Assumption*), it's really the rich marble-work that steals the show, from the polished marble patterned floors to the baptismal font ornately carved from an enormous single block. Don't expect to find this magnificent cathedral in the centre – unlike most Italian cities, Verona's Duomo is on a tiny square near the river; however, in the great Italian tradition of church-building, it was constructed atop an Early Christian church and a Roman temple.

Romeo + Juliet 4 real?

Most visitors to Verona seem intent on doing an itinerary that takes in a combination of places that are thought to provide settings for Shakespeare's *Romeo and Juliet*, and other sites where the 'real' lovers had been. A balcony at the **Casa di Giulietta** *(via Cappello 23, T045-803 4303,* Mon 1330-1930, Tue-Sun 0830-1930, courtyard free, house €4) is one of Verona's most popular attractions.

However, it's quite the magical mystery tour because the existence of a real life Romeo and Juliet is highly doubtful. It's widely felt that Shakespeare's inspiration for the play was *The Tragicall Historye of Romeus and Juliet*, a poem written by an Englishman, Arthur Brooke, in 1562. However, Brooke's inspiration was in turn a French translation of a tale by Italian writer Matteo Bandello. Bandello himself wasn't even the original source for the story either, which goes back further still. The earliest version of the story has been traced back to *Mariotto and Gianozza*, a short story by Masuccio Salernitano published in 1476. While this took inspiration from an earlier fictional story based around a tragic romance, this was the first time it was set in Italy, yet it contains many of the elements that went into Shakespeare's version, including the secret marriage. Luigi da Porto later adapted the story, giving the characters the name *Giulietta e Romeo* and fleshing out more details including the names of the feuding families, Montecchi and Capuleti (Montague and Capulet) and the location of Verona.

An amble around romantic Verona

THERE IS NO WORLD WITHOVT VERONA WALLS,
BVT PVRGATORY, TORTVRE, HELL ITSELF,
HENCE BANISHED IS BANISH'D FROM THE WORLD,
AND WORLD'S EXILE IS DEATH; . . . . "

"NON ESISTE MONDO FVOR DALLE MVRA DI VERONA;
MA SOLO PVRGATORIO, TORTVRA, INFERNO.
CHI È BANDITO DI QVI, È BANDITO DAL MONDO
E L'ESILIO DAL MONDO È MORTE; . . . . "

(SHAKESPEARE, "ROMEO AND JVLIET", ATTO III, SCENA III)

Verona is romantic whichever way you look at it – a city made for unhurried ambles hand-in-hand – and you don't need to have read Shakespeare's *Romeo and Juliet*, nor visited the famous balcony where the fictional characters allegedly declared their love, to discern it. This easy-going stroll takes you along the most atmospheric streets to see the key sights, such as the monumental **Roman Arena** and commanding citadel **Castelvecchio**, and to savour truly sublime views, such as those from hilltop **Castel San Pietro**, a perfect picnic spot. Do-able in two hours for a taste of Verona, you can extend this walk to a full day if adding museum visits and a lunch stop on the way.

Set off from **piazza Brà**, Verona's vast semi-circular square that is home to the ancient **Roman Arena** (see page 243), which dominates the piazza. The curved row of alfresco cafés and wide polished marble footpath is known as the **Listone**. While the apricot, lemon and tangerine-coloured buildings make for an attractive photo op, the over-priced cafés cater mainly to tourists. Do a lap of the piazza's perimeter in a clockwise direction around the Arena to appreciate its immensity. Note the four three-storey-high limestone arches – this is the only part of the Arena's outer wall to survive two 12th-century earthquakes; the rest of the structure is actually the internal tiered seating, restored in the 15th century.

At via Leoncino you'll see the imposing 19th-century neoclassical **Palazzo Barbieri** on your left, with its enormous Corinthian columns, now Verona's House of Representatives. Next on your left is the regal **Palazzo Gran Guardia** with gracious arcades, which serves as the city's civic centre and auditorium. Adjoining it is the restored double-arched **Portoni della Brà** (Brà's 'little door'), boasting a gold-faced clock at its centre. Next on the left is Verona's main opera house, the 18th-century **Teatro Filarmonico** (see page 260)which hosts the winter opera season, while the Arena provides a spectacular setting for summer performances.

Directly ahead is via Roma, which leads to the crenellated, red-brick **Castelvecchio** (see page 244), a striking sight with its stout towers and ramparts. Beside it, the lovely white limestone first-century **Arco dei Gavi** crossed via Postumia until the French destroyed it in 1805 and it was rebuilt here in 1932. There's an impressive view of the castle and city from the other side of the splendid brick **Ponte Scaligero**, which spans the fast-flowing Adige. While you're there take a quick look at the august Austrian-built **Arsenale**, which has a dignified quadrangle garden dotted with trees, before wandering along Lungadige Campagnola to **Ponte Vittorio**. Linger on the bridge for a brilliant view of Castelvecchio and Ponte Scaligero.

From here, walk a block along via Armando Diaz to the wonderful limestone **Porta dei Borsari** (door of the bursars) with its rows of arches and windows. Dating to the first century, it was the entrance to the Roman city; an inscription on the architrave commemorates Emperor Gallieno's restoration of the city walls in AD 265. Amble under the arches and along corso Porta Borsari, the *cardus decumanus* (main east-west road), which becomes corso Sant'Anastasia. Turn left on via San Pietra which turns into via Duomo to visit the pink and white-striped Romanesque **Duomo** (see page 245).

From piazza del Duomo, head for the river and over the tri-arched **Ponte del Pietra**. Cross the road and hike up the stairs snaking up to the gardens of **Castel San Pietro** for mesmerizing vistas of Verona.

Fom this vantage point, it's all spires and towers prettily framed by trees; could there be a more romantic spot for a picnic? The brick wall serves adequately as both table and chairs.

Return via the path but once over the bridge, swing left onto via Ponte di Pietra to visit the Gothic **Chiesa di Sant'Anastasia**, dating to 1290, which has a 14th-century portal, black, white and red marble columns and a fresco-covered chapel. Turn left onto via San Pietro, then right onto via Santa Maria in Chiavi for the exquisite **Arche Scaligere** (see page 241) and **piazza dei Signori** (see page 241). Join Dante at the piazza's centre to admire the stunning square before slipping beneath the arch to beautiful **piazza Erbe** (see page 241). Browse the boutiques of **via Giuseppe Mazzini**, Verona's main pedestrian shopping thoroughfare, on your way back to piazza Brà.

Below: View of piazza Erbe from the heights of Torre dei Lamberti.

Sleeping

If you are driving and staying in the *città alta* (upper town) be aware that parking can be a nightmare on weekends and during the warmer months. Many hotels will provide a permit to park for free: arrange this when you book, and get clear directions as to where to park.

Excelsior San Marco €€€
Piazza della Repubblica 6, T035-366111, hotelsanmarco.com.
This modern property is the best choice in the lower town, with a good location close to the upper town walls. Well appointed rooms get more elegant (or fussy, depending on your taste) as you pay more. Rooftop restaurant.

Mercure Bergamo Palazzo Dolci €€€
Viale Papa Giovanni XXIII 100, T035-227411, mercure.com.
Belying its elegant old exterior, this is a very contemporary-styled hotel, with modern art and sleek furniture. Rooms have all mod cons including satellite TV and Wi-Fi, and it's well positioned for the train station and has ample parking.

Agnello d'Oro €€
Via Gombito 2, T035-249883.
It's a squeeze in the reception of this charming hotel in a tall, narrow building on a tiny square in the upper town. The rooms,

while cosy, are a little less snug once you're ensconced. The enchanting and atmospheric downstairs tavern dates back to the 17th century (see page 252).

Hotel Ristorante Il Gourmet €€
Via S Vigilio 1, T035-437 3004, gourmet-bg.it.
Close to the historic centre, this former mansion has only 10 rooms and one two-bedroom suite. The rooms are a little dated, but the public areas, restaurant and terrace are pleasant. Private parking.

Hotel Piazza Vecchia €€
Via Colleoni 3, T035-428 4211, hotelpiazzavecchia.it.
A prime location in the middle of the charismatic main thoroughfare of the old town is just one of the attractions of this small hotel. Exposed wood

Bed & Breakfast Bergamo
bedandbergamo.it
A good website and association if you're looking for B&Bs in Bergamo and surrounds. Some possess oodles of rustic charm with vine-covered exteriors, exposed beams, and balconies with views of the lower town, while others are very modern in style with chic contemporary furniture. Bookings can be made online.

beams and a slightly arty feel are also compelling. Only the sometimes-standoffish staff and parking headaches dim the romanticism.

San Lorenzo €€
Piazza Lorenzo Mascheroni 9/A, T035-237383, hotelsanlorenzobg.it.
With a prime location at the top of the *città alta*, this four-star hotel is a good option for those who want to enjoy the old town in real comfort. With 25 rooms, it's an intimate property and a renovation has refreshed the mod cons without losing the character of the building.

Hotel S Giorgio €
Via S Giorgio 10, T035-212043 sangiorgioalbergo.it.
A convenient choice if you're travelling by train (one block from the station) or driving and find driving through the upper town daunting, this old-

fashioned place may look like it's been decorated by *nonna* (lots of floral fabric and dried flowers); however, the service is also old-fashioned and welcoming. Fortunately there are modern amenities, with Wi-Fi in the rooms, as well as a computer in the hallway.

Brescia

Hotel Vittoria €€€
Via X Giornate 20, T030-280061, hotelvittoria.com.
The only real choice in the historic centre, but thankfully it's an admirable one, with a handsome exterior and an elegant neoclassical interior. The rooms are in very good condition and the suites are enormous; all are well-equipped, including fast internet.

Hotel Ambasciatori €€
Via S Crocifissa Di Rosa 92, T030-399114, ambasciatori.net.
Located just outside the historic centre (about a 10-minute walk), this hotel is popular with business travellers and the rooms and friendly service make up for the rather mundane exterior. A small gym and Wi-Fi keeps guests happy as does the better than average breakfast offerings.

Jolly Hotel Igea €€
Viale Stazione 15, T030-44221, jollyhotels.it.
This modern four-star hotel, part of the Spanish NH chain, is typical of their style of hotel, being contemporary with good attention to detail and an excellent level of service and amenities. The hotel is around 10 minutes walk from the historic centre and has a good restaurant and bar.

Cremona

Dellearti Design Hotel €€
Via Bonomelli 8, T0372-23131, dellearti.com.
The 'design hotel' craze saw some interesting designs as well as some that didn't work or age so well. This hotel tips towards the latter category, with the industrial theme and dim lighting a little off-putting. The unbeatable location (less than a block from the main square), secure parking, and friendly reception staff more than make up for it. Great discounts off-season.

Agriturismo Cremona

Tourist office, piazza del Comune, T0372-23233, aptcremona.it
Cremona's tourist office has a long list of B&Bs and *agriturismo* properties on their books, ranging from simple and sparse, to rustic and cosy. The helpful staff can arrange accommodation for you. Most are in the countryside outside Bergamo, so you'll require transport.

Hotel Continental €€
Piazza della Libertà 26, T0372-434141, hotelcontinentalcremona.it
This modern hotel is a safe choice, with 62 rooms and a four-star rating. Rooms are comfortable and quiet and it's in an okay location if you don't wish to drive through the historic centre.

Dellearti Design Hotel.

Mantua

Hotel San Lorenzo €€
Piazza Concordia 14, T0376-220500 hotelsanlorenzo.it.
This central hotel is a bit of a charmer, with 19th-century furnishings and a family-run atmosphere. Some of the spacious and well-kept rooms have piazza views and the breakfasts are excellent.

Albergo Bianchi Stazione €€
Piazza Don E Leoni 24, T0376-326465, albergobianchi.com.
A welcoming, friendly and family-run hotel across from the train station and a 10-minute stroll from the historic centre, some of the 53 well-kept rooms overlook the hotel's private garden.

Hotel Broletto €
Via Accademia 1, T037-223678.
A great location is the prime attraction of this small but somewhat dated hotel but it's quite cosy all the same.

Agriturismo Mantua

Largo Porta Pradella 1, T0376-324889, agriturismomantova.it.
Mantua has a consortium that features a wide selection of *agriturismo* accommodation; as most are in the countryside, you'll need a car to get there and get around.

Alfresco dining in Verona.

Armellino B&B €
Via Cavour 67, T346-314 8060, bebarmellino.it.
This modish B&B is right in the heart of the old town, set in an 18th-century palace with a lovely blend of antique and contemporary touches. There are only three rooms, two standard rooms and a larger suite, and all are excellent value – but cash only.

Corte San Girolamo €
Strada San Girolamo 1, T0376-391018, agriturismo-sangirolamo.it.
Located 3 km from the old town, this *agriturismo* estate has 14 simply decorated rooms in rustic style with exposed wooden beam ceilings and tiled floors. There is plenty of wildlife to spot and the place has bicycles that you can use to ride the 40 km of tracks around the region.

Verona

Due Torri Hotel Baglioni €€€€
Piazza S Anastasia 4, T045-595044, baglionihotels.com.
Easily the swishest accommodation in town, this medieval building is home to a supremely luxurious hotel with lavish furnishings, Murano chandeliers, and acres of marble. Unless you're in a suite, the public areas, restaurant and bar (both recommended) are more elegant than the rooms, but it's certainly a charming address within walking distance of the sights.

Hotel Accademia €€€
Via Scala 12, T045-596222, accademiavr.it.
This elegant old hotel has been taking guests since 1880 and provides a superior level of service for a four-star. It's in an unbeatable location in the centre of the shopping district and close to the arena if you're here for a concert. Fantastic discounts off season.

Appartamenti L'Ospite di Federica De Rossi €€
Via XX Settembre 3, T045-803 6994, lospite.com.
Set in a small 19th-century building, this self-catering accommodation is cosy and comfortable. The studios are just larger than your average hotel room, but have a small kitchenette, while the apartments have a separate

bedroom. The location is better suited to a longer stay as it's over the bridge, Ponte Aleardi.

Hotel Europa €€
Via Roma 8, T045-594744, veronahoteleuropa.com.
Hotel Europa is a good value three-star in a city that has few bargains, with an excellent location, all the usual mod cons, and a continental breakfast. Rooms are on the smallish side, but Verona isn't a city where you hang out in your room.

Residence Antico San Zeno €
Via A Rosmini 15, T045-800 3463 residenceanticosanzeno.it.
An elegant and tastefully decorated residence and apartments situated in a relatively quiet location that's a pleasant walk to the sights. The apartments, which can sleep several people, have a fully-equipped kitchen. Parking available.

Hotel Torcolo €
Vicolo Listone 3, T045-800 7512, hoteltorcolo.it.
Just one block from piazza Brà, this small hotel has 19 individually decorated rooms, with lovely details including 19th-century furnishings. The owners and hosts Silvia and Diana are tremendously knowledgeable and helpful, and the double-glazed windows and elevator demonstrate that they care about guest comfort.

Around Verona

Hotel Villa del Quar €€€
Via Quar 12, T045-680 0681, hotelvilladelquar.it.
This Relais & Châteaux property is a charming five-star converted villa around 11 km from Verona in the heart of the Valpolicella wine-growing region. The villa has touches of the Renaissance, although the swimming pool and nearby golf course keep things modern. Chef Bruno Barbieri commands the kitchen of the Arquade restaurant and you may want to sign up for their cooking courses after sampling the cuisine.

Ca del Rocolo €€
Via Gaspari 3, T045-870 0879, cadelrocolo.com.
Located 11 km from Verona, this delightful *agriturismo* B&B has two rooms available in a villa dating back to 1800. A must for foodies, the property is a working farm with olive trees, fresh fruit and vegetables, and hand-crafted extra virgin olive oil, honey, jams and preserved vegetables, all produced on the premises or locally. Children might like the riding school available at a nearby property.

Asino (donkey) features regularly in northern Italian cuisine.

Eating

The restaurants of Bergamo, Brescia, Cremona, Mantua and Verona are open pretty much all year around, the better restaurants closing only for a Christmas season break and in summer for a month. Opening times can vary so a phone call ahead is recommended, although most restaurants and trattorias open for lunch (1200-1500) and dinner (1900-2300) at least six days a week, closing one night a week, often Monday or Tuesday.

Bergamo

L'Osteria di Via Solata €€€€
Via Solata 8, T035-271993, osteriaviasolata.it.
The only Michelin-starred restaurant in the upper town,

it's a charmingly old-fashioned restaurant that makes for a romantic setting. Fish and meat dishes dominate the menu and the creativity is apparent in the use of chocolate- and caramel-infused sauces.

Colleoni & Dell'Angelo €€€
Piazza Vecchia 7, T035-232596, colleonidellangelo.com.
The white, vaulted-ceiling rooms of this elegant restaurant are filled with diners enjoying the refined and modish versions of classic local dishes such as *casoncelli* – ravioli, here with sage, butter and Parmesan. A fascinating wine list and knowledgeable staff.

Al Donizetti €€
Via Gombito 17a, T035-242661, donizetti.it.
Probably the most popular casual eatery in town, it's one of the best. When the weather is fine, the tables on the terrace are so busy there's often a wait, the reason being the wooden platters piled high with local cold cuts and cheeses.

Vineria Cozzi €€
Via B Colleoni 22, T035-238836, vineriacozzi.it.
This wine bar is charming but unassuming; however, the food is outstanding. They also do a wonderful version of the local speciality *casoncelli*. There are tables in the bar and more formal seating out the back.

La Colombina €€
Via Borgo Canale 12,
T035-261402.
Another local eatery (a trattoria this time) offering seasonal local speciality dishes in rustic, yet handsome surroundings. It affords you an opportunity that you shouldn't ignore – they too do a wonderful *casoncelli* – ravioli stuffed with meat and herbs on this occasion.

Da Ornella €
Via Gombito 15, T035-232736.
This fine trattoria is popular with locals and visitors who come for the rustic handmade pastas and roasted meats, but the must-do dish here is certainly the rabbit with polenta, a local speciality.

Ristorante Castello Malvezzi €€€€
Via Colle S Giuseppe 1,
T030-200 4224,
castellomalvezzi.it.
It's not often that you get to dine on the terrace of a 16th-century hunting lodge, and it's more of a castle really. Expect creative, refined local cuisine and considerate service.

Osteria Al Bianchi €€
Via Gasparo da Salò 32,
T030-292328, osteriaalbianchi.it.
This simple, no-nonsense osteria in the heart of the old centre serves up honest, hearty fare.

Try their spinach and ricotta dumplings or, for the more brave, their *brasato d'asino* (braised donkey), a rustic local speciality. Being an osteria the wines are excellent too.

Vasco Da Gama €€
Via Musei 4 (alternative entrance on via Beccaria), T030-375 4039.
A restaurant brimming with character, this has rustic charm but also a more modern, glassed-in area overlooking via Beccaria. The cuisine is unapologetically Brescian with that hearty, no-compromise style and laden with the well-loved local butter.

Locanda Dei Guasconi €€
Via C Beccaria 11, T030-377 1605,
locandadeiguasconi.it.
Down this busy 'eat street' Locanda Dei Guasconi has a cosy rustic Italian interior but a glassed-in 'outside' dining area reminiscent of a classic French bistro. The food, however, is very Brescian. Expect plenty of polenta dishes (try the wild boar stew if it's on the menu) and excellent local wines.

Osteria La Grotta €
Vicolo del Prezzemelo 10,
T030-44068, osterialagrotta.it.
One of the oldest in town, it's also one of the most endearing, with frescoes on the walls, well-worn wooden furniture, and hams hanging from the ceiling.

Clearly their hams are excellent, as are the cheeses, and there are some cherished local dishes that are hard to find in many restaurants such as *trippa in brodo* – tripe in consommé.

Il Violino €€€
Via Sicardo 3 (off piazza Duomo),
T037-246 1010, ilviolino.it.
While it's not a very original name for a restaurant in the home of the violin, we'll forgive it as it's such a handsome one. There's plenty of pasta and risotto dishes – try their house special *risotto con zucca, mostarda ed amaretti* (risotto with pumpkin and local mustard fruits), while main courses are filling meat or fish options. A strong wine list and good service.

La Sosta €€
Via Vescovo Sicardo 9, T037-245 6656, osterialasosta.it.
Not far from the main plaza, this local favourite is everything a good Italian eatery should be. It has a warm and inviting atmosphere, handmade pasta (try the gnocchi), excellent salami and hams, and local seasonal specialities such as *tartufo freschi d'Alba* (fresh truffles from Alba). Great regional wines and fine service.

La Botte €€
*Via Porta Marzia 5/a,
T037-229640.*
This wonderful old tavern has atmosphere by the barrel load, from the exposed wooden ceiling to the old wine casks transformed into chairs and tables. It has delicious food too, with some wonderful dishes such as *malfatti con funghi porcini* (dumplings with porcini mushrooms), lots of seafood, and plates of cured meats and cheeses.

Centrale €
Vicolo Pertusio 4, T037-228701.
Just as it says, this traditional trattoria is centrally located, and has a firm following for its straightforward fare of regional favourites. Among others, try their *tortelli di zucca* (pasta with pumpkin filling) – it'll require a couple of laps around the main square to work off!

Mantua

Aquila Nigra €€€€
Vicolo Bonacolsi 4, T0376-366751/327180, aquilanigra.it.
This former convent near the Palazzo Ducale is still a place of virtue and worship, but it's now about the delightful rendering of Mantua's best dishes. The *saltarelli e frittata di zucchine* (freshwater shrimps with zucchini) is a must, but try their greatest hits with the degustation menu. They also

have a more casual osteria next door, La Porta Accanto, but be sure to book ahead for the restaurant.

Fragoletta Antica €€
Piazza Arche 5a, T0376-323300.
One of the oldest osterias in town, it serves up local classics with a modern sense of style and presentation. Try the tortelli filled with pumpkin.

Grifone Bianco €
Piazza dell'Erbe 6, T0376-365423, grifonebianco.it.
If you're wandering around this lovely square trying to decide where to eat, this is the place to head – great local salami, scrumptious risotto, and handmade *gnocchetti* (small dumplings), and it's all good value too.

Ochina Bianca €
Via Finzi 2, T0376-323700.
This osteria is elegant, while being cosy and inviting. Also inviting is the menu, packed full of local specialities but updated with flair. Try their signature slow-cooked donkey dish, *stracotto d'asino al lambrusco con polenta.*

Around Mantua

The area around Mantua is famous for its cuisine. One of the first complete cookbooks, *L'Arte di Ben Cucinare* was penned here by Bartolomeo Stefani in 1662. While

others had published recipes, Stefani included 'ordinary' dishes, not just those served at fancy banquets. Today the region is just as influential as there are many highly regarded restaurants in the area around Mantua – led by the trio featured below. Remember to book ahead.

Dal Pescatore €€€€
38 km west of Mantua in Canneto sull'Oglio, just off SS10, T0376-723001, dalpescatore.com.
For most diners, Michelin three-star restaurants are daunting and formal affairs, with stuffy waiters and sommeliers trying to steer you towards a bottle of something you'll need a second mortgage to pay off. Inspired by French country restaurants that Antonio Santini and his wife Nadia (now the main chef) saw on their honeymoon, this restaurant, located between Mantua and Cremona, has become the Italian equivalent of what they saw. The food is approachable, with plenty of the best *tortelli* (filled pasta) you will ever try, and their sea bass and duck dishes are legendary.

Al Bersagliere €€€€
18 km northwest of Mantua in Goito, on SS236, T0376-60007.
While Goito is a cute hamlet, the main reason to come here is to try the cuisine at Al Bersagliere – and you won't be sorry. If their amazing *tortelli di zucca* or the equally stunning *agnolini* in

Wines local to Verona are certainly worth sampling.

capon broth is on you'll be happy. Follow them up with one of their game or fish main courses and you'll be in heaven. Well worth the diversion.

Ambasciata €€€€
30 km southeast of Mantua in Quistello, via Martiri di Belfiore 33, T0376-619169, ristoranteambasciata.it.
Foodies and critics love Ambasciata, not just because the food is sublime (it is), but because there is a real sense of passion for food and life here. Romano Tamani might have two Michelin stars, but the elegance of his restaurant is underplayed by the quirkiness of an antique store in some of the decoration. Whatever you order make sure you try the pasta dishes – Tamani is a master pasta-maker.

Verona

Il Desco €€€€
Via Dietro San Sebastiano 7, T045-595358, ildesco.com.
Chef Elia Rizzo has earned himself two Michelin stars for his extremely creative cuisine – and rightly so. Excellent produce with respect for the past, and an eye on the future, is what makes the food here stand out. Seafood and meat have equal billing, while the service, wine list and desserts are all stunning.

La Fontanina €€€
Via Portichetti Fontanelle 3, T045-913305, ristorantelafontanina.com.
Cosy, elegant and very romantic, La Fontanina has been a standout restaurant for years. The attention to detail and the brilliant tasting menus of seafood or meat keep people coming back. The ravioli stuffed with chestnut and pumpkin with guinea-fowl ragù, or their presentation of scallops are both equally flavoursome.

Ristorante Arche €€€
Via Arche Scaligere 6, T045-800 7415, ristorantearche.com.
This elegant restaurant is the best choice in town for seafood because the menu and kitchen stay true to the traditional way of preparing seafood in the Veneto. There are red-meat-based dishes on the menu, but their shellfish-based dishes are the pick of the list.

La Bottega del Vino €€
Vicolo Scudo di Francia 3, T045-800 4535.
While this sounds as if it's a wine shop, it is actually one of the city's best restaurants disguised as a large osteria. *Caval* and *cavallo* (horse meat) feature heavily on the menu, giving visitors the perfect chance to pair it with the excellent wine cellars' big reds from the north of Italy. This is an eatery and wine cellar that's legendary for very good reason.

Trattoria Tre Marchetti €€
Vicolo Tre Marchetti 19/b, T045-803 0463.
Regional favourites are what keep locals coming back to this cosy, friendly restaurant that is rumoured to be one of the oldest trattorias in Italy. The duck is a firm favourite.

Ristorante Greppia €€
Vicolo Samaritana 3, T045-800 4577, ristorantegreppia.com.
The first of many decisions you'll make at this lovely restaurant is whether to dine alfresco or in the elegant interior with vaulted ceilings. The other challenge comes with the excellent, authentic menu of local favourites. Here's a hint: the homemade pasta is brilliant.

Enoteca Al Bersagliere €€
Via Dietro Pallone 1, T045-800 4824, trattoriaalbersagliere.it.
This friendly enoteca provides a great introduction to the region's cooking. A favourite of the house is their excellent *baccalà* (cod) with polenta as well as *caval* (horse). An excellent wine list and outdoor patio dining area in summer make this a great year-round choice.

Antica Osteria Al Duomo €
Via Duomo 7a, T045-800 4505.
This simple osteria is a gem for its pared back, music-focused atmosphere as well as its authentic local vibe and friendly service. The staff will like you even more if you go for the donkey and horse dishes – they're a speciality.

Osteria al Duca €
Via Arche Scaligere 2, T045-594474.
Overlook the boast of the Bard's tenuous connection (Romeo's birthplace?!) to this osteria because the casual and raucous atmosphere is as comforting as the pasta and polenta dishes coming out of the kitchen.

There are many elegant restaurants in Verona.

Five of the best

Veronese dishes

❶ **Sfilacci di cavallo** Shredded horse meat with oil and lemon dressing.

❷ **Pastissada de caval** Horse meat stew served with polenta.

❸ **Trippa alla Parmiggiana** Tripe with Parmesan cheese.

❹ **Risotto all'Amarone** Risotto with the local Amarone wine.

❺ **Gnocchi con ragù di asino** Dumplings with donkey ragù (also with horse, *caval*).

Entertainment

Bergamo, Brescia, Cremona, Mantua and Verona all boast lively entertainment scenes. The late afternoon/early evening ritual of aperitivo is popular, and each town boasts café-bars on the main piazzas and atmospheric *enotecas* tucked away on their cobbled lanes. Wine bars and pubs won't open until 1200 and will close at some point from 2400-0200. Clubs won't open until at least 2000 and close in the early hours of the morning.

Unlike many other parts of Italy, summer is actually quite vibrant here, with plenty of cultural events; Verona in particular has a full programme of opera, as well as rock and pop concerts, in the Arena. There are also many smaller musical events, many held in churches around towns and cities – ask what's on at the local tourism office and you might catch a sublime string quartet playing in an atmospheric Gothic church.

Bergamo

Bars & clubs

Cooperativa Città Alta
Vicolo Sant'Agata, T035-218568.
This café, bar and trattoria ran by a local cooperative can get fairly raucous during Thursday's happy hours; however, on other nights a quiet drink is in order on the lovely garden terrace enjoying views of the surrounding hills.

Pozzo Bianco
Via Porta Dipinta 30b, T035-247694.
Slide onto one of the wooden benches and join the local students for a beer at this popular (albeit off-the-beaten-track) *birreria* (beer hall).

Vineria Cozzi
Via Colleoni 22, T035-238836, vineriacozzi.it.
You can choose from several hundred wines at this popular *enoteca* – and you can also get something scrumptious to snack on (see page 252).

Bobino
Piazza della Libertà, T035-1990 4056.
Dress up for this rather elegant-looking club in the *città bassa* (lower town), which attracts a well-dressed crowd for its house music.

Cantinaccia
Via Quinto Alpini 6/a, T0393-336 3727.
This popular venue in the *città bassa* sees an international set coming for the Latin American music.

Classical music, opera & theatre

Arturo Benedetti Michelangeli International Piano Festival
Donizetti Theatre, piazza Cavour 15, T035-240140, festivalmichelangeli.it.

This annual piano festival is one of the highlights of Bergamo's cultural calendar.

Rassenga Organistica
Centro Culturale Nicolò Rezzara, via S Elisabetta 5, T035-243539, centrorezzara.it.
Organ concerts, organized by the Centro Culturale Nicolò Rezzara and held in churches in Bergamo and surrounding towns, such as Carravaggio and Martinengo, celebrated its 25th year in 2008. Check with tourist offices for details.

Teatro Donizetti
Donizetti Theatre, piazza Cavour 15, T035-240140.
Bergamo's main theatre plays host to a full programme of concerts, theatrical productions, music festivals and events throughout the year, from rock and folk to jazz and blues bands.

Brescia

Bars & clubs

There are lots of bars between piazza della Loggia and piazza Paolo and the surrounding streets in the *centro storico* that start to hot up around aperitivo time and stay open late, especially at weekends. Also popular for aperitivo is the piazzale Arnaldo area which boasts views over the countryside.

Caffè Duomo Pasticceria

Opposite Duomo Vecchio.
The alfresco tables on the piazza are a lovely place for a quiet afternoon drink.

Osteria Al Bianchi

Via Gasparo de Salò 42, T030-292328.
Thu-Mon.
This is one of the most popular bars for a drink in this busy area; great wines by the glass, with good local options.

Osteria Vecchio Botticino

Piazzale Arnaldo 6, T030-48103.
Mon-Sat until 0100.
Just east of the old centre, this cool low-lit bar attracts locals who like to sit with a glass of wine for a while as they take in the scene.

Muse e Musei

Piazza Brusato 24, T030-45048.
Thu-Tue until 0200.
This popular jazz club gets crowded late at night with local students and musos piling in and sinking in to the sofas to listen to live music.

Classical music, opera & theatre

Brescia is home to the Brixia Symphony Orchestra with a woman conductor – Giovanna Sorbi. She's also the Artistic director of the Festival di Musica Sacra (Sacred Music Festival), held in various churches in the city from February through to June. Check the Comune di Brescia website (comune.brescia.it) for details or visit the tourist office.

Cremona

Bars & clubs

There are several café-bars on the main squares of piazza del Comune and piazza del Pace, overlooking the colossal Duomo, that are wonderful for a gelato or an aperitivo in the evening. **Portici del Comune** (piazza del Comune 2, T0372-21295), an atmospheric old place tucked under the arcades, is popular with locals, with tables spread right out into the square at night.

Classical music, opera & theatre

Teatro Amilcare Ponchielli

Corso Vittorio Emanuele 52, T0372-022010, teatroponchielli.it.
This superb theatre hosts the Festival di Cremona every May,

Restaurants line the perimeter of piazza Broletto, Mantua.

along with a full programme of orchestras and concerts, from Gregorian Chant to Byzantine music.

Bars & clubs
Buca del Gabbia
Via Cavour 98, T0376-366901.
This wine bar gets especially crowded and cosy on a winter's evening when it's a great place to warm the bones.

Tiratappi
piazza Alberti 30, T376-322366.
Tucked away down a little laneway off Piazza Mantegna, right near Sant'Andrea church, this wonderful old wine bar has a loyal following who flock here for the local wines and short menu of tasty regional snacks.

Classical music, opera & theatre
The awe-inspiring **Palazzo Te** (via Giovanni Acerbi) plays host to performances and recitals of classical and other music but see the tourist office for details of events organised by other musical associations and sponsors, not the Palazzo itself.

Bars & clubs
Osteria Al Carroarmato
Vicolo Gatto 2a, T045-803 0175.
Thu-Tue until 0200.
Appealing laid-back atmosphere, a mixed crowd, friendly waiters, and occasional live music.

Al Ponte
Via Ponte Pietra 26, T045-569608.
Thu-Tue until 0300.
The good wine list and wonderful river views make this garden bar a favourite for watching the sun go down over the hills with a glass of *vino* in hand.

Caffè delle Erbe
Piazza delle Erbe 32.
Tue-Sun until late.
On a square boasting several late-night bars, this one attracts a local, lively, and occasional raucous young crowd.
Lots of fun!

Cappa
Piazza Brà Mollinari 1, T045-800 4549.
Daily until 0200.
With its oriental decor and scattered cushions about the place, this bar has great views over the Adige. Good cocktails and occasionally live jazz.

Tip...
To find out what's happening in Verona, check out Veronalive (veronalive.it) which has its finger on the pulse of what's cool in the city.

Cinema
Teatro Stimate
Piazza Cittadella, T045-800 0878.
Sink into a comfy seat at this arthouse cinema and delight in some Italian (or world cinema) with subtitles, a rarity in Italy.

Classical music, opera & theatre
Arena di Verona
Piazza Brà.
Box office: 6/b via Dietro Anfiteatro, Mon-Fri 0900-1200, 1515-1745, Sat 0900-1200, performance days 1000-2100, non-performance days 1000-1745, T045-800 5151 (bookings), arena.it.
Nothing says summer in the city like seeing an opera or concert at this famous Roman amphitheatre. Just make sure to get your tickets early to avoid the ruthless scalpers. You can purchase tickets through the website.

Shopping

Teatro Filarmonico
Via dei Mutilati 4, T045-805 1891.
Box office: via Roma 3,
1000-1200, 1630-1930, or until
2100 on performance days,
Booking line T045-800 5151,
arena.it.
Despite bombings and fires in
its long history, this is a theatre
that won't say die. An excellent
concert space, it's a far more
intimate experience than
the Arena.

Teatro Romano
*Regaste Redentore 2,
T045-800 0360.*
Box office: Palazzo Barbieri, via
Degli Alpini 2, Mon-Sat (Sun if a
performance is on), 1030-1300,
1600-1900, T045-806 6485,
estateteatraleveronese.it.
A summer theatre festival is held
here, with the highlight being
English language performances
of Shakespeare, including, of
course, Romeo and Juliet.

Browsing the shops in Bergamo,
Brescia, Cremona, Mantua
and Verona is infinitely more
enjoyable than shopping the
lakes. There's far less tourist tat
(except in Verona where piazza
Erbe's market stalls have given
over to tacky tourist trinkets)
and more small, interesting
specialized stores. Locals hit
the streets to shop in the late
afternoon and early evenings,
especially on summer weekends,
when the town centres have a
real buzz about them and are fun
to wander even if you're not a

shopper. Opening hours
vary enormously, from the
fashion emporiums and global
franchises which tend to do
business from Monday-
Saturday 0900-1930, to the
smaller independent shops
which will close for lunch around
1230 and reopen around 1530.
Shops opening on Sunday
during summer, in Bergamo and
Verona for instance, will close
one weekday (usually Monday)
and/or open late another
afternoon (often Tuesday).

The largest range of shops are to be found in the *città bassa* (lower town), in the streets around piazza Matteotti and piazza Vittorio Veneto, on Il Sentierone, via Torquato Tasso, via XX Settembre and via Tiraboschi. Although the little shops lining the hilly cobblestone streets of via Gombito and via Colleoni in the *città alta* (upper town) are a lot older, have more character, and are more fun to browse.

Clothing & accessories

Tiziana Fausti
Piazza Dante 1A, T035-224142 & piazza Libertà 10, T035-210535, tizianafausti.com.
If you only have time for one *città bassa* shop (as many making the mad dash to the airport do), try Tiziana Fausti's two sleek stores for impeccable Italian and international fashion labels for men and women, as well as emerging regional designers, including Alaia, Alberta Ferretti, Bottega Veneta, Bruno Manetti, Etro and Chiara Boni.

Trussardi
Via Milano 40, T035-634111.
Trussardi was born in Bergamo and has a house in the *città alta*, which locals like to brag about, and this Trussardi store is the place to head for the chic men's and women's wear, leather goods and accessories, at discounted prices.

Food & drink

One of the delights of shopping in Bergamo is to follow your nose to its many delicious bakeries, pastry shops and gourmet food stores. In the *città alta*, via Gombito and via Colleoni are the streets to look for gifts to take back home, such as jars of *mostarda* (pickled fruit relish, wonderful with cheese) or picnic basket fillers.

Ol Formager

Piazzale Oberdan 2, T035-380162.
Bergamo's best cheese shop could very well be one of Italy's finest. The Signorelli family have been in the business since grandfather Alessandro starting making cheese in 1920. Let them guide you and don't be afraid to try!

Pasticceria Cavour Caffetteria 1850

Via Gombito 7/A T035-243418.
The windows of this historic shop display the delicious *Polenta e Osèi* cakes that Bergamo is famous for. Made from sponge cake with hazelnut butter cream inside, covered in polenta and marzipan, and dusted with sugar crystals, these tasty treats get their names from the little chocolate birds on top (see box, page 220 and picture, page 216).

Pasticceria Sant'Anna

Via Borgo Palazzo 43, T035-238406.
Head here for homemade cakes and pastries to stock the picnic basket before heading out for a bike ride in the Bergamo hills.

Tresoldi Alberto Panificio

Via B. Colleoni 13, T035-243960.
Look for the green shopfront of the 'three coins' bakery (a hint that what's inside won't cost more than a few coins) for wonderfully fresh bread, the best in town.

Furniture & design

900 Design
Via Broseto 18, T035-077 0109, 900design.it.
This vintage Italian furniture and lighting design store, owned by architect Carlo Piccinelli, is where you'll find those cool collectibles you couldn't afford in Milan, such as an Artemide Omega hanging light or a Flos Foglio wall lamp, or – if you're happy to ship (the airport is close!) – a funky Zanotta sofa or Brunati 1970s lounge chair. Alternatively, pop a retro plexiglass magazine rack in the carry on.

Shopping Centre

Orio Centre
Via Portico 71, Orio al Serio, T035-459 6201, oriocenter.it.
Mon-Fri 0900-2200, Sat & Sun 0900-2100.
One of Italy's largest malls, this sleek, chic shopping centre is

La Bottega del Vino, Verona.

home to some of the country's best brands, including Benetton, Stefanel, Nara Camiche, Oysho, Replay, Intimissimi, Calzedonia and Breil. There's even a Frette store. Close to Bergamo's airport, it makes a good stop if you have to kill time before your flight.

Brescia

Brescia has a lively and fascinating shopping scene, which should be no surprise considering it's a centre for industry and manufacturing with a large immigrant population. The best shopping is on and around corsos Zanardelli and Magenta in the centre of the old town, and between there and piazza Vittoria and piazza Loggia.

Clothing & accessories
Interno 5
Contrada Cavaletto 5,
T030-375 7436.
One for the guys, this cool store stocks casual men's clothes. Expect anything from printed Commes des Garcons t-shirts to Ugo Cacciatori's baroque-meets-Damien Hirst jewellery.

Penelope
Via A Gramsci 16/A, T03-46902.
One of Italy's most eclectically-and adventurously-curated women's fashion stores stocking clothes, shoes and accessories labels that err on the audacious side, including Azzedine Alaia, Martin Margiela, and Sigourney.

Food & drink

Piazza del Mercato is home to a bustling food market. In the darkness under the porticos there are dozens of delicatessens. If you're looking for an *alimentari*, *salumeria*, *panetteria*, *pasticceria* or *enoteca*, so you can stock up on those picnic supplies, this is where to find it!

Cremona

Il Consorzio Liutai Antonio Stradivari

Piazza Stradivari 1, T0372-463503, cremonaviolins.it.
The Consortium of Antonio Stradivari Violinmakers has exquisite handmade violins for sale in their showroom, starting from €5,000 to €14,000 for a concert-standard instrument. If you're serious about buying a violin and you want to order one, the Consortium is happy to advise and organize a visit to a violin-maker's workshop.

Food & drink

Negozio Sperlari

Via Solferino 25, T0372-22346, sperlari1836.com.
Visit the historic 'Antica Bottega di Strada Solferino' for gourmet foods (over 3,500 items apparently!), including confectionery, nuts, sweet wines, liqueurs, and Cremona's specialty *torrone* (nougat), and you'll see why they were made purveyors to the Royal Family in 1921. Take something home by **Agusto**

Fieschi (*fieschi1867.com*), manufacturers of *mostarda* and *torrone* since 1867. Maximus is the *torrone* to get, reputedly cooked for 10 hours and hand cut. Enjoy it with a bottle of winemaker Beppe Bassi's *Sol* dessert wine, created from Picolit and Molinelli grapes grown a few kilometres away and produced by the Fregoni family – they're very proud of it!

Mantua

Mantua's best shopping is to be found in the streets around piazza Broletto and piazza Erbe, and along corsos Umberto I and Vittorio Emanuele II. You'll find plenty of chic boutiques, shoes and accessories shops, along with gourmet food stores.

Clothing & accessories

Folli Follie

Corso Vittorio Emanuele II 21-27, T0376-360390, follifollie.it.
Giuseppe and Lucia Galli opened their first Folli Follie store here in Mantova in 1970, and now own some seven stores across northern Italy, specialising in stylish Italian clothes, shoes and accessories.

Lubiam

Viale Fiume 55, T039-376 3091, lubiam.it.
A favourite with fashion-conscious guys, this is the outlet store for one of Italy's most notable, and in recent years

more stylish, men's labels, which has been in the business of making tailored suits since 1911.

Verona

Crammed with fabulous shops, via Mazzini (between the Arena and piazza delle Erbe) is the place to head for stylish clothes, especially designer wear, leather handbags and shoes, perfume, cosmetics and books. But it's in the side streets off Mazzini such as via Cappello where you'll find some of the more interesting stores.

Food & drink

Antica Salumeria Albertini

Corso Sant'Anastasia 41/a, T045-803 1074, salumeriaalbertini.it.
Regional cheeses, cured meats, olive oils, balsamics, and local wines… it's all hanging up here in this fragrant shop and it's all delicious – the place to head in Verona for picnic supplies or tasty souvenirs.

Cantina Oreste dal Zovo

Vicolo San Marco in Foro 7, T045-803 4369, enotecadalzovo.it.
If you can't decide what to buy in this atmospheric wine shop, in operation since 1958, ask qualified sommelier and owner Oreste for advice.

Activities & tours

Bergamo

Cycling & walking

A new cycling and walking path established in 2008 begins at via Baioni then meanders through the beautiful hills, passing the city walls. Other cycle paths in the area run along old train routes passing through villages in the Brembana and Seriana valleys. The tourist office (via Gombito 13, T035-242226, turismo.provincia.bergamo.it) has maps and details.

Qualified guides from City of Bergamo Tourist Guide Group (contact details as above) offer engaging two-hour guided 'discovery tours' of Bergamo's Città Alta starting from piazza Mercato. Wednesday, Saturday & Sunday 1500 (English & Italian), Saturday 1030 (Italian & German), €10, no bookings.

Sightseeing
CitySightSeeing Bus
bergamo.city-sightseeing.it.
3 Apr-1 Nov, daily,
€13 (24-hr ticket).
This hop-on-hop-off bus does one 60-minute route around the city, beginning and ending at Stazione piazza Marconi with pre-recorded commentary in English, Italian, German, Spanish. Wheelchair access.

Historical Villa Tours
T035-233350,
tourdimorestoriche.it.
Apr-Jun, Sun, times vary, see website for details. 1 palace €5-7.50, 3 palaces €13, 5 palaces €17.
These guided tours visit five beautiful Bergamo mansions, Palazzos Agliardi, Moroni, Terzi, Palma Cavozzi Vertova, and Grismondi Finardi, and can be done altogether or individually. A companion event offers five jazz concerts at each villa on different afternoons (Mar, Sun 1600-1800).

Brescia

Cycling
Brescia has a free bike-borrowing scheme during summer. Bikes can be collected and returned from outside the main train station (0730-1930) but visit the tourist office (piazza Loggia 6, T030-240 0357, comune.brescia. it) for cycling route suggestions.

Food & wine
The Associazione Strada del Vino Franciacorta (via Verdi 53, Erbusco, near Brescia, T307-760870, stradadelfranciacorta.it) organizes a range of activities in the Franciacorta wine region near Brescia, including the wine-focused Festival del Franciacorta, dozens of wine events, cellar-door tasting and vineyard tours throughout the year. They also offer themed walking, cycling, and horseriding tours and can arrange tailor-made excursions to wineries.

Cremona

Food & wine
Strada Del Gusto Cremonese
Piazza del Comune 5,
T0372-23233,
stradadelgustocremonese.it.
The 'Cremonese Taste Route', the group that promotes Cremona's gastronomic traditions and products, organizes a range of festivals, events, tours and activities held throughout the year.

Sightseeing
Associazione Guide Turistiche ed Interpreti di Cremona
Piazza Giovanni XXIII,
T0372-37970.
Summer Mon-Fri 1000-1200, rest of year Mon-Wed 1500-1700, cremonatour.net.
Cremona has its act together when it comes to guides with a top-notch organisation of highly qualified multi-lingual guides offering city walking tours to themed excursions. Groups of six preferred, personalised tours can be arranged.

Walking
The tourist office (see page 231) produces an excellent brochure and map – *Cremona City of Art and Music: Six Itineraries to Discover the City* – outlining self-guided walks on the following themes: The Roman & early Middle Ages; The Middle Ages;
The Renaissance City; The Spanish & the 18th Century; The City and Music; and The City and Po River.

Mantua is a wonderful city to cycle around.

Romeo Bus Tour
AMT Bus Company,
T045-840 1160, amt.it.
Jun-Sep Tue-Sun at 1000, 1130,
1300, 1530; 90 mins; €15, tickets
sold on board & at the tabacchi
on piazza Brà.

Departing and returning to
piazza Brà, this 1.5 hour tour on
a small air-conditioned bus takes
in the main sights accompanied
by a headset commentary, apart
from on a Saturday afternoon,
when a real, live guide can
answer the inevitable questions
about the truth of the *Romeo &
Juliet* story.

Guide Verona
*Associazione Culturale Guide
Center Verona, vicolo Scala Santa
14, T045 8018175,
guideverona.com.*
Half-day tour €105,
full-day €210.

These culturally-focused tours
have a variety of programmes,
from walking tours of the city to
visits to the local wine districts of
Valpolicella and Soave.

Juliet & Co Walking Tours
T045-810 3173, julietandco.com.
Apr-Nov daily 1730;
75 mins, €10.

These recommended tours
depart from the Vittorio
Emanuele II equestrian statue on
piazza Brà and take in the major
sights. Longer tours, including
half- and full-day excursions are
also available.

Mantua

Boating
Several boat companies offer
cruises on Mantua's placid lakes
during the warmer months,
but Motonavi Andes Negrini
(via San Giorgio 2, T0376-322875,
motonaviandes.it) is the most
popular, offering several options of
60- or 90-minute cruises on Lago
di Mezza, Lago Inferiore and Lago
Vallazza, departing around eight
times a day from its jetty on Lago
Inferiore. €8-10, book in advance.

Cycling
There are several sign-posted
cycling routes around Mantua, a
wonderful town to bike around.
See the tourist office (piazza
Mantenga 6, T0376-432432
turismo.mantova.it) for details.
You can hire bikes from **Mantua
Bike Di Busselli Giovanni** (viale
Piave 22b, T0376-220 909) for €2
hour/€8 day.

Verona

Cycling & walking
Passeggiando per Verona
Mon-Sat 0900-1900,
Sun 0900-1500.

The commune has established
four self-guided walking routes
of 3-4 hours each. Pick up the
brochure *Passeggiando per
Verona* from the tourist office
(degli Alpini 9, piazza Brà,
T045-806 8680) or get details
online (comune.verona.it/
turismo/passeggiando).

Amici della
Bicicletta di Verona
*T045-800 4443,
amicidellabicicletta.it.*
This cycling club has a variety of
cycling trips and excursions on
its calendar that riders can join.

Contents

268 Getting there
270 Introduction
272 Directory
276 Language

Practicalities

Getting there

Air

From UK and Ireland
Access to the lakes is gained by overland travel after arriving in the following cities: Milan (closest to Maggiore and Como), Bergamo (Como), Brescia (Como, Garda), Verona (Garda) and Lugano in Switzerland (Maggiore, Como).

From North America
Alitalia, American Airlines, British Airways and **Delta** are some of the airlines offering direct flights from the states to **Milan Malpensa Airport**. Canadian travellers will have to either change in the US, or fly to another European city for a connection. **Alitalia** fly directly from Toronto to Rome. A popular route from North America to Milan is via Dubai, travelling with **Emirates**.

From Rest of Europe
Direct flights to the airports serving northern Italy depart from all major European cities. There are direct passenger trains to Milano Centrale from many points of departure including Munich, Paris and Amsterdam. A **Motorail** service carries passengers and their vehicles from Düsseldorf to Verona (see Going green box).

Airport information

Milan Malpensa Airport (T02-748 5220 sea-aeroportimilano.it), just 15 km from Lake Maggiore, is well placed for access to the western lakes. There's a bus to central Milan every 20 minutes (journey time 50 mins, €5) and the Malpensa Express train every 30 minutes (40 mins to Cadorna station, €11). Change midway at Saronno for lines heading north to Como and Maggiore. **Linate Airport** (T02-748 5220 sea-aeroportimilano.it), 15 km east of Milan is connected to San Babila station by city bus 73 every 10 minutes (30 mins, €1). **Orio al Serio Airport** (sacbo.it), 8 km southeast of Bergamo, is a gateway to Como and Garda.

A shuttle bus to Bergamo runs every half hour (€3.50). Frequent trains leave Bergamo on a 60 minute journey to Milan Centrale.

Garda is easily reached from Verona and Brescia. **Verona Villafranca** (T045-809 5666 aeroportoverona.it), 18 km southwest of the city, is served by **APTV** (apt.vr.it) buses running to the centre every 20 minutess. A **Ryanair** hub in the region, **Brescia Montichiari** (T030-965 6599 aeroportobrescia.it), is 18 km southeast of Brescia and closer to Garda than Verona. Buses run to Verona (€11) and Brescia (€7.50). Trains run from Brescia to Desenzano del Garda roughly every half hour. Budget airline **Darwin** fly from the UK, Italy and France to **Lugano Airport** (lugano-airport.ch). It's in Switzerland, 5 km west of Lugano, convenient for Como and Maggiore. Italian budget airline **MyAir** flies from a number of European destinations into Milan's **Orio al Serio** (orioaeroporto.it).

Rail

You can travel with **Eurostar** (eurostar.com) from London to Paris before joining an overnight sleeper from Paris Bercy to Verona Porta Nuova. Book tickets at **raileurope.com** (T0870-584 8848) searching for trains after 1900. When making transfers to the lakes, the major towns are: Como/Varenna/Lecco for Lake Como; Desenzano/Peschiera for Lake Garda; Arona/Stresa/Verbania for Lake Maggiore.

Road

It's a 1,200 km journey from London to the most westerly lake, Orta, but you'll be treated to some amazing scenery. If it's high-octane you're after, take the Stelvio Pass, 100 km north of Garda: with 48 hairpin turns, Jeremy Clarkson rates it as the

Going green

The **Motorail** (raileurope.co.uk/frenchmotorail) service – a car-carrying train – has advantages over combining a flight with car hire. You can carry as much luggage as you want and bring *back* as much as you like. An overnight long distance motorail journey can be time effective compared with a flight and the sleeper can even save on a hotel bill or two. There aren't yet any direct motorail trains to Italy from France, but a service departs from Calais to Nice, leaving about a four hour drive along the Southern French coast and up to the Italian lakes.

best drive in the world. EU nationals taking their own car need an International Insurance Certificate (also known as a Green Card). Those holding a non-EU licence also need to take an International Driving Permit. **Autostrade** (T055-420 3200 autostrade.it) provides information on Italian motorways and **Automobile Club Italiana** (T06-49981 aci.it) gives general driving information.

Bus/coach

Eurolines (T0870-580 8080 nationalexpress.co.uk) operate three services per week from London Victoria to Milan with a travel time of around 28 hours. Prices start at £95 return. Coaches arrive and depart in Milan at the new bus station Milano Lampugnano.

Getting around

There are several options for getting around Milan and the Lakes – if you want to do plenty of sightseeing, visiting many of the towns covered in the book, by car is the best way to do it. If you are planning on driving, a good map to take is the *AA Road Map Italy: Italian Lakes & Milan*. If you just want to go from say, Milan to Lake Como and hang out, it's easy to just catch the train and do sightseeing by ferry. If you're planning on doing some hiking or off-road mountain biking, it's best to get trail maps from the actual destination, either from the tourist office or a climbing/biking shop.

Rail

Italy has an extensive rail network, and it's the best way to get around the country on a city-based trip. It's often quicker than a domestic flight, when you include check-in times and waiting for baggage. Milan to Rome, for instance, takes just over four hours. There is good rail coverage in the north of Italy and you can cover many of the places listed in this book by train.

It's worth knowing that there are several different train services running in Italy: air-conditioned and splendid Eurostar Italia, direct and convenient InterCity, and the slightly less regular Regional trains. All can be booked at trenitalia.com, where the type of train is indicated with the initials ES, IC or REG. 'Amica' fares are cheaper advance tickets (if you can find one), flexi fare costs more but is – you guessed it – flexible, and standard fare is just that.

In general, it's cheaper and more convenient to book online or at ticket machines for the journeys you need to take than it is to buy a pass. When using a service such as Eurostar Italia or InterCity, booking is advised and a surcharge in addition to a pass will often be required; passes therefore lose their thrift factor for tourists. On many Italian trains it's possible to travel 'ticketless', meaning you get on the train and quote your booking reference when the conductor comes round.

Booking and buying tickets at the counter or via machines in train stations is convenient if you can't access the internet. Remember, you must validate train tickets at the yellow stamping machines before boarding.

Road

EU nationals taking their own car need to have an International Insurance Certificate (also known as a *Carte Verde*). Those holding a non-EU licence also need to take an International Driving Permit with them. Unleaded petrol is *benzina*, diesel is *gasolio*.

Italy has strict laws on drink driving – steer clear of alcohol to be safe. The use of mobile telephones while driving is illegal. Other nuances of Italian road law include children under 1.5 m being required to be in the back of the car and a reflective jacket must be worn if your car breaks down on the carriageway in poor visibility. Make sure you've got one. Since July 2007 on-the-spot fines for minor traffic offences have been in operation – typically €150-250. Always get a receipt if you incur one.

Speed limits are 130 kph (motorway), 110 kph (dual carriageway) and 50 kph (town). Limits are 20 kph *lower* on motorways and dual carriageways when the road is wet. *Autostrade* (motorways) are toll roads, so keep cash in the car as a backup even though you can use credit cards on the blue 'viacard' gates. **Autostrade** (T055-420 3200, autostrade.it) provides information on motorways in Italy and **Automobile Club d'Italia** (T06-49981, aci.it) provides general driving information. ACI offers roadside assistance with English-speaking operators on T116.

Be aware that there are restrictions on driving in historic city centres, indicated by signs with black letters ZTL (*zona a traffico limitato*) on a yellow background. If you pass these signs, your registration number may be caught and a fine winging its way to you. If your hotel is in the centre of town, you may be entitled to an official pass –

contact your hotel or car hire company. However, this pass is not universal and only allows access to the hotel.

Car hire

Car hire is available at all of Italy's international airports and many domestic airports. You will probably wish to book the car hire before you arrive in the country, and it's best to do so for popular destinations and at busy times of year. Check in advance the opening times of the car hire office.

Car hire comparison websites and agents are a good place to start a search for the best deals. Try easycar.com, carrentals.co.uk.

Check what each hire company requires from you. Some companies will ask for an International Driving Licence, alongside your normal driving licence, if the language of your driving licence is different to the country you're renting the car in. Others are content with an EU licence. You'll need to produce a credit card for virtually all companies. If you book ahead, make sure that the named credit card holder is the same as the person renting and driving the car to avoid any problems. Most companies have a lower age limit of 21 years and require that you've held your licence for at least a year. Many have a young driver surcharge for those under 25. Confirm insurance and any damage waiver charges and keep all your documents with you when you drive. Always take a printed copy of the contract with you, regardless of whether you have a booking number and a 'confirmed' booking.

Bicycle

While Milan itself is not the easiest city to ride a bike in, thankfully the rest of the areas covered by this book are. While the roads are narrow, Italians love their bike-riding and are well used to passing cyclists. Bikes can be hired everywhere on the lakes and mountain bikes are available at the popular mountain-biking destinations, such as Lake Garda.

Bus/coach

While you can use buses to get around, trains (often with a convenient link to the city centres by bus) are more popular.

Directory

Customs & immigration

UK and EU citizens do not need a visa, but will need a valid passport to enter Italy. A standard tourist visa for those outside of the EU is valid for up to 90 days.

Disabled travellers

Italy is a bit behind when it comes to catering for disabled travellers, where access is sometimes very difficult or ill thought out. Contact an association or agency before departure for more details such as **Accessible Italy** (aacessibleitaly.com) or **Society for Accessible Travel and Hospitality** (sath.org). Locally, **Milano Per Tutti** (milanopertutti.it) has an extensive database (available in English or Italian) of sights in the city and important information such as door widths. A non-profit organization, A.I.A.S. di Milano ONLUS (via Mantegazza Paolo 10, T02-330 2021, aiasmilano.it), runs the website.

Emergency numbers

Police T112 (with English-speaking operators), T113 (*carabinieri*); Ambulance T118; Fire T115; Roadside assistance T116.

Etiquette

Bella figura – projecting a good image – is important to Italians. Smart casual dress at the very least is expected, even in summer when other countries dress down. Take note of public notices about conduct: sitting on steps or eating and drinking in certain historic areas is not allowed. Covering arms and legs is necessary for admission into some churches – in some cases shorts are not permitted. Punctuality is apparently not mandatory in Italy, so be prepared to wait on occasion – even at government-run sights where opening times are often treated as a suggestion.

Families

Whether for a traditional beach break or an afternoon in a gelateria, families are well accommodated in Italy. The family is highly regarded in Italy and *bambini* are indulged, and there's plenty to do for children besides endless museum visits. Do note that sometimes lone parents or adults accompanying children of a different surname may need evidence before taking children in and out of the country. Contact your Italian embassy for current details (Italian embassy in London, T020-7312 2200).

Health

Comprehensive travel and medical insurance is strongly recommended for all travel. EU citizens should apply for a free European Health Insurance Card (ehic.org) which replaced the E111 form and offers reduced-cost medical treatment. Late-night pharmacies are identified by a large green cross outside. T1100 for addresses of three nearest open pharmacies. The accident and emergency department of a hospital is the *pronto soccorso*. Local hospital details are in the Essentials boxes for each destination.

Insurance

Comprehensive travel and medical insurance is strongly recommended for all travel – the EHIC is not a replacement for insurance. You should check any exclusions, and that your policy covers you for all the activities you want to undertake. Keep details of your insurance documents separately; emailing yourself with the details is a good way to keep the information safe and accessible. Ensure

you have full insurance if hiring a car, and you might need an international insurance certificate if taking your own car (contact your current insurers).

Money

The Italian currency is the euro. There are ATMs throughout Italy that accept major credit and debit cards. To change cash or travellers' cheques, look for a *cambio*. Most restaurants, shops, museums and art galleries take major credit cards. Paying directly with debit cards such as Cirrus is less easy in some places, so withdrawing from an ATM and paying cash is the better option. Keep plenty of cash for toll roads if you're driving. ATMs are everywhere in the region and locations are listed in the Essentials boxes for each destination for streets and piazzas where you'll generally find several ATMs.

Police

While it appears that there are several different types of police in Italy (and several dozen uniforms for each!), there are two types of police forces that you will see most often: the *polizia* (T113) and the *carabinieri* (T112). The *polizia* are the 'normal' police under the control of the Interior Ministry, while the *carabinieri* are a defacto military force. However both will respond if you need help.

Post

Italian post has a not entirely undeserved reputation for being unreliable, particularly for handling postcards. Overseas post will require *posta prioritaria* (priority mail) and a postcard stamp will start at €0.60. You can buy *francobolli* (stamps) at post offices and *tabacchi* (look for T signs). Post office locations are listed in the Essentials boxes for each destination.

Safety

The crime rate in Italy is generally low, but rates of petty crime higher. Of all the areas mentioned in this book, Stazione Centrale and the metro in Milan are the most likely locations for pickpockets to be operating. Take general care when travelling: don't flaunt your valuables, take only what money you need and split it, and don't take risks you wouldn't at home. Beware of scams and con artists, and don't expect things to go smoothly if you partake in fake goods. Car break-ins are common, so always remove valuables and never leave anything that looks valuable in the car.
Take care on public transport where pickpockets or bag-cutters might operate. Do not make it clear which stop you're getting off at – it gives potential thieves a timeframe to work in (most work in groups). Female travellers with find the north of Italy quite safe, apart from some attention from local Lotharios, who are generally harmless.

Telephone

The dialling codes for the main towns in the region are: **Bergamo** 035; **Brescia** 030; **Como** 031; **Cremona** 0372; **Mantua** 0376; **Milan** 02; **Orta San Giulio** 0322; **Sirmione** 030; **Stresa** 0323; **Verona** 045.

You need to use the local codes below even when dialling from within the city or region. The prefix for Italy is +39. You no longer need to drop the initial '0' from area codes when calling from abroad. For directory enquiries call T12.

Time difference

Italy uses Central European Time, GMT+1.

Tipping

Most waiters in the region expect a tip from foreigners; 10-15% is the norm if you're really happy with the service. Leaving change from the bill is appropriate for cheaper *enotecas* and osterias. Taxis may add on extra costs for luggage etc but an additional tip is always appreciated. Rounding up prices always goes down well, especially if it means avoiding having to give change – not a favourite Italian habit.

Tourist information

Tourist information for the individual towns is listed in the Essentials boxes for each destination.

Voltage

Italy functions on a 220V mains supply and the standard European two-pin plug.

Language

In hotels and bigger restaurants, you'll usually find English is spoken. The further you go from the tourist centres, however, the more trouble you may have, unless you have at least a smattering of Italian. Around the northern shores German is spoken nearly as often as English as a second language.

You'll find that the heavy Veronese dialect is spoken in the east of the region. A slight variant on the Veneto dialect, the dialect spoken today in and around Verona has changed little in centuries and exhibits Germanic influences. Characteristic sounds are short, clipped and nasal, from the back of the mouth. Lombard dialects are scarcely spoken and the few people who keep the language alive will, in most instances, use standard Italian when speaking to someone unfamiliar.

Stress in spoken Italian usually falls on the penultimate syllable. Italian has standard sounds: unlike English you can work out how it sounds from how it's written and vice versa.

Vowels

a like 'a' in cat
e like 'e' in vet, or slightly more open, like the 'ai' in air (except after c or g, see consonants below)
i like 'i' in sip (except after c or g, see below)
o like 'o' in fox
u like 'ou' in soup

Consonants

Generally consonants sound the same as in English, though 'e' and 'i' after 'c' or 'g' make them soft (a 'ch' or a 'j' sound) and are silent themselves, whereas 'h' makes them hard (a 'k' or 'g' sound), the opposite to English. So ciao is pronounced 'chaow', but chiesa (church) is pronounced 'kee-ay-sa'.

The combination 'gli' is pronounced like the 'lli' in million, and 'gn' like 'ny' in Tanya.

Basics

thank you	*grazie*
hi/goodbye	*ciao* (informal)
good day (until after lunch/ mid-afternoon)	*buongiorno*
good evening (after lunch)	*buonasera*
goodnight	*buonanotte*
goodbye	*arrivederci*
please	*per favore*
I'm sorry	*mi dispiace*
excuse me	*permesso*
yes	*si*
no	*no*

Numbers

one	*uno*	17	*diciassette*
two	*due*	18	*diciotto*
three	*tre*	19	*diciannove*
four	*quattro*	20	*venti*
five	*cinque*	21	*ventuno*
six	*sei*	22	*ventidue*
seven	*sette*	30	*trenta*
eight	*otto*	40	*quaranta*
nine	*nove*	50	*cinquanta*
10	*dieci*	60	*sessanta*
11	*undici*	70	*settanta*
12	*dodici*	80	*ottanta*
13	*tredici*	90	*novanta*
14	*quattordici*	100	*cento*
15	*quindici*	200	*due cento*
16	*sedici*	1000	*mille*

Gestures

Italians are famously theatrical and animated in dialogue and use a variety of gestures.

Side of left palm on side of right wrist as right wrist is flicked up   Go away

Hunched shoulders and arms lifted with palms of hands outwards   What am I supposed to do?

Thumb, index and middle finger of hand together, wrist upturned and shaking
What are you doing/what's going on?

Both palms together and moved up and down in front of stomach   Same as above

All fingers of hand squeezed together   To signify a place is packed full of people

Front or side of hand to chin   'Nothing', as in 'I don't understand' or 'I've had enough'

Flicking back of right ear   To signify someone is gay

Index finger in cheek   To signify good food

Questions

how?   *come?*

how much?   *quanto?*

when?   *quando?*

where?   *dove?*

why?   *perché?*

what?   *che cosa?*

Problems

I don't understand   *non capisco*

I don't know   *non lo so*

I don't speak Italian   *non parlo italiano*

How do you say ... (in Italian)?
   come si dice ... (in italiano)?

Is there anyone who speaks English?
   c'è qualcuno che parla inglese?

Shopping

this one/that one   *questo/quello*
less   *meno*
more   *di più*
how much is it/are they?
    quanto costa/costano?
can I have …?   *posso avere …?*

Travelling

one ticket for...   *un biglietto per...*
single   *solo andata*
return   *andata e ritorno*
does this go to Verona?
    questo va a Verona?
airport   *aeroporto*
bus stop   *fermata*
train   *treno*
car   *macchina*
taxi   *tassi*

Hotels

a double/single room
una camera doppia/singola
a double bed   *un letto matrimoniale*
bathroom   *bagno*
Is there a view?   *c'è un bel panorama?*
can I see the room?   *posso vedere la camera?*
when is breakfast?   *a che ora è la colazione?*
can I have the key?   *posso avere la chiave?*

Time

morning   *mattina*
afternoon   *pomeriggio*
evening   *sera*
night   *notte*
soon   *presto/fra poco*
later   *più tardi*
what time is it?   *che ore sono?*
today/tomorrow/yesterday   *oggi/domani/ieri*

Days

Monday   *lunedi*
Tuesday   *martedi*
Wednesday   *mercoledi*
Thursday   *giovedi*
Friday   *venerdi*
Saturday   *sabato*
Sunday   *domenica*

Conversation

alright   *va bene*
right then   *allora*
who knows!   *bo! / chi sa*
good luck!   *in bocca al lupo!* (literally, 'in the
    mouth of the wolf')
one moment   *un attimo*
hello (when answering a phone)
    pronto (literally, 'ready')
let's go!   *andiamo!*
enough/stop   *basta!*
give up!   *dai!*
I like ...   *mi piace ...*
how's it going?   (well, thanks) *come va?* (*bene, grazie*)
how are you?   *come sta/stai?* (polite/informal)

Index

A

about the authors 4
about the book 4
About the region 26-75
acknowledgements 4
Accademia Carrara, Bergamo 223
activities & tours 72
  Milan 138
  Lake Como 191
  Lake Garda 213
  Lakes Maggiore & Orta 161
  Towns of the Po Valley 164
agriculture 50
agriturismo 58
air 268
airport information 268
albergo 58
Alto Garda, Lake Garda 200
antique show 53
Antonio Citterio 107, 121
Arca della Pace, Milan 111
Arche Scaligere, Verona 241
Archi di Porta Nuova, Milan 111
architectural glossary 117
architecture 38
Arco dei Gavi, Verona 243
Arco della Pace, Milan 111
Arena di Verona, Verona 243
Arona 149
Arsenale, Verona 247
art 38
Ascona, Switzerland 149

B

Bagolino, Lake Garda 203
Baptistery, Bergamo 221
Baptistery, Cremona 232
Baptistery, Milan 85
Barbarossa 31
bars & clubs 66

Basilica di Saint Giulio,
  Lake Orta 153
Basilica di San Andrea,
  Mantua 237
Basilica di Sant'Ambrogio,
  Milan 115
Basilica di Sant'Abbondio,
  Como 171
Basilica Santa Maria Maggiore,
  Bergamo 221
Basso Garda, Lake Garda 196
Bellagio, Lake Como 16, 178
Bellano, Lake Como 182
Bergamo 13, 16, 218
Bergamo Alta 219
Bergamo Bassa 222
Berlusconi, Silvio 37, 45
Biblioteca Ambrosiana,
  Milan 145
birds 50, 183
Borgo Pignolo, Bergamo 222
Borromean Islands,
  Lake Maggiore 146
    Isola Bella 146
    Isola Madre 146
    Isola dei Pescatori 146
Borromeo family 145
Botticelli 87, 92, 108
Brera, Milan 107
Brescia 13, 224
Brigate Rosse 37
Brixia, Brescia 228
Broletto, Brescia 227
Brutalist Modernism 42

C

Ca'Grande, Milan 41
Callas, Maria 91, 175,
Campanone, Bergamo 220
Cannero Riviera,
  Lake Maggiore 149

Cannobio, Lake Maggiore 150
Cappella Colleoni, Bergamo 221
Caravaggio 87, 107, 223
Carnevale di Verona 52
Carnevale Ambrosiano 52
Casa degli Omenoni, Milan 95
Casa del Fascio, Como 42
Casa del Manzoni, Milan 87
Casa di Giulietta , Verona 245
Casino Royale
  (Martin Campbell) 24
Castello, Bergamo 222
Castello, Brescia 229
Castello di San Giorgio,
  Mantua 237
Castello di Vezio 183
Castello Sforzesco 14, 96
Castel San Pietro, Verona 247
Castelvecchio, Verona 244, 247
Cattedrale di
  Santa Maria Assunta 17, 231
Cattedrale San Pietro,
  Mantua 238
Cernobbio, Lake Como 175
Certosa di Pavia, Pavia 15, 118
Charlemagne 30
children 66
cinema 66
Cisalpine Gaul 29
Civica Biblioticha Angelo May,
  Bergamo 220
Civici Musei del
  Castello Sforzesco 98
Clooney, George 185
Colico, Lake Como 182
Collezione Gli Archi in Sala
  dei Violini, Cremona 232
Colonno, Lake Como 175
Como 16, 168
Corteo dei Re Magi 52
Cremona 13, 17, 230
customs & immigration 272
cycling 73

 D

d'Annunzio, Gabriele 202
d'Este Isabella 238
DH Lawrence 25
da Vinci, Leonardo 41, 87, 96, 98,
  102, 108, 114, 115
Dante 241
della Scala family 243
Desenzano, Lake Garda 199
design 44, 45, 70, 105, 106, 114, 135
disabled travellers 272
Domaso, Lake Como 182
drinking 60
driving
  Four lakes' drive 203
  Great Valley National Park
    circuit 151
  Lake Maggiore circuit 149
Duomo, Bergamo 221
Duomo, Como 169
Duomo, Desenzano 199
Duomo, Salò 201
Duomo, Mantua 238
Duomo, Milan 14, 84
Duomo Nuovo, Brescia 226
Duomo Vecchio, Brescia 229
Duomo, Verona 245

E

eating & drinking 60
  Lakes Maggiore & Orta 156
  Milan 124
  price codes 5
  Lake Como 187
  Lake Garda 210
  Towns of the Po Valley 252
Eco, Umberto 25
Edict of Milan 29, 116
emergency Numbers 272
Emperor Constantine 116

enoteca 61
entertainment 66
environment 48
  Milan 128
  Lake Como 190
  Lake Garda 212
  Lakes Maggiore & Orta 159
  Towns of the Po Valley 257
etiquette 272

 F

families 272
Farewell to Arms,
  A (Ernest Hemingway) 25
Fascism 35, 42
fashion 69, 104
fashion show 53
Ferragosto 20, 54
Festa del Naviglio 20, 53
Festa di San Giovanni 54
Festa di Sant'Ambrogio 21, 55
Festival Latino Americando 54
Festival Milano 55
Festival Mix 53
film 22
Film Festival 53
Fontana Contarini, Bergamo 220
food & wine 73
football 73, 138
Formula One 55, 74, 138
Fototeca (Musei Civci di Lecco),
  Lecco 185
Foucault's Pendulum
  (Umberto Eco) 25
Funicolare per Brunate,
  Como 173
Futurism 42, 110, 171, 172, 223

G

Galleria Comunale d'Arte
  (Musei Civci di Lecco), Lecco 185
Galleria d'Arte Moderna e
  Contemporanea/GAMEC,
  Bergamo 223
Galleria Vittorio Emanuele II 86
Garda Jazz Festival 53
Garda, Lake Garda 205
Gardone Riviera, Lake Garda 201
Gargnano, Lake Garda 203
gay & lesbian 67
George Clooney 185
getting around
  bicycle 271
  bus/coach 271
  car hire 271
  rail 270
  road 270
getting there
  air 268
  airport Information 268
  bus/coach 269
  rail 269
  road 269
Gian Galeazzo Visconti 84
Giardini Pubblici, Milan 111
Giardino Botanico Hruska,
  Lake Garda 202
Giò Ponte 114
glossary 276
  architectural 117
  food & drink 64
Gothic 38, 84, 102, 118
Grand Prix 20
Grand Tour, The 37
Gravedona 182
Great Days Out
  An amble around Verona 246
  Certosa di Pavia 118
  Island Hopping:
    Lake Maggiore 146

Lake Como Gardens 180
Lakeside Promenade 172
Milan's centro storico 94
Milan fashion walk 104
Outdoor activities:
  Lake Como 176
Outdoor activities:
  Lake Garda 206
Great Night Out
  Milan's Navigli 130
Grotte di Catullo, Lake Garda 197

H

health 272
Hemingway, Ernest 25
hike 49

I

I Promessi Sposi
  (Alessandro Manzoni) 24
Il Cenacolo 15, 102
Il Vittoriale, Lake Garda 202
Innocents Abroad,
  The (Mark Twain) 24
insurance 272
Introducing the region 6-25
Isola Bella 146
Isola Comacina 175
Isola dei Pescatori 146
Isola di San Giulio 153
Isola Madre 146
Italian Wars, The 32

J

Jazz festival 53

L

La Notte
  (Michelangelo Antonioni) 22
La Punta Spartivento,
  Bellagio 178
La Scala 90
Lago d'Idro 203
Lago di Ledro 203
Lago di Valvestino 203
Lake Como 164-191
  activities & tours 191
  ATMs 169
  bus station 169
  eating & drinking 187
  entertainment 190
  hospital 169
  itinerary 167
  pharmacy 169
  post office 169
  shopping 190
  sleeping 186
  tourist information 169
  train station 169
Lake Garda 192-213
  activities & tours 213
  ATMs 197
  bus station 197
  eating & drinking 210
  entertainment 212
  hospital 197
  itinerary 195
  pharmacy 197
  post office 197
  shopping 212
  sleeping 208
  tourist information 197
  train station 197

Lake Iseo 203
Lakes Maggiore & Orta 140-163
  activities & tours 152
  eating 156
  entertainment 159
  Lake Maggiore 144
  Lake Orta 152
  sleeping 154
  shopping 160
language courses 73
La Piazze dei Sapori 53
La Rocca, Bergamo 222
La Scala 90
La Scala Season Opening 55
Lecco 185
Lenno 175
Le Piazze dei Sapori 20, 53
Liberation Day 53
Lido della Bionde,
  Lake Garda 197
Limone sul Garda,
  Lake Garda 205
Listone, Verona 246
kiterature 24
locanda 58
Locarno, Switzerland 149
Loggia dei Militi 231
Lombard League, The 30
Lombardy 15

M

Mafia 47
Malcesine, Lake Garda 205
Manerba, Lake Garda 200
Mantua 13, 17, 236
Manzoni, Alessandro 24
  Casa del Manzoni 87
  Villa Manzoni 185

Markets 63
  Lake Como 190
  Lake Garda 212
  Lakes Maggiore & Orta 160
  Milan 137
Medieval 38
Mediolanum 29
Menaggio 178
Menu reader 64
Metro, Milan 80
Mezzanotte Di Fiaba 18, 55
Mezzegra, Lake Como 175
Michelangelo 98
Michelin stars 201
Michelin-starred restaurants
  Ambasciata
    (around Mantua) 255
  Dal Pescatore
    (around Mantua) 254
  Joia (Milan) 125
  Il Desco (Verona) 255
  Il Ristorante Cracco (Milan) 124
  L'Osteria di Via Solata
    (Bergamo) 252
  La Rucola (Sirmione) 210
  Mistral (Bellagio) 180
  Trussardi alla Scala (Milan) 124
  Villa Crespi
    (Orta San Giulio) 157
  Villa Fiordaliso
    (Gardone Riviera) 211
Milan 76-139
  activities & tours 138
  ATMs 81
  bus station 80
  eating 124
  entertainment 128
  hospital 81
  itinerary 79
  map 82, 88
  pharmacy 81
  picnic 127
  post office 81

  shopping 135
  sleeping 120
  tourist information 81
  train stations 80
Milano d'Estate 20, 54
Milano International
  Film Festival 55
Milano Internazionale
  Antiquariato 53
Milano Marathon 21, 55
Milano Moda
  Donna Autunno/Inverno 53
Mille Miglia 20, 53
Miracle in Milan
  (Vittorio De Sica) 22
money 274
Moniga, Lake Garda 200
Monte Mottarone 162
motor racing 74
Mura di Gallieno, Verona 243
Murano glass 92
Musei Civici Como, Como 171
Musei Civci di Lecco, Lecco 185
Museo Archeologico
  (Musei Civci di Lecco, Lecco) 185
Museo Archeologico
  (Musei Civici Como), Como 171
Museo Archeologico,
  Bergamo 222
Museo Bagatti Valsecchi,
  Milan 109
Museo Civico Ala Ponzone,
  Cremona 234
Museo Civico di Storia Naturale,
  Milan 111
Museo d'Arte Antica
  (Civici Musei del
  Castello Sforzesco) 98
Museo degli Strumenti Musicali
  (Civici Musei del
  Castello Sforzesco) 100

Index

Museo del Cinema, Milan 112
Museo dell'Ottocento, Milan 110
Museo Della Preistoria e
  Protostoria (Civici Musei del
  Castello Sforzesco) 98
Museo delle Arti Decorative
  (Civici Musei del Castello
  Sforzesco) 99
Museo di Milano, Milan 109
Museo di Risorgimento,
  Milan 109
Museo di Storia Contemporanea,
  Milan 109
Museo di Storia Naturale
  (Musei Civci di Lecco), Lecco 185
Museo Donizetti, Bergamo 222
Museo Egizio
  (Civici Musei del Castello
  Sforzesco) 98
Museo Nazionale della Scienza
  e della Tecnica Leonardo
  da Vinci, Milan 114
Museo Poldi Pezzoli, Milan 92
Museo Teatrale alla Scala 91
Museo Scienze Naturali,
  Bergamo 222
Museo Storico
  (Musei Civici Como), Como 171
Museo Storico (Musei Civci
  di Lecco), Lecco 185
Museo Stradivariano
  (Museo Civico Ala Ponzone),
  Cremona 235
music 67
Mussolini 42, 175, 202

Napoleon 84, 96, 110
national parks 49
nature 48
Navigli 15, 130
Nicolò Amati 232
Nordic walking 48
Notturni in Villa 20, 54

O

Ocean's Twelve
  (Steven Soderbergh) 23
Omegna 152
opera and classical 54, 67,
  90, 222, 243
Orta San Giulio 153
osteria 63

P

Padiglione d'Arte
  Contemporanea, Milan 111
Palazzo Arcivescovile 94
Palazzo Barbieri, Verona 247
Palazzo Belgioioso, Milan 95
Palazzo Belgiojoso 185
Palazzo Comunale, Cremona 232
Palazzo della Loggia, Brescia 226
Palazzo della Ragione,
  Bergamo 220
Palazzo della Ragione,
  Mantua 237
Palazzo della Ragione, Milan 95
Palazzo della Ragione,
  Verona 241
Palazzo Ducale, Mantua 237
Palazzo Gran Guardia,
  Verona 247
Palazzo Maffei, Verona 241

Palazzo Marino, Milan 95
Palazzo Reale, Milan 86
Palazzo Te, Mantua 239
Parco Baia delle Sirene,
  Lake Garda 205
Parco Comunale 178
Parco Maria Callas,
  Lake Garda 197
Parco Nazionale
  del Gran Paradiso 49
Parco Nazionale della
  Val Grande 151
Parco Sempione, Milan 100
Passa Ampola, Lake Garda 203
Pavia 119
Peck 137
pensione 58
Peschiera del Garda,
  Lake Garda 199
piazza Brà, Verona 241
piazza dei Signori, Verona 241
piazza del Carmine, Milan 95
piazza del Comune 231
piazza del Duomo, Milan 94, 84
piazza della Scala, Milan 95
piazza Erbe, Verona 241
piazza Mercanti, Milan 95
Pinacoteca
  (Musei Civici Como) Como 171
Pinacoteca (Civici Musei del
  Castello Sforzesco) Milan 99
Pinacoteca Ambrosiana 87
Pinacoteca di Brera 107
Pirelli Tower, Milan 113
Planetario Ulrico Hoepli,
  Milan 112
Po Basin 49
Poldi Pezzoli, Gian Giacomo 92
police 274
Porta dei Borsari, Verona 243
Porta Sant'Alessandro,
  Bergamo 222
Porta Ticinese, Milan 111, 131

Porta Venezia, Milan   111
post   274
Practicalities   266-279
price codes   5
language   276
Pre, Lake Garda   203
Puccini, Giacomo   91
Punta San Vigilio, Lake Garda   205

Q

Quadrilatero d'Oro   15, 69, 104

R

Renaissance   40
ristorante   61
Risorgimento   34
Riva del Garda   203, 205
Rocca di Angera   149
Rocca Scaligera, Lake Garda   197
Roman Empire   29
Romanesque   38
Rotonda di via Besana, Milan   116
Rotonda San Lorenzo, Mantua   239
Rustico Medioevo   20, 54

S

Sacro Monte di San Francisco   153
safety   274
Sala Comacina, Lake Como   175
Salò, Lake Garda   201
Salone Internazionale del Mobile   18, 53
San Babila, Milan   116
San Bartolomeo, Bergamo   222
San Fedele, Milan   95

San Fedele, Como   171
San Maurizio, Milan   116
San Rocco, Lake Como   175
San Sepolcro, Milan   116
Santa Anastasia, Verona   247
Santa Caterina del Sasso   149
San Lorenzo Maggiore, Milan   116
Santa Maria del Carmine, Milan   95
Santa Maria delle Grazie, Milan   102
Santa Maria del Tiglio   182
Santa Maria presso San Celso, Milan   116
Sant'Agostino, Como   171
Sant'Eustorgio, Milan   116
San Vigilio Funicular, Bergamo   222
Scaligeri family   243
Sforza family   96
shopping   68
    Lake Como   190
    Lake Garda   212
    Lakes Maggiore & Orta   160
    Milan   135
    Towns of the Po Valley   260
Sirmione, Lake Garda   197
sleeping   56
    Lake Como   186
    Lake Garda   208
    Lakes Maggiore & Orta   154
    Milan   120
    price codes   5
    Towns of the Po Valley   248
Sognando Shakespeare   54
Spider's Strategem, The (Bernardo Bertolucci)   23
Stalls of Santa Lucia   55
Star Wars Episode II: Attack of the Clones (George Lucas)   23
St Ambrose   115
Stazione Centrale, Milan   112

Storo, Lake Garda   203
Strada del Vina Franciacorta, Brescia   229
Stradivarius   100, 232
Stresa, Lake Maggiore   145

T

Teatro alla Scala, Milan   14, 90, 134
Teatro Donizetti, Bergamo   222
Teatro Filamonico, Verona   247
Teatro Romano, Verona   243
Teatro Sociale, Mantua   237
telephone   274
Tempio della Vittoria, Milan   111
Teorema (Pier Paolo Pasolini)   23
The Last Supper   102
theme parks   213
time difference   274
Tintoretto   108
tipping   275
Titian   87, 108
Torrazzo, Cremona   232
Torre Civica, Bergamo   220
Torre dell'Orologio, Brescia   226
Torre dell'Orologio, Lake Garda   201
Torre Velasca, Milan   112
Torri del Benaco, Lake Garda   205
tourist information   275
    Como   169
    Cremona   231
    Lake Garda   197
    Lake Maggiore   145
    Lake Orta   153
    Milan   81
Towns of the Po Valley   214-265
    Bergamo   218
    Brescia   224
    Cremona   230
    Mantua   236
    Verona   240

trattoria 61
Tremezzina Riviera,
  Lake Como 175
Tremezzo, Lake Como 175
Triennale, Milan 106
Tutti Santi 21, 55
Twain, Mark 24

 U

Unification of Italy 35

V

Valtenesi, Lake Garda 200
Varenna, Lake Como 183
Verbania, Lake Maggiore 148
Verdi, Giuseppe 91
Verona 13, 17, 240
Verona Opera Festival 54
Veronia 241
Villas, hotels
  Villa Crespi (Orta San Giulio) 155
  Villa d'Este (Cernobbio) 187
  Villa Fiordaliso
    (Gardone Riviera) 208
  Villa Serbelloni (Bellagio) 178
Villas, museums & gardens
  Il Vittoriale
    (Gardona Riviera) 202
  Villa del Balbianello
    (Lenno) 180
  Villa Carlotta (Tremezzo) 181
  Villa Geno (Como) 173
  Villa Olmo (Como) 172
  Villa Melzi (Bellagio) 179
  Villa Manzoni (Lecco) 185
  Villa Monastero (Varenna) 183

Villa Pallavicino (Stresa) 145
Villa Romana (Desenzano) 199
Villa Taranto (Verbania) 148
Visconti family 86, 96, 118, 175
voltage 275

W

walking 74
  Historical city itineraries,
    Bergamo 231
  Lakeside Promenade,
    Como 172
  centro storico walk, Milan 94
  fashion walk, Milan 104
  Navigli, Milan 130
  Roman Brixia, Brescia 228
  Verona 246
water quality 51
water sports
  & boating 74, 176, 206
well-being 75
what the locals say 81, 103,
  126, 183
winter sports 75
World Wars, First & Second 35

Another slice of Italy

Footprint Lifestyle guides

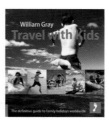

Books to inspire and plan some of the world's most compelling travel experiences. Written by experts and presented to appeal to popular travel themes and pursuits.

66 99

A great book to have on your shelves when planning your next European escapade
Sunday Telegraph

Footprint Activity guides

These acclaimed guides have broken new ground, bringing together adventure sports and activities with relevant travel content, stunningly presented to help enthusiasts get the most from their pastimes.

66 99

This awesome guide has been hailed as 'the new surfer's bible'
Extreme Sports Channel

footprintbooks.com

Credits

Footprint credits

Text editor: Alice Jell
Picture editor: Kassia Gawronski
Layout & production: Angus Dawson
Maps: Compass Maps Ltd

Managing Director: Andy Riddle
Commercial Director: Patrick Dawson
Publisher: Alan Murphy
Editorial: Sara Chare, Ria Gane,
Jenny Haddington, Felicity Laughton,
Nicola Gibbs
Design: Mytton Williams
Cartography: Sarah Sorenson, Rob Lunn,
Kevin Feeney, Emma Bryers
Sales & marketing: Liz Harper,
Hannah Bonnell
Advertising: Renu Sibal
Business Development: Zoë Jackson
Finance & Administration: Elizabeth Taylor

Print
Manufactured in Italy by EuroGrafica
Pulp from sustainable forests

Footprint Feedback
We try as hard as we can to make each
Footprint guide as up to date as possible
but, of course, things always change.
If you want to let us know about your
experiences – good, bad or ugly – then
don't delay, go to footprintbooks.com
and send in your comments.

Every effort has been made to ensure
that the facts in this guidebook are
accurate. However, travellers should still
obtain advice from consulates, airlines etc
about travel and visa requirements before
travelling. The authors and publishers
cannot accept responsibility for any loss,
injury or inconvenience however caused.

Publishing information

FootprintItalia Italian Lakes
1st edition
© Footprint Handbooks Ltd
May 2009

ISBN 978-1-906098-61-2
CIP DATA: A catalogue record for this
book is available from the British Library

® Footprint Handbooks and the Footprint
mark are a registered trademark of
Footprint Handbooks Ltd

Published by Footprint
6 Riverside Court
Lower Bristol Road
Bath BA2 3DZ, UK
T +44 (0)1225 469141
F +44 (0)1225 469461
www.footprintbooks.com

Distributed in North America by
Globe Pequot Press